PSYCHOANALYTIC OBJECT RELATIONS THEORY AND THE STUDY OF RELIGION

On Faith and the Imaging of God

John McDargh

UNIVERSITY
PRESS OF
AMERICA

LANHAM • NEW YORK • LONDON

Copyright © 1983 by

University Press of America,™ Inc.

4720 Boston Way
Lanham, MD 20706

3 Henrietta Street
London WC2E 8LU England

Library of Congress Cataloging in Publication Data

McDargh, John.
  Psychoanalytic object relations theory and the study
of religion.

  Based on the author's thesis (Ph.D.—Harvard
University, 1981)
  Bibliography: p.
  1. Faith. 2. God. 3. Psychoanalysis and religion.
4. Psychology, Religious. I. Title.
BV4637.M37   1983   200'.1'9   83-14776
ISBN 0-8191-3510-0 (alk. paper)
ISBN 0-8191-3511-9 (pbk. : alk. paper)

To my family,
and to all new families of every form,
being created today in hope and with courage
that the future may find faith on earth.

ACKNOWLEDGEMENTS

This book is, in the main, a revision of the doctoral dissertation completed in 1981 in the Program for the Study of Religion, Harvard University Graduate School of Arts and Sciences. To Professor Robert L. Moore, Chicago Theological Seminary, and others of my colleagues in the Person, Culture and Religion group of the American Academy of Religion I am endebted for the encouragement to bring this work to print - not as the adequate final statement of its problematic, but rather as a stimulus to further investigation of the relevance of modern psychoanalytic theory for the study of religion and as an introduction into the dialogue between religion and psychology of the hitherto under-investigated resources of object relations theory in psychoanalysis.

Because this book began its life as a dissertation, it is appropriate to acknowledge some special debts of friendship and collegiality, a review of which is also an autobiographical summary of the major intellectual influences that find expression in this work.

From the very beginning until the very end, Dr. William Rogers, then Parkman Professor of Divinity, Harvard Divinity School, now president of Guilford College, has been mentor, colleague and friend. The discussion of methodology in Chapter Three owes its inspiration to Dr. Rogers, but his influence on this project and indeed on the entire course of my graduate education cannot be measured in footnotes. Behind Dr. Rogers' methodological program is a deeper concern for the spirit of interdisciplinary study characterized by an uncompromising reverence for the integrity and irreducibility of the data of human experience. It is this total approach to work "on the boundary" of theology and psychology which I count as Dr. Rogers' most enduring gift to those of us fortunate to have studied with him.

The seminal intellectual experience of my first years at Harvard was the year long graduate seminar in psychoanalytic theory conducted in 1975-76 by Dr. George Goethals, Department of Psychology and Social Relations. It was Dr. Goethals who first introduced me to psychoanalytic object relations theory and much of my curiosity about the implications of this development in psychoanalysis stems from the powerful impact of that first encounter.

The other key influence from my first several years at Harvard was the work and the person of Dr. James Fowler, Candler School of Theology, Emory University. The degree to which I draw upon his pioneering work in the theory of faith development should be evidence for the stimulation which this later has given my own thinking. The extent to which I feel free to propose correction and offer alternatives is evidence of Dr. Fowler's objectivity of mind and generosity of spirit that has encouraged criticism and invited dialogue from the very beginning.

Professor Lee Helena Perry, Program in Counseling and Consulting Psychology, Harvard Graduate School of Education, was the counselor, consultant, colleague and confessor through the longest and most arduous stage of the dissertation research. The interviews which form the clinical data for this dissertation were conducted as part of a larger research project designed with and supervised by Dr. Perry. Her superb clinical skills and judgment were invaluable in the execution of the empirical portion of this project.

Outside of the Harvard community, the single most sustained and significant source of intellectual stimulation and personal inspiration has been Dr. Ana-Maria Rizzuto, Clinical Professor of Psychiatry at Tufts Medical School. Dr. Rizzuto's landmark research, published in 1979 as The Birth of the Living God, is one of the central points of theoretical reference for this book. It was my unusual privilege and great joy to have been invited to follow the progress of that work in manuscript, and to consult with her on this investigation as it took form. Like Dr. Fowler, Dr. Rizzuto is one of those rare scholars whose generous sense of sponsorship and conviction that "truth belongs to the Spirit" invites and encourages the new colleague in the field.

No researcher could have asked for a more challenging, supportive and unfailingly interesting group of colleagues than those who have pursued with me the study of religion and psychology at Harvard and elsewhere: Dr. Michael Rush; Dr. Sharon Parks; Dr. David Barnard; Dr. Dorothy Austin; Dr. Herbert Lovett; and Fr. Gary Dorrien.

To Dr. Robert Daly, S.J., and my present colleagues in the Department of Theology, Boston College, I am grateful for the opportunity to teach and to pursue this interdisciplinary research in a collegial environment where theological issues can be pursued in a spirit of inquiry open to the resources of every branch of human knowledge.

The long labor of transforming ideas into words and words into finished copy would have been impossible without the efforts of a loyal and talented friend, Tim Dunn, who help proofread this manuscript and saw it through its final stages.

Finally, I am deeply and humbly endebted to the many men and women who generously and courageously shared their life stories in the process of the empirical research that undergirds this project. In particular I am daily appreciative of the opportunity to have met and to have learned from the two remarkable women who are referred to in this dissertation as "Stacy R." and "Ann B." Their willingness to risk, at many levels, made the research a rich and productive process for all of us.

Special acknowledgement is made to the following for permission to quote from their copyrighted material: to Macmillan Publishers, Inc. for excerpts from H. Richard Niebuhr, The Meaning of Revelation (copyright, 1941); and to The Journal of Religion and Health, for excerpts from William Meissner's "Notes on a Psychology of Faith" (vol. 8, 1969).

TABLE OF CONTENTS

PREFACE xiii

INTRODUCTION .xv

CHAPTER ONE   PSYCHOANALYTIC OBJECT RELATIONS THEORY:
               A NEW RESOURCE FOR AN OLD DEBATE

  I. The Emergence of the Topic from
      The Problem of Defining Religion. 2

  II. The Functional Approach to the Study of Religion. . 6

  III. The Substantive Approach to the Study of Religion . .9

  IV. Point and Counterpoint:
       Psychoanalytic Theory in the Between. 14

  V. The Iool of Mediation: A Revised Depth Psychology. 15

  VI. What is Psychoanalytic Object Relations Theory. . . 17

CHAPTER TWO   FAITH: THE THEOLOGICAL VANTAGE

  I. Faith as a Borrowed Term. 23

  II. H. Richard Niebuhr and the Protestant Contribution
       to the Definition of Faith: The Protestant Question
       and the Niebuhrian Dilemma. 24

       The Point of Beginning: The Fragmented Self
       The Goal of Development: Integrated Selfhood
       Political and Psychological Dimensions
          of the Unified Self
       The Means of Faith: A Revolution of Imagery
       Summary

  III. The Operationalization of a Definition of Faith:
        The Contributions of James Fowler 34

        The Niebuhr Legacy
        Taking up the Task: The Faith Development Model
        Fowler's Definition(s) of Faith

The Research Project
"From Where" and "Towards What" in
  Faith Development Theory
Summary

IV. The Catholic Vantage on Faith:
    Development and Distinctiveness 45

    The "Fides Qua" and the "Fides Quae" Distinction
    The Second Vatican Council and the Problem of Faith
    The Point of Beginning: The Quest for the Real
    The Goal of Development:
      The Overcoming of Concupiscence

V. William W. Meissner: Psychoanalysis Looks at Faith 52

    Faith: From Primal Trauma to Ego Integration
    The Double Paradox of Faith
    A Proposed Methodology for the
      Study of Religious Experience

CHAPTER THREE   FAITH: A THEORETICAL ANALYSIS

   I. Working on the Boundary. 67

  II. The From Whence of Faith 72

    Faith is involved in the development
      of the sense of being real
    Faith is involved in the growth of a sense of being
      in relationship to a real and meaningful world
    Faith is integrally related to the development
      of the capacity to be alone
    Faith is to be found in the processes involved in
      the development of the capacity to tolerate
      dependency

 III. The To Where of Faith. 87

    Faith is involved in the development of
      the capacity to tolerate ambivalence
    Faith undergirds the sense of oneself as
      available for loving self-donation

CHAPTER FOUR   HOW DOES FAITH FUNCTION?
               ENTER THE MATTER OF CONTENT

   I. The Questions in the Margin 104

x

II. From Personal Images to the Transcendent. 105

III. From the Transcendent to "God". 114

IV. Object Representations Revisited. 117

V. The Object Representation of God
   and the Conceptualization of God. 124

VI. Summary 133

CHAPTER FIVE   REVIEW AND PROSPECTIVE OF RESEARCH
                METHODS ON THE IMAGING OF GOD

I. Introduction. 137

II. Freud and his Forebearers on Religion 137

III. Post-Freudian Investigation of the Image of God . 140

IV. Psychological Studies of the Image of God:
    Psychoanalytic Perspective. 141

V. Psychoanalytic Object Relations Theory
   and Research on Religion. 144

CHAPTER SIX   PRESENTATION OF CASE MATERIAL

I. Method of Collection of Data 153

II. The Case of Ann B.: A Retreat to Advance 155

Introduction
Early Childhood and Family Structure
Earliest Interaction with God
Adolescence: The Expansion of the World
    and the Contraction of the Family
The God Relationship in Adolescence
College Years: Religious Moratorium and Return
Finding a Future and Beginning a Marriage
The First Mission Assignment and Personal Tragedy
The Middle Years and the Onset of Depression
Return, Reconsolidation and Recovery
The Object Representation of God
    through the Depression and Beyond
Towards the Future:
    Personal and Professional Horizons

III. The Case of Stacy R.:
      Learning to Care for the Inner Child. 182

          Introduction
          Early Childhood and Family Structure
          Double Bind
          Handling Aloneness in Childhood
          God in Early Childhood
          Parental Divorce and Aftermath
          Early Adulthood and Marriage
          Inner Work and Outer Transformations
          The Dream of the Truncated Baby
          Towards the Future: Personal and Professional
             Horizons

CHAPTER SEVEN   AN OBJECT RELATIONS ANALYSIS
                   OF FAITH DEVELOPMENT. 203

    I. The Emergence of a Psychoanalytic
        Theory of Object Relations. 204

          Two Stories of Failure and a Revolution in Theory
          Fairbairn and Winnicott: Internalization
             for Defense vs. Primary Creativity

   II. Case Analysis: Infancy and Early Childhood . . .214

          Prelude to the Drama: Setting the Stage
          Birth and the Origins of Basic Trust
          The Separation Individuation Process
          Traditional Object Phenomena, Play and God

  III. Play Age Through Adolescence 230

          Stacy: God and the Judgmental Factor
          Ann: God the Controller

   IV. The Crises of Adult Life 237

          Ann and the Long Way Home
          Stacy and the Child of the Dream

    V. Concluding Reflections 245

APPENDIX A
APPENDIX B
BIBLIOGRAPHY

PREFACE

At one point several years ago, while the ideas presented in this book were still taking shape, a colleague of mine struggling to understand this research challenged me with the question: "Are you trying to say that God is nothing but a cosmic teddy bear?" "No," I replied, "but I am arguing that we cannot understand fully what compels human beings to seek after that which they name 'God' until and unless we understand something about our relationship to our teddy bears."

Today it would make this same claim, understanding, of course, that "teddy bear" is only a convenient short-hand for the rich complex of early childhood experiences which involve every human begin in attempting to symbolize a meaningful world of secure relationship. Now as then, however, I recognize the concern behind my colleague's query, namely that I am involved in some form of psychological reductionism, the sort of "nothing-but-ism" which has contributed to the religious community's periodic mistrust of psychology and the psychological community's reputation in some quarters for impoverished thinking. The concern is not misplaced, but it may be outdated - a quarrel carried on with an older body of psychoanalytic doctrine regarding religious origins that is itself being called into question from within the psychoanalytic community by the emergence of new clinical data and new theoretical perspectives on the structure of mental life. One reason that the development within modern psychoanalytic thought of object relations theory so quickly captured my own interest and scholarly imagination is that it appears to offer a way of understanding the origins of human religious sensibility, and in particular the creation and elaboration of our images of the divine that finally does justice to religious maturation as well as religious pathology, adult faith as well as childhood fantasy.

For the student of the psychology of religion presently unfamiliar with psychoanalytic object relations theory, this text may serve as an introduction to its principal theoretical innovations. For those already aware of this development this book attempts to show the resource which an object relations perspective is for addressing a central problem in the psychology of faith development: the role of the representation of God in the life of faith.

It is my hope that this text may be a fruitful stimulus for further thought and investigation across a number of different academic disciplines and professional commitments. Theologians concerned to work out the linkages between human development on the natural order and the life of faith may find in object relations theory a way of thinking about how revelation is grounded in the actual processes of human self becoming. Secular psychologists and psychotherapists will, I hope, find in the clinical portions of this book of basis for listening with renewed interest and attention to the religious contents of their client's sharing as offering another "royal road" to the inner world. Finally, pastors, religious educators, and spiritual directors should see in this material an affirmation and a theoretical elucidation at the psychological level of what they have already observed and testified to throughout the ages: that the human being's relationship to his or her God can be as lively, as changeable, as dynamic and as open-ended as the most intimate and spontaneous of human relationships.

John McDargh
Boston College
June 10, 1983

"Come," my heart has said,
"Seek His face."
I will seek Thy face, O Lord;
do not hide it from me.

Psalm 27: 8-9

Have mercy on us therefore, O deep God of the void
Spare this race in this your earth still in our free
choice...
And make the eyes of our hearts,
And the voice of our hearts in speech,
Honest and lovely within the fences of our nature,
And a little more clear.

James Agee, 1935
from Permit the Voyage

INTRODUCTION

Nowhere is the project of this book more succinctly set out than in the words of the psalmist above. The research and reflection that have culminated in this text have converged upon a single question, "How is it that human beings are constituted by their development to 'seek the face of God'?" Nothing has seemed clearer to me than that as a species we are, as Berdyaev put it, "incurably religious." Something in our fundamental nature, something in our heart, compels us to face the faceless universe. I intend "face" in both of its senses. We come upon ourselves both drawn and driven to face outwards to the limits of our lives and ask the questions of ultimacy. But, further, the intent behind those questions is to find the face of that ultimate reality, to discern its intention towards us and our own place before it.

The form in which I have posed this central question reveals the bent of my own Catholic formation which holds that gratia perficit naturam, the activity of grace builds upon or perfects nature. Even before I found this insight eloquently updated in Karl Rahner's arguments for a theological anthropology, I had already been drawn to look for answers in what can be known about early childhood development from the resources of the social and behavioral sciences. This work is the initial fruit of that inquiry.

xv

In broadest terms, to use the words of James Agee, it is an effort to become "a little more clear" and honest about "the fences of our nature," this nature that is our one and only arena for salvation. More specifically it examines the resources offered towards our understanding of human faith by one particular perspective on human development, the psychoanalytic, and more precisely that broad ranging movement within psychoanalysis know as object relations theory.

The contribution of psychoanalytic object relations theory is seen to have two related aspects. First it offers a coherent psychological account of the "humanward" side of faith which articulates with significant aspects of faith as identified by certain Protestant and Catholic theologians. Second, it draws into a consideration of the psychological dynamics of faith one signal element of content, the thematization of the object of faith as "God." An object relational perspective on faith shows how it is that "God" as an internalized object can, under some circumstances of development, be available to mediate the processes of faith and under other circumstances will not be. Furthermore, by examining the essential relationship that obtains between the process of self and object representation and the process whereby human beings achieve the faith that undergirds self-becoming, we are enabled finally to understand why it is so inescapably human to seek for the face of the divine, the face that makes faith possible. This book has been structured to present these dual dimensions of object relations theory's offering to the study of religion.

Chapter One takes bearings upon the study of religion broadly in order to fix the position of this work as a potential contribution to an ongoing debate between substantive and functional definitions of religion. Chapter One explains how the problematic of this project emerged for me out of the tension between these two approaches to the subject matter of religion. In this chapter I identify faith as the subject of the book and contemporary psychoanalytic theory as the psychological science which I will utilize to dialogue with theology.

Chapter Two examines in a selective fashion theological sources for the category of faith. This examination is divided in two parts, each presenting a theologian and a psychologist who has specifically made faith the object of empirical investigation. In the first part I consider a Protestant vantage on faith and choose as an exemplar of that perspective H. Richard Niebuhr. I then look at the work of James Fowler, a psychologist of faith who has explicitly used the Niebuhrian formulation of faith to direct a psychological investigation

based upon structural developmental theory. The second part of
this chapter takes up a contemporary Catholic perspective on
faith, specifically illustrated in the writings of Karl Rahner.
The psychologist of faith who is considered under this column
is psychoanalyst and Jesuit, William W. Meissner. In Chapter
Three various aspects of faith identified by these theologians
and psychologists are combined to present a composite
definition and analysis of faith.

Chapter Three and Chapter Four are the core of the book.
Chapter Three opens with a brief methodological preface that
uses a model developed by William Rogers to discuss my approach
to the integration of psychological and theological perspectives. The bulk of the chapter is devoted to a
presentation of six dimensions of faith analyzed from a
psychoanalytic object relations perspective. These six lines
of development are organized under two rubrics. Four are
regarded as aspects of what I will discuss as the "from whence"
of faith, the foundational human problem which defines the
starting point of faith development. This fons et origo of
faith is identified,following H. Richard Niebuhr, as the
problem of becoming a self. The four aspects of self-becoming
most clearly implicated in human faith are: (1) the capacity to
be alone; (2) the sense of being real; (3) the capacity to
tolerate dependence; and (4) the sense of being in relationship
to a real and meaningful world.
    The other general category under which I have organized
the dimensions of faith is what I have termed the "to where" of
faith, a psycho-theological statement of the goal of human
development in faith. This I name love or radical community
and within that identify two aspects: (1) the capacity to
tolerate ambivalence; and (2) the sense of oneself as available
for loving self-donation.

    Chapter Four takes up the "how" question of faith and
begins with a clue, again from H. Richard Niebuhr, that faith
involves the reasoning of the heart by means of personal
images. This discussion is then transposed into the terms of
psychoanalytic object relations to analyze (1) the human
requirement for images of the transcendent in order to sustain
the integrative activity of faith; and (2) the unique availability of images of "God" to serve for the object of faith
because of their developmental origin in pre-oedipal and
oedipal struggles with self-becoming. Utilizing the
theoretical and clinical work of Ana-Maria Rizzuto we present a
theoretical statement on the origins of the object
representation of God and its relationship to the processes of
faith. The chapter concludes be developing a distinction
between ideas about God and object representations of God. The

xvii

remainder of the book then is an effort to illustrate the explicative power of an object relational analysis of faith by using it as a "tool to think with" when considering two human lives.

Chapter Five is an over view of various efforts to study the object representation of God from a variety of theoretical and methodological positions. The specific clinical tools used in my own research approach are briefly discussed.

Chapter Six presents extended case studies of two women in their midfifties, code named Ann B. and Stacy R. An extended semi-clinical interview was conducted with both women. Additionally, each completed a number of questionnaires and projective instruments and submitted autobiographical work. The cases are by design presented in some detail and with minimal interpretive commentary. It is hoped that the reader will thereby form his or her own independent clinical judgments in the course of reading this very rich and suggestive material. When reading the analysis I offer in the subsequent chapter the reader will therefore be better able to enter into a critical dialogue with my position.

Chapter Seven completes the book with an analysis of the two case studies presented in Chapter Six. These analyses do not presume to be exhaustive of the material nor do they develop systematically each of the six developmental dimensions of faith discussed in Chapter Three. They do focus on key aspects of the faith developmental process and in particular serve to introduce to the study of faith the concepts of True-Self/False-Self and transitional object phenomena as these have been developed by British psychoanalyst, D.W. Winnicott.

CHAPTER ONE

PSYCHOANALYTIC OBJECT RELATIONS THEORY:
A NEW RESOURCE FOR AN OLD DEBATE

I. The Emergence of the Topic from
the Problem of Defining Religion . . . . p. 2

II. The Functional Approach to
The Study of Religion. . . . . p. 6

III. The Substantive Approach to
The Study of Religion. . . . . p. 9

IV. Point and Counterpoint:
Psychoanalytic Theory in the Between . . . . . p. 14

V. The Tool of Mediation:
A Revised Depth Psychology . . . . p. 15

VI. What is Psychoanalytic Object Relations Theory? p. 17

1

CHAPTER ONE

PSYCHOANALYTIC OBJECT RELATIONS THEORY:
A NEW RESOURCE FOR AN OLD DEBATE

I. The Emergence of the Topic from the Problem of Defining
    Religion

    I think that it is not unfair to characterize the history
of the relationship between psychoanalytic theorists and
theologians as less a dialogue than a protracted litigation
over the value and the validity of one another's ways of
managing the world. Classical psychoanalysis for its part
pressed the case that religion was the "universal obsessional
neurosis of humankind," a developmental fixation in the service
of enabling persons to evade the harsh facts of their
helplessness before fate and their aloneness in the universe.
According to this critique, now become quite familiar to us,
the maturity of the individual and the race at large
necessarily requires setting aside the illusion that is
religion (Freud, 1927, 1930). Theologians for their part
presented a variety of rebuttals. [1] Some argued that Freud's
critiques of religion did not touch the substance of religion
because religion dealt with spiritual realities while
psychoanalysis was mired in materialism (Maritain, 1958).
Alternatively, others dismissed Freud's views on religion, even
while maintaining a respect for psychoanalysis as a therapy, on
the grounds that Freud's religious judgments were a function of
his atheism and the bias of his early experience with Christian
anti-Semitism (Zilboorg, 1962). Finally some theologians
accepted with better or worse grace the validity of the
Freudian analysis of religion but only in so far as it applied
to "lower" or less developed forms of religion (most recently,
Kung, 1979). This last and likely most sophisticated sort of
response Peter Homans, in his book Theology After Freud,
identifies with the concerns of a peculiarly Protestant
theological existentialism with its determination to "protect
what it conceives to be the theological dimension of human life
from reduction to psychological processes and psychological
understandings" (Homans, 1970, p. 20).

    The approach of theological existentialism by Homans'
account acknowledges the validity of psychoanalytic critiques
of what Tillich called "the God of theological theism," or what
Homans prefers to call the "transference God." According to
this view psychoanalysis describes well the blocks and
fixations which prevent the individual from moving beyond the
transference aspects of God. In that sense psychoanalysis can

serve, to use Jurgen Moltmann's phrase, as "a bulldozer in the way of the gospel" (Moltmann, 1974, p. 296). However, this particular vantage on psychoanalysis limits its usefulness to this propadeutic, unmasking function. Psychoanalysis is not seen to offer anything towards understanding the further processes of self-transcendence. In other words, it can not on its own terms account for how religion can outgrow its infantile origins. It can be descriptive but not prescriptive except in a negative sense. It is Homans' suggestion that what is needed is a "higher" reading of Freud which would have a positive contribution to make in interpreting the processes of creativity and integration operative "beyond the transference God."

I would propose that just such a higher reading of Freud is now available and as a consequence the way is opening for a new and more constructive dialogue between religion and psychoanalysis. This reading is to be found in a broad-based theoretical development within psychoanalysis which is commonly referred to as object relations theory (Friedman, L.J., 1975; Friedman, L., 1978; Mendez and Fine, 1976; Sugerman, 1977; Kanzer, 1979). Rather than a single cohesive school of thought, object relations theory represents the convergence of a number of discoveries made in the clinical practice of psychoanalysis, the study of early childhood development, family theory and ethology.

Those points of convergence form a pattern that draws attention to some key insights in Freud which Freud himself was unable to grasp in their full significance. Among those insights which have been developed and advanced by an object-relational perspective, and which appear to have great potential relevance for the study of religion, are: 1) the unparalleled importance of the character of early parent-child interaction for the future development of personality and psychic structure, 2) the potential value for adaptation of so-called "regressive" phenomena, 3) the primacy of relation-seeking throughout life, 4) the central significance over the entire life cycle of fantasy and the imaginative processes, and 5) the "immortal" character of our significant early relationships through the memorializing functions of the human psyche.

Simply as a distinctive theoretical perspective that has exercised considerable influence in Britain and begun to make its impact in the United States, object relations theory in psychoanalysis deserves the serious attention of students of the psychology of religion concerned to remain in contact with advancements in depth psychology. Already a number of scholars have begun to suggest that object relations theory has the

3

potential to move the psychoanalytic study of religion into a new era (Meissner, 1977; Pruyser, 1974). Only a few writers, however, have used an object relational perspective in considering particular religious issues (Henderson, 1975, 1976; Sugerman, 1976) or in analyzing specific clinical data of a religious nature (Klauber, 1974; Lubin, 1959; Taylor, 1978). The only large scale clinical application of object relations theory to a problem central to the study of religion is the very significant recent work of Ana-Maria Rizzuto (Rizzuto, 1979) which has been a major inspiration for this project and which I will discuss at some length later. The task which has not been undertaken to date is to introduce the resources of psychoanalytic object relations theory to the study of religion in a more systematic way.

In its broadest intent this book aims to develop some of the possibilities of that partnership. This is a difficult task to do "in general," so I have chosen to illustrate the potential contribution of psychoanalytic object relations theory to the study of religion by bringing that body of theory to bear on what appears to me to be a particularly important and vexing problem, "In the dynamics of human faith, what is the role played by those psychological processes whereby individuals come to develop their own personal representations of God?"

Two prefacing questions immediately present themselves. First, "How is this a problem, let alone an important one?" Second, "Why is psychoanalytic object relations theory a suitable resource for dealing with it?" Answers to both questions must be in some sense autobiographical. In this first chapter I would like to introduce this problem by first showing how it identified itself to me in the process of trying to negotiate opposing general approaches to the subject matter of the study of religion.

The problem of understanding human faith, and within faith the function of a person's conscious and unconscious imagings of God, arose for me out of the dialogue between what I shall call a functional and a substantive approach to the study of religion.

A functionalist perspective on the psychology of religion I take to refer to any methodology which begins with a definition of religion as that which serves a particular purpose or function in the psychic economy of the individual or the society, and then proceeds to identify certain actions or patterns of action as religious or not depending on whether they play that role. My own early encounter with functionalist thinking during my doctoral study at Harvard was an exciting

4

and intellectually liberating experience, as it was for many. In such efforts as the work of sociologist Robert Bellah or the application of structural-developmental theory to the study of faith by James Fowler we saw a model that appeared to free the psychology of religion from the confining definitions in which it had become bound. To regard religion - or better, faith - as a universal human dynamic cuts across lines of belief and barriers of culture and greatly extends the scope of the discipline. Functionalism offered an interpretative tool with which one could labor in long neglected areas of life and with segments of the human population hitherto regarded as "unreligious" and hence outside the area of our study.

At the same time experiences began to accumulate in the process of clinical work, counseling and further research which suggested that for all its welcomed inclusiveness, a functional approach to the study of religion perhaps neglected some crucial data. It was data that the religious traditions have long understood is not accidental to the processes of faith. I observed in myself and in others - clients, friends, counselees and my students - that regardless of our formal religious or irreligious designation we carry on a lively relationship with our own very private, very personal images of God. It is a relationship that might be sporadic, not always conscious or consistent, and often more deeply ambivalent than our self-professed creeds would give evidence of. Yet, these relationships are clearly of psychological and religious significance. These relationships when they can be observed seem to have a more than casual bearing upon those processes of comprehensive meaning-making and self-orientation to an "ultimate environment" which describes the activity of faith (Fowler, 1978).

With the accumulation of such observations I was brought to wonder, "How does our relationship to these internalized images of God relate to the dynamic of faith?" Is it incidental content, or is there something fundamental and in some sense essential about the need to relate to a personal object of faith which can account for the persistent influence in faith activity of our representations of God?

It was these sorts of questions which conducted me back to consider with new respect the claims of an alternative approach to the definition of religion which might be termed the substantive approach. From this perspective religion is defined in terms of a particular content regarded as normative. This content can vary widely. It may be as commonsensical as "whatever beliefs, practices or observances are commonly held to be religious in a given culture" or it may be as particular as Milton Spiro's definition of religion as "an institution consisting of culturally patterned interactions with culturally postulated superhuman beings"(Spiro, 1966, p. 96). A substantive approach may subsequently investigate the function of certain religious beliefs or acts in a given life or culture, but it does not identify the object of its inquiry in terms of that function.

In the succeeding sections we shall set out in greater detail what appear to be the relative strengths and weaknesses of these approaches; this for one purpose. The issues raised by these approaches direct us back to the contributions of psychoanalysis and at the same time display the necessity for revision within psychoanalytic theory. In the rest of the book then we hope to demonstrate that psychoanalytic object relations theory is just such a revision as can seriously attend to religious "content," specifically as individual's object representations of God, while offering a non-reductive explication of their role and function within the overall process of human faith.

II. The Functional Approach to the Study of Religion

The outlines of a functional approach to the subject of religion can be early discerned in the work of William James, the man who stands at the head of the psychology of religion tradition in this country. James begins The Varieties of Religious Experience with a definition of religion which seems to have a particular "content" and hence might be fairly called a substantive definition. "Religion," he writes, ". . .shall mean for us the feelings, acts and experiences of individual men in their solitude, so far as they apprehend themselves to stand in relationship to whatever they may consider the divine" (James, 1904/1958, p. 42). Having laid out this definition, however, James goes on to describe the religious function in a human life in a way that makes it clear that his primary concern is with what religion does for the individual. "Religion," he continues, "whatever it is, is a man's total reaction upon life" (James, 1904/1958, p. 46). He further proposes that this reaction is identified as religious primarily by what it accomplishes, namely, "to make easy and felicitous what in any case is necessary," that is, the accommodation of the person to the total reality of life as it besets him or her (James, 1904/1958, p. 56).

This highly condensed discussion demonstrates the features common to all functional definitions of religion that have followed upon James' initiative. First religion is identified as some fundamental or constitutive human activity that engages

6

the whole person. Second, that activity is distinguished by the role or function which it plays in the "life economy of the individual" (Allport). Third, that function pertains to the human process of adaptation and response to the most ultimate problems of living. The functional approach represents a shift away from regarding religion chiefly as a set of certain readily identifiable cultural products (religion as a noun), and towards a concept of "religious function" (religion as an adjective or adverb). This movement, general but by no means universal across the psychology of religion, has been described as a shift from the old question, "What are the significant data of religious experience?" to a new question: "Which data of experience are of religious significance?" (Pruyser, 1960, p. 109).

Within the sociology of religion the functional approach draws on the formulations of Emile Durkheim and Bronislaw Malinowski. The Durkheimian influence, combined with American structural functionalism and a touch of Tillich, is found in the definitions of religion offered by Robert Bellah: religion is "a set of symbolic forms and acts which relate man to the ultimate condition of his existence" (Bellah, 1964, p. 358). Clifford Geertz proposes another definition of religion which displays a similar functional perspective: "Religion is a system of symbols which acts to establish powerful, pervasive and long-lasting moods and motivations in men by formulating conceptions of a general order of existence and clothing these conceptions with such an aura of factuality that the moods and motivations seem uniquely realistic" (Geertz, 1966, p. 4).

As these definitions illustrate, a functional approach no longer assumes that the subject matter of religion is a set of discrete beliefs that can be clearly identified by the administration of pen and pencil tests. What the functionalist looks for are the symbols, practices, forms - both shared and private - which integrate meaning and motivation (Bellah, 1964). Another way of saying this is that in a functional approach there is an attention to knowing, but knowing of a different sort than concerned psychological researchers who interrogated people about the explicit contents of their religious knowledge. From a functional vantage "knowing" is not an intellectual or notional assent to a set of propositions of a special sort, but a profoundly affective process involving the construction of a system of meaning, a comprehensive orientation to reality, in terms of which one is moved to.act in the world and is guided in that action. Building on this key insight there has begun a fundamental redefinition of the very subject matter of the study of religion.

7

Within the academic study of religion, Wilfred Cantwell Smith has provided perhaps the most careful scholarly warrant for this approach. He has systematically advanced the argument that the study of religion has been trammelled in misunderstanding by taking for its subject matter a reified entity called "religion" presumed to have a propositional content that was its whole meaning and significance (Smith, 1962). In his study of the linguistic confusion that has historically obscured the meaning of "belief" and "believing," Smith points out that religion was originally a term that meant to describe a total human attitude towards that which was perceived to be the divine (Smith, 1977).

Religio in the beginning referred to the worshipful "recognition" of the holy and not to systems of doctrine which could be intellectually evaluated as true or false. In order to recover the proper perspective Professor Smith urges that we regard the object of our inquiry not as religion but religious persons, individuals characterized by their personal faith. Again, faith here does not refer to a set of ideas or concepts which one opines are true in the absence of the usual data of proof. Rather, faith is defined as "a quality of the person, not of the system. . .an orientation of the personality, to oneself, to one's neighbor, to the universe; a total response; a way of seeing whatever one sees and of handling whatever one handles, a capacity to live at a more than mundane level; to see, to feel, to act in terms of a transcendent dimension" (Smith, 1979, p. 12).

As psychologists of religion begin to adopt the concept "faith" rather than "religion" to identify the focus of their study, the discipline begins to stretch its imagination with respect to what counts as legitimate areas of investigation. [2] From counting heads in pews and tallying questionnaires on belief, the psychology of religion moves to take on the universal and more subtle problem of meaning making and life construction in a theoretically unlimited population. The creative work of James Fowler which sets out explicitly to study the development of faith is an example of this approach to which I shall have frequent reference. Because Fowler also uses for his purposes a structural developmental model with its own characteristic concern for formal structure over particular contents, his work usefully demonstrates, as we shall see, both the merits and the limitations of a functional perspective. What is of concern to us more proximately, however, is Fowler's definition of religion which illustrates the functional paradigm: "Faith. . .is a person's or a community's way-of-being-in-relation to an ultimate environment. . .(which) involves - for individuals and communities - acts of knowing,

8

construing, or composing an apprehension of an ultimate environment" (Fowler, 1978, p. 24).

The functional approach to the study of religion possesses some obvious strengths. It allows us to view faith as a universal human phenomenon operating even in the lives of persons conventionally regarded as "non-religious." As a lens through which to examine conventionally religious persons it permits the researcher to make some very important but hitherto hard to draw discriminations. Studies of religion till now have been conceptually handicapped by the fact that even after investigating the beliefs and practices of individuals there has been something left out of the analysis which accounts for how it is that a religious conviction or identification in fact makes a difference in the actual life and activity of the person in the world. Gordon Allport's influential distinction between "intrinsic" and "extrinsic" religion was only an attempt to grapple with this problem by identifying the level at which religious beliefs took hold of and organized a person's life. When faith is made the fundamental life process to be studies it subsumes the problem of how "religion" fits into a life. One can then ask how a particular belief or ritual practice is or is not part of the total "faith constructive activity" (Fowler) of the individual.

As I suggested above, the functional approach to the psychological study of religion rescues the enterprise from some of the trivialization and confinement of an approach that only concerns itself with persons' stated religious beliefs or attitudes, observable practices and rituals, church attendance, doctrinal orthodoxy, etc. Yet as proposed earlier, from a number of sources the intuition gathers that perhaps functional definitions in their drift towards inclusiveness have blurred crucial features of the phenomenon and have obscured what is unique and distinctive about human religiousness. This might be the position of persons for whom religion is substantively defined. It is to that alternative current in the study of religion that I now direct our attention.

III. The Substantive Approach to the Study of Religion

A substantive approach to defining religion would identify religion in terms of the "meaning contents" of the phenomenon (Berger, 1974, p. 126). Among theorists themselves there is a great diversity in terms of what "meaning contents" are regarded as salient for an understanding of religion "in its essence." On the one hand we have what might be termed "high"

9

substantive definitions represented by the phenomenological school of Religionwissenschaft, and in particular the work of scholars such as Rudolf Otto, Gerardus Van der Leeuw, and Mircea Eliade. For these thinkers the controlling concern is to identify within religious rituals and beliefs that underlying element which makes them uniquely religious.

The "low" practice of substantive definition I would associate with the research of perhaps the majority of American and British social psychologists who have confined themselves almost exclusively to a behavioral definition of religion as "a cultural product analyzable in terms of specific cognitive beliefs or observable behaviors, attitudes testable, practices, etc., and important for its consequential effects on non-religious behaviors, morals, attitudes, etc." (Brown, 1973). Not surprisingly the latter are the group which appropriates exclusively to itself the distinction of doing "empirical research in the study of religion" (Warren, 1976).

Most relevant for the purposes of this book would be the work of those researchers who, adopting a substantive approach, further argue that human religiousness not only involves a necessary content (as, for example, an intention towards the transcendent), but that this content in order to be genuinely religious must somehow be configured as personal. We have already cited one such definition from the side of the sociology of religion, Milton Spiro's definition of religion as "an institution consisting of culturally patterned interactions with culturally postulated superhuman beings" (Spiro, 1966, p. 96). [3] A comparable definition proposed by a psychologist of religion would be R.H. Thouless' suggestion that religion is "a felt practical relationship with what is believed in as supernatural being or beings" (Thouless, 1961, p. 4).

Antoine Vergote, the Belgian psychologist of religious development, offers a more nuanced version of the same definition:

> In spite of the fact that in certain religious quests
> there is a dominant tendency to absorbative union, we
> can only conceive of religion when the sacred pole
> appears as superhuman, or, to use the metaphysical word,
> transcendent. And we consider that there is only
> transcendence when the sacred is thought of as a being
> in some way personal, a center of consciousness and
> will. The importance of salvation presented by the
> sacred lies in a lived relationship with the
> transcendent center of salvific will; though as in human
> love, any other impersonal factors can also play a part
> in the religious quest.
> (Vergote, 1969, p. 14)

10

Even where there is resistance to so explicit a personalization of the object of religious knowing and intending, there is often a conviction that to be religious an individual's <u>relationship</u> to his or her sense of the ultimate must somehow follow the model of the interpersonal. Paul Pruyser represents this setting of the issue of the personal at one remove. He raises the sort of question that follows from the substantive approach: "How much personalization of any God is needed to make belief religious? Or still differently put, where is the borderline between religious beliefs embedded in creed and cult, and philosophical beliefs which function as assumptions or hypotheses even though fervently held?" (Pruyser, 1974, p. 83). [4]

Despite the force of the functional perspective increasingly a substantive approach appears to be exerting a fresh appeal, catching up as it does a number of reigning concerns within the study of religion and the culture at large. There is first of all a certain negative reaction to the functional approach to religion on the grounds that it hides a measure of "bad faith," a loss of interest or a loss of nerve with respect to the radical content of religious believing. Peter Berger fires this salvo from the substantive position with typical forcefulness if debatable accuracy:

> The functional approach to religion, whatever the original theoretical intentions of its authors, serves to provide quasi-scientific legitimations of a secularized world view. It achieves this purpose by an essentially simple cognitive procedure. The specificity of the religious phenomenon is avoided by equating it with other phenomena. The religious phenomenon is "flattened out." Finally it is no longer perceived. Religion is absorbed into the night in which all cats are grey. The greyness is the secularized view of reality in which any manifestations of transcendence are strictly speaking meaningless, and <u>therefore</u> can only be dealt with in terms of social or psychological functions that can be understood without reference to transcendence. (Berger, 1974, pp. 128-129)

Berger's voice is an alert to the possibility that functionalists may have missed or overlooked a concern for content and the accompanying caveats which might be found in their own original theorists. [5] William James, for example, who was cited earlier as a forerunning functionalist, also warned that while religion represented a "total reaction upon life,"not every total reaction upon life deserved to be designated religious. Religious belief for James has a certain "thickness" or positive content. There was "something there"

11

towards which the religious human being pointed him or herself, and that "something" often seemed only adequately considered in personalized terms. Accordingly he wrote, "The universe is no longer a mere it to us, but a Thou, if we are religious; and any relations that may be possible from person to person might be possible here" (James, 1897/1967, p. 211).

A more constructive motive for a concern with identifying a substantive definition of religion is a renewed concern for the way in which faith is mediated through concrete images and symbols. In part this concern reflects the distress attending the collapse of traditional images of the transcendent which has left many modern persons adrift without a way of organizing and speaking their sense of the ultimate. There is a sense that the loss of these images and symbols that in the past were the stay and anchor of a cohesive sense of identity and connection may account for the restless, preoccupying longing and sense of nostalgia that haunts the age (Wheelis, 1958; Homans, 1970). Yet it is not only the decay and dissolution of religion that provokes attention. Perhaps more remarkable is the evidence in our day that the resourcefulness and the creativity of the religious imagination will not be capped. Something there is that both calls into question the adequacy of old imaginings of the transcendent and yet is constantly producing new ones (Bowker, 1973).

A further development that perhaps as much as any other has directed our interest to religious contents has been the experience of contemporary women for whom the traditional Christian images of God as Father have been rendered radically problematic by the emergence of a feminist theological consciousness - the recognition of the political, social and psychological dangers that have attended the hegemony of that imagery. These experiences spotlight a pressing need to try and understand in what way the faith process may or may not require the imaging of a personal transcendent, and that in terms that are familial and parental. What kind of freedom is there to leave behind these configurations of the sacred, with what losses and what sorts of new possibilities?

Finally there are a host of questions which simply get raised in attempting to apply a functional definition of faith like that of Fowler to the actual data of complex human lives, questions which seem to call for some analysis in terms of content. For example, why is it that for some people faith is possible in terms of the inherited structures and images of traditional religion while for others, often from the self-same family or tradition, these symbols must be left behind, rejected, or repressed in order to accomplish the work of

12

faith? Or how does it happen that some images of the transcendent exercise particular power and have a special valence at different periods of history or for different persons? Why do some images of faith endure under one guise or another and others do not survive a generation?

At least in the West, the content that most urgently demands analysis is the persistent presence in the faithing process of our conscious and unconscious images of God. In the lives of persons who maintain a faith thematized in terms of religious symbols these images are unavoidable. They powerfully mediate the spoken and unspoken sense of the individual regarding what is to be trusted and mistrusted, valued or avoided. Yet even for individuals who claim no explicit religious faith or whose faith has apparently moved beyond the mediation of a consciously held representation of God, it is uncanny how often slips of the tongue, unexpected crises, or the candid telling of a life story will reveal the presence of a representation of God that was operative at one time in life and that seems to wait still in some not-quite-forgotten corner where it was left behind, exiled, banished or simply misplaced.

All these are questions which argue that an adequate approach to the study of religion must look at the what of faith and not just the how. Or to put the matter in its most positive form: that all of our many real concerns can only be met in an approach that combines the gifts of both a substantive and a functional understanding of human religion, or, as I shall prefer to say, of human faith.

Logically, the first place to look for this combination of gifts was the psychoanalytic tradition. It was Freud after all who early took seriously the role of the figure of God in the religious development of the individual. However, if one went no further than Freud and the classical psychoanalytic formulations on religion one would also likely not get any further than the stand-off arguments discussed at the beginning of the chapter. Freud attends to personal religious content but assigns it a function that is strictly defensive and necessarily to be outgrown. Fortunately psychoanalytic theory has itself grown beyond the positions which made this sort of reductionism inevitable. It is one purpose of this book to demonstrate how these contemporary developments in psychoanalytic theory make it a prime resource for exploring both the what and the how of faith. In order to appreciate more fully the potential contributions of these developments it would be useful to see how the limitations of psychoanalysis have traditionally been regarded from both the structural and functional perspectives, and hence what the object relations

13

revision within psychoanalysis will have to accommodate if it is to be responsive to the concerns of both positions.

IV.

Point and Counterpoint: Psychoanalytic Theory in the Between

If we assume, contra Berger, that the proponents of the functionalist perspective are not in the main covert secularists, are there other motives to which we might attribute their resistance to the notion that faith must involve in some way an active symbolization or imaging of the transcendent Other? There is one motive that appears to be key, and especially for those who far from being "secularizers" are committed to the recovery of religious faith. For many functionalists it is the shadow of Freud that falls upon the discussion of the "objects" of faith. Wary of the human tendency to project human characteristics on to other entities, real or imagined, psychologists following Freud usually recommend the withdrawal of such projections. This is either done on the epistemological premise that there is no "object" out there to correspond to the projection or to act as a screen for it, or it is done on the therapeutic premise that such projections represent a "splitting" of the psychic structure and a diminishment of the capacity to relate to the "real world." The functionalist position attempts to side step this problem by concentrating its attention on the faith activity of the human subject and avoiding consideration of religion as a unitary phenomenon with a discrete content. Freud, seen from this vantage, falls into the ranks of the substantivists. He follows Freurbach again in promoting the "mischief of reification" whereby it is accepted that religion is a something with a definite and fixed form if only one could find it" (Smith, 1962, p. 47).

There is a sense in which the association of Freud with the Religionwissenschaft tradition is perfectly appropriate. Freud, like Otto, Eliade and others, operated within the same 19th century certainty that religion was a singular or unidimensional "something" and that one could name that "something" by locating the unitary source of religion in some primary historical or psychological reality. [6] Yet from another point of view, Freud fits uneasily in the substantive school. He switches sides on the crucial issue of how it is that the student of religion comes to know his subject, or how it is that religious persons are to be understood. For at least some scholars the method of the substantive approach to the study of religion is to look for the human meaning that

14

must be understood "from within." It is the approach of Weber's Verstehen. W.C. Smith's proposal for understanding a religious statement displays this strategy: "To endeavor not to see what its words and clauses mean. . .but to see what they meant to the man who first uttered them, and what they have meant to those since for whom they have served as expressions of faith" (Smith, 1962, p. 183).

At least in the classical Freudian tradition this "knowing from within" only partially describes the process of achieving a "scientific" understanding of religion Religion as "the universal obsessional neurosis of mankind" represents an act of unconscious self-deception, the exact meaning of which the religious individual can not be aware of until he is able to face those aspects of himself and his world against which religion has served as a defense (Freud, 1927). In this sense Freud is the consumate functionalist outsider whose achievement was to clearly pose the question, "What role or function does such and such a religious action, attitude or affect play within the total economy of the individual psyche?" It was, of course, Freud's conviction, proceeding from a 19th century rationalism, that religion's function would be comprehensible to the extent that it could be demonstrated to be epiphenomenal to other more fundamental but rationally explicable psychic processes. This is the basis for the hope that is his Comtean inheritance, that the power and influence of religion might at least diminish with the advance of reason and scientific thought.

V.   The Tool of Mediation: A Revised Depth Psychology

The fact of the matter is that Freud, or more properly, psychoanalytic theory, does show up on both sides of the substantive-functional conflict. Psychoanalysis took an early and sustained interest in the specific contents of religion, pre-eminently in the individual's and the society's images of the divine. At the same time psychoanalytic theory was primarily concerned with the function these religious contents had in the process of adaptation and defense throughout the human life cycle. Psychoanalytic theory is already, as it were, "in the middle", and as such may be in a unique position to unite the virtues of both the substantive and the functional understanding of human religiousness. To do so, however, it must be demonstrated that psychoanalytic theory has developed to the point that it has incorporated the critiques derived from both positions. Both a functional and a substantive approach to the study of religion come to the Freudian

15

tradition with their respective intellectual demands. These together offer the terms whereby psychoanalytic thought might again be seen as a welcomed partner in the study of religion.

1. A revised psychoanalytic psychology would need to show that it can handle the full range of religious contents. By "full range" I mean that there would need to be a recognition within the theory of a) both maternal and paternal aspects of religious imagery, and b) religious development that moves beyond the images towards, on the one hand, the most sophisticated labors of the theologians, and on the other, the most profound experiences of the named and unnamed saints of the tradition.

2. These contents would have to be treated in a non-reductionistic fashion. That is to say, the role of the symbolic and the imaginative in human development would have to be conceived in such a way as to show how religion outgrows the archaism of its developmental origins and achieves an independent and integral place in the human life and culture.

3. The above calls for a revision of the notion of projection and projective mechanisms that does not foreclose on the question either of the ontic status of these "objects" of projection or on the role of these mechanisms in the ordinary maintenance of the healthy, well-functioning human being.

4. Psychoanalytic investigation needs to demonstrate that it has incorporated the values of "knowing from within" that is the strength of the phenomenological approach to the study of religion. In other words, that in its theory building, particularly with respect to religion and the symbolic life, it has permitted the phenomena to speak for itself.

5. Finally, as the psychological function of faith is more inclusively identified so that it covers the full range of human development, one must be able to show how the processes whereby particular conscious and unconscious religious contents are generated positively relates to the integrating activity of faith.

These are substantial demands, but it is our contention that they are potentially satisfied in what has begun to emerge as a pervasive and influential current within contemporary psychoanalytic thinking object relations theory. In the presentation of the object-relational perspective beginning in Chapter Three it should begin to become apparent how this revision of Freud with its greater attention to preoedipal life history and the role of processes of fantasy and imagination in development meets these requirements. For the present, because of the general unfamiliarity of the term "object relations theory" and because of the confusion that surround the term even within the field, it would be useful to pause and offer a preliminary definition anticipating our later discussion.

VI. What is Psychoanalytic Object Relations Theory?

Object relations theory is not properly a discrete school within psychoanalytic thought though it clearly involves a revision of some of Freud's work and does have implications for the practice of psychoanalysis and psychoanalytic psychotherapy. I take the term to refer to a broad ranging development within psychoanalytic theory which has turned away from the more physicalist or "energy" models of mental operation that characterized early Freud in particular, and appropriated instead those insights in Freud which give pride of place to personal relationship as the matrix within which the human psyche is formed, and as the model for its subsequent operation. The insight central to this perspective is that the person is not constituted by the isolated play of impersonal instinctual energies, but by the inter-play of human persons - both as those relationships actually occur in the world and as they are carried on in conscious and unconscious fantasy or, we might say, as they are internalized. Otto Kernberg, an American exponent of this perspective, offers this description of the approach:

> In broadest terms, psychoanalytic object-relations theory represents the psychoanalytic study of the nature and origins of interpersonal relations, and of the nature and origins of intrapsychic structures deriving from, fixating, modifying and reactivating past internalized relations with others in the context of present interpersonal relationships. Psychoanalytic object-relations theory focuses upon the internalization of interpersonal relations, their contribution to normal and pathological ego and superego developments, and the mutual influences of intrapsychic and interpersonal object-relations.
> (Kernberg, 1976, p. 56)

One question which inevitably arises at this point is the reasonable one, "Since what is evidently at issue in this theory is our relationships, real or imagined, conscious or unconscious, with persons, why employ the term 'object'

17

relations?" In part one could respond that the term is a technical one original to Freud that has become fixed in psychoanalytic discourse in English and therefore is useful for communication within the discipline. More positively it could be pointed out in defense of this language that indeed the human infant's first relationship is not with a "whole person" but with fragmentary perceptions of the person, primally with the mother's breast and eyes. It is precisely as these "part objects" become identified and consolidated in the child's experience that a relationship with the full reality of a whole object (person) begins to become a possibility. Despite this defense of the accepted usage, it must be admitted that "object relations" can be a misleading term if it suggests discrete, statis images that are somehow the fixed possession of the individual. As we shall emphasize repeatedly, what is of concern in this perspective is the dynamic, affective relationship which an individual carries on throughout life with the complex of memories, images and mental representations which arise from the earliest experiences of human relations.

It is a major thesis of this book that one of the most significant object representations with which an individual is in life-long relationship is the object representation of God. The factors which compound to form this representation are many and varied, "the preoedipal psychic situation, the beginning state of the oedipal complex, the characteristics of the parents, the predicaments of the child with each of his parents and siblings, the general religious, social and intellectual background of the household," and even the unique circumstances in which the child may have been first introduced to the possibility of God by parents, neighbors or teachers (Rizzuto, 1979, p. 45). When we shall refer in this dissertation to the "image of God" we shall not mean by that any single "picture" or mental entity, but rather the individual's very personal dynamic relationship to this conscious and unconscious constellation of values, impressions, memories and images. What shall concern us about this object-representation of God is how the individual's relationship to it may make it available or unavailable for the activity of faith.

Gordon Allport once remarked that "a narrowly conceived science can never do business with a narrowly conceived religion. . .only when both parties broaden their perspective will the way to understanding and cooperation open" (Allport, 1950). Object relations theory is one such broadening of a psychological perspective which is ready to do business with a comparably expanded understanding of religion. This enlarged understanding seems to me to be available in the formulations on faith developed first within the Christian theological community but subsequently appropriated by theorists working on the boundaries of psychology and theology.

It is to these definitions of faith that we turn in the next chapter. These understandings of faith and their appropriations by certain psychologists of religion are the intellectual background for an object-relational analysis of faith. It is fitting therefore that some time be devoted to a review of the sources within the Catholic and Protestant traditions which are foundational for the definition and analysis of faith which we shall be elaborating in Chapter Three and Four of this work.

FOOTNOTES CHAPTER ONE

1. For other examples of the Protestant theological response to Freud see Albert C. Outler, Psychotherapy and the Christian Message (New York: Harper, 1954); David E. Roberts, Psychotherapy and the Christian Message (New York: Scribner's, 1953); Reinhold Niebuhr, "Human Creativity and Self-Concern in Freud's Thought,' in Benjamin Nelson, Ed., Freud and the Twentieth Century (New York: Meridian, 1958). For illustrative responses from the Roman Catholic tradition see Roland Dalbiez, Psychoanalytic Method and the Doctrine of Freud, Trans. T.F. Lindsay (London: Longmans, Green, 1941); P. Dempsey, Freud, Psychoanalysis and Catholicism (Cork: Mercier, 1956); Albert Ple, Chastity and the Affective Life, Trans. Marie-Claude Thompson (New York: Herder and Herder, 1966).

2. This shift of terms from "religion" to "faith" parallels developments within the theological community as well. An eloquent example of a definition of faith is found in the work of Richard R. Niebuhr who identifies faith as "a man's whole way of behaving or going out of himself and returning. It includes his whole method of taking hold - intellectually, morally and aesthetically - of the known and 'paying deference' to the unknown" (Niebuhr, 1972, p. 38).

3. Spiro's definition operates within a long tradition of sociological and anthropological definitions that emphasize the relationship to a supernatural Other as the heart of religion. One of the earliest and most influential substantive definitions of religion of this order was proposed by Edward Tylor who declared that religion is "belief in Spiritual Beings" (Tylor, 1871). Tylor's definition or variations thereon have been reasserted down to the present. See Goody, 1961; Horton, 1960; Williams, 1962.

4. Having posed the question, Pruyser himself draws back from defining the divine in personal terms while insisting that our relationship to the images or concepts we develop of the transcendent will, if religious, "partake of the emotional quality of human-object relations" (Pruyser, 1974).

5. It is instructive to note that Berger is addressing what might be called the "second generation" of students of religion who have adopted uncritically the pioneering formulations of Bellad and others. Bellah himself, for whom Berger claims great respect, believed that Freud, Marx and Durkheim, and the "cybernetic theorists" (Parsons, Langer, Cassirer, and presumably Bellah, too) represent a synthesis of the phenomenology of religion school and the rationalist-functionalist view (Freurbach, Hume, etc) (Bellah, 1970, pp. 3-19).

7. The attempt to isolate and distill the "essence" of religion has come under considerable criticism quite apart from the substantive-functional debate. Within the psychology of religion there has been a strong movement, influenced by scholars such as Charles Glock and Ninian Smart to recognize the "multidimensionality" of religion. (For a survey discussion of this issue see Capps, 1974.)

CHAPTER TWO
FAITH: THE THEOLOGICAL VANTAGE

I.   Faith as a Borrowed Term. . . . . p. 23

II.   H. Richard Niebuhr and the Protestant Contri-
      bution to the Definition of Faith: The Protestant
      Question and the Niebuhrian Dilemma . . . . . p. 24

      The Point of Beginning: The Fragmented Self . . .p. 27

      The Goal of Development: Integrated Selfhood. . .p. 30

      Political and Psychological
      Dimensions of the Unified Self. . . . . .p. 31

      The Means of Faith: A Revolution of Imagery . . .p. 32

      Summary. p. 34

III. The Operationalization of a Definition of
      Faith: The Contributions of James Fowler

      The Niebuhr Legacy . . . . p. 34

      Taking up the Task:
      The Faith Development Model. . . . . p. 35

      Fowler's Definition(s) of Faith. . . . . p. 37

      The Research Project . . . . p. 38

      "From Where" and "Towards What"
      in Faith Development Theory. . . . . p. 40

      Summary. p. 44

IV.   The Catholic Vantage on Faith:
      Development and Distinctiveness

      The "Fides Qua" and the "Fides Quae" Distinction p. 45

      The Second Vatican Council
      and the Problem of Faith . . . . p. 46
      The Point of Beginning:
      The Quest for the Real . . . . p. 47

      The Goal of Development:
      The Overcoming of Concupiscence. . . . . p. 50

21

V. William W. Meissner:
A Psychoanalyst Looks at Faith

Deciding on Terms - Grace or Faith? . . . . . p. 52

Faith: From Primal Trauma to Ego Integration   p. 53

The Double Paradox of Faith . . . . p. 56

A Proposed Methodology for the
Study of Religious Experience . . . . p. 58

CHAPTER TWO
FAITH: THE THEOLOGICAL VANTAGE

I.   Faith as a Borrowed Term

As long as a psychology of religion confines the subject of its study to "religion," however controverted the definition of that word may be, conversation can perhaps be contained within the charmed circle of psychological discourse. But when "faith" is made the focus of study we are dealing with a borrowed term. That debt must be acknowledged and repaid in the coin of a respectful hearing of everything the original owners of the concept had to say about its meaning and usage. Faith is a term which derives from the language of a religious community. More particularly, as Gerhard Ebling shows, it derives from Old Testament and later Judaism which passed it into the Christian scriptures where it attained its "unusual intensity" and centrality (Ebling, 1963, p. 207). Any study in the psychology of religion which chooses to use the language of "faith" is therefore working on that vaguely defined, eminently perilous, but hopefully productive boundary area between theology and psychology. As creditors to the Christian theological tradition, psychologists of "faith" necessarily must be in conversation with that tradition. This chapter is about that conversation, its specific content and some of the rules that govern the dialogue.

The major aim of this chapter is to identify the resources for a definition of faith to guide our total investigation. That requires returning first to the religious sources of the term and from there to current contributions of psychologist studying religion who have adopted from those sources the category "faith" to describe the subject matter of their study.

When we examine the Christian tradition we find two distinct though converging strands of reflection on faith which might be very roughly characterized as "Protestant" and "Catholic" approaches. From the former perspective we will look at the uses of faith in the work of H. Richard Niebuhr. Niebuhr is the theologian who perhaps more than any other in modern Protestantism seems to have been aware of problems central to our inquiry: the conflict between a structural analysis and a content analysis, the tension between idolatry and devotion, the necessity for speaking about the personal "object" of faith and yet the inherent religious dangers in that language. When we then turn to James Fowler's empirical inquiry into the structure of faith we will see how it builds upon the Niebuhrian paradigm.

The Catholic approach to faith we will describe by reference to the work of Karl Rahner, contemporary Catholic theologian, whose thought has so powerfully influenced the post-Vatican II Church. Though the influence of Rahner on the thought of Jesuit psychoanalyst William W. Meissner can not be see as directly as that of Niebuhr upon Fowler, nevertheless one can observe certain "family resemblances" which justify the alignment, and the examination of Meissner's contructive study of the psychodynamics of faith.

The assumption that directs our interrogation of both Protestant and Catholic theologians and psychologists of religion is that every definition of faith has behind it a basic understanding of the nature of the human person under two aspects. First, what it is that is seen as the dominant life problem or dilemma with which human beings have to contend in the course of development. In traditional religious language, what is "original sin"? Second, what it is that represents the telos or goal of human development, the optimal human life, the end point of maturation. In religious terms, what is the sanctified life, genuine holiness, spiritual adulthood? One might view these as the "from whence" and the "to where" questions. Every theologian who takes seriously the necessity of having a theological anthropology, and every psychologist asking non-trivial questions of human development, must work implicitly or explicitly from his or her answers to these questions.

II. H. Richard Niebuhr and the Protestant Contribution to the Definition of Faith: The Protestant Question and the Niebuhrian Dilemma

A good number of years ago I attended an ecumenical conference at which a lecturer on the topic of faith began his address with the bold assertion - "I mean to tell you the Protestants have won this one." At a multi-religious gathering it hardly seemed appropriate that a speaker would be trying to score points for one side's orthodoxy or heterodoxy and so I was a bit defensive and puzzled over the meaning of the statement. It actually was several years before I think I finally understood the import of the observation, and more time yet before I realized that I agreed.

What I believe the lecturer meant with his calculated-to-awaken opening line was that with respect to faith, it is the Protestant question that has come to be the dominant form in which the problem of faith is raised in our own day. The statement assumes that in some sense the

24

"Catholic" approach to faith typically begins with the metaphysical question, "Does God exist?" while the Protestant way of coming at the matter is to pose the more existential and life derived question, "How is faith in God possible?" Later in the chapter I will discuss why I believe that the Protestant question has come to be the question of the age, even for those of us nurtured in the Catholic Christian tradition. For now I hold up this question because H. Richard Niebuhr himself begins his investigation of faith by aligning himself with its implicit method and intent (Niebuhr, 1960a, p. 115). What are these?

Posed in the form "How is faith in God possible?," the Protestant question already carries a series of crucial assumptions. The first is that faith is a reality in human life, experienced antecedent even to the explicit evocation of "God". Hence the problem is not posed "How shall we have faith" but precisely, "How shall we have faith in God?" If faith is somehow a fundamental fact of life, then it must have to do with the most basic problems of human existence. The quest for faith begins directly for Niebuhr with his answers to the "from whence" question, the question of what is the foundational human dilemma.

As Niebuhr saw it, the life problem is how to become a self. Human selfhood, he would argue, and not alone, is not simply given with physical existence like the sensory equipment or certain instinctual functions. Becoming a self is an accomplishment and not simply an individual one. It is a social accomplishment. It occurs as a human person, living from birth in a community of other selves, comes to develop a coherent sense of him or herself as a whole, integral agent capable of entering into enduring relationships of loyalty and fidelity with other individuals and with an expanding circle of other persons and communities. Instructed by George Herbert Mead, Harry Stack Sullivan and other theorists of the "social self," Niebuhr continually evoked the commanding idea that to become a self requires the individual to be received from birth into a matrix of relationships with persons that present themselves as trustworthy, that genuinely love him or her as a unique person, and that can receive the love and esteem of the growing child.

Niebuhr's name for that total relational stance towards the reality that supports one's sense of self is faith. Specifically, he defines faith as:

> . . .the attitude and action of confidence in, and fidelity to, certain realities as the sources of value and the objects of loyalty. This personal

25

attitude or action is ambivalent; it involves reference to the value that attaches to the self and to the value towards which the self is directed. On the one hand it is trust in that which gives value to the self; on the other hand it is loyalty to that which the self values.   (Ibid., p. 16)

When Niebuhr uses the word "ambivalent" in the preceding passage he is not using the term in its usual meaning of a mixed attitude of love and hate, like and dislike (although as we shall observe later in the clinical materials, this sort of ambivalence often does characterize our relationship to those object representations that stand behind our faith). In this particular passage Niebuhr means by ambivalence a double movement or valence in the phenomenon of faith. On the one hand faith describes one's trust in and loyalty to that which, or the One who, has a value objective to oneself. On the other hand that same person or reality is significant as that which gives meaning and value to the self. What human persons yearn for is a sense of themselves as good, a sense of themselves as prized, valued and recognized as of worth for being who they are and simply as they are. Yet alone this is not enough, or more accurately it is important for one's sense of being valued that this be extended by another who is herself regarded as being of great value. The human being also desires to locate value, preserve goodness, assign worth in that by which one hopes to be known and recognized. [1]

Consistent with the relational character of faith for Niebuhr is his insistence that this process of trusting and valuing is directed towards an object which is <u>personal</u>, though not necessarily <u>personalized</u>. In other words, the response which is evoked by the object of faith is the response of a self receiving and accepting recognition from another self, regardless of whether the locus of value and trust is conceived of as a person. For example, an individual who has given his loyalty to and received his sense of ultimate value from "the country" will sometimes speak of his sense of gratitude in terms that in other situations would be appropriately applied to an interpersonal relationship. Conversely, we are not surprised to hear persons express feeling of anger, hurt and betrayal towards the institutions or causes which had been the repositories of their trust but which have proven unworthy or inadequate to that trust.

It is the personal character of the initiative and response of faith that is precisely its distinguishing feature. For this reason Niebuhr aligns himself with Luther in asserting that "trust and faith of the heart alone make both God and idol. . . For the two, faith and God, hold close together.

Whatever then thy heart clings to. . .and relies upon, that properly is thy God" (Ibid., p. 119). Niebuhr puts the point even more succinctly in his own words, "Now to have faith and to have a God is one and the same thing. We never merely believe that life is worth living, but always think of it as made worth living by something on which we rely. And this being, whatever it be, is properly termed our God" (Ibid.).

Now the problem with the valued something(s) on which we rely to give meaning and worth to our existence is that they are finite. This means two things. First it means that we are constantly experiencing throughout life the disappointment and betrayal of our successive gods. As children we discover the fallibility and limitations of the omnipotent parents. Later we become disillusioned by turns with favorite teachers, avowed causes, philosophical systems, chosen vocations and careers. In the limit situations of our lives, pre-eminently in the encounter with suffering and death, all gods are tested and sooner or later found wanting. The second vexing difficulty with finite centers of loyalty and value is that they are multitudinous, not only sequentially but simultaneously. As a consequence we find ourselves organizing our lives in terms of a number of different gods, often with competing and conflicting claims upon our fidelity.

The Point of Beginning: The Fragmented Self

We are now closer to being able to state in a useful way Niebuhr's understanding of the dilemma with which faith has to deal. Broadly, the all-commanding life task is the continuous creation of the self, but existentially the way this is experienced is in the ever present struggle to maintain the integrity and unity of the self, the effort to integrate the multiple conflicting aspects of the self. Niebuhr seems to have been profoundly impressed with the problem he termed "inner manyness." He quotes a poem that captures well this sense:

I have too many selves to know the one.
In too complex a schooling was I bred,
Child of too many cities who have gone
Down all bright crossroads of the world's desires,
And at too many altars bowed my head
To light too many fires.
(Niebuhr, 1963, p. 137)

Niebuhr described this situation of the disunity of the self under two discrete but related aspects which I would term the "political" and the "psychological". The political problem of

27

the self is the problem of responding to competing demands for action, all of which come at one with equal moral weight. The underlying yearning for unity and integration in the self prompts the search for some principle by which one can rightly order one's loyalties and energies so as to respond in as comprehensive and inclusive a way as possible. The dilemma is an ethical one or, more accurately, a political one since it can be viewed as a problem in negotiating priorities, aligning loyalties, and effecting an equitable governance of one's resources for action. [2] Niebuhr discusses the problem in his lectures on Christian ethics published as The Responsible Self (Ibid., p. 139):

In this, our personal and social manifoldness, we have been left with a small seed of integrity, a haunting sense of unity and of universal responsibility. But there seems to be nothing in the world of forces acting upon us which makes that internal world actual. There seems to be no One among all the many corresponding to that hidden self which is not free to act integrally amidst the many systems to which it responds.

This political dimension of integrated selfhood is one that keys well to a structural developmentalist paradigm in psychology. If one looks at Niebuhr's statement of the human problem though that particular psychological lens, then it may be appropriately described as the situation of individuals attempting to become disembedded from one set of loyalties, social expectations or ways of viewing obligation in order to respond to wider and more extensive demands for action. Development thus understood is the process of making more and more adequate (i.e., universal, comprehensive, inclusive) cognitive maps whereby one can make meaning out of moral appeals that are presently experienced as hopelessly in conflict. When we later examine the work of James Fowler, who builds his psychological analysis of faith upon a structural-developmental model, we will observe that this political metaphor is predominate, though not exclusive, particularly in his earlier formulations of faith development theory.

The other side of "personal manifoldness" as sketched by Niebuhr could be termed the "psychological", or perhaps more precisely, the intrapsychic. Viewed under this aspect, attention shifts away from the multiple centers of meaning external to the person and concentrates instead on the phenomenon of inner manyness. The emphasis here is on the invisible loyalties which are distributed throughout the self system so that there is not one coherent and cohesive self but

28

rather the experience of many warring "selves" which withdraw from any central self the energies available for relationship and commitment. The phenomenon Niebuhr points to was also well described by theologian David Miller (1974, p.5):

It is a matter of the radical experience of equally real but mutually exclusive aspects of the self. Personal identity cannot be fixed. Normalcy cannot be defined. The person experiences himself as many selves each of which is felt to have autonomous power, a life of its own, coming and going on its own and without regard to the centered will of a single ego. [3]

If the political metaphor for manyness correlates with a structural developmental model of the person, Niebuhr's descriptions of the intrapsychic expressions of personal manifoldness are on first inspection most strongly evocative of the discussion of ego-splitting and fragmentation of the self found within the psychoanalytic literature, and particularly psychoanalytic object relations theory. Niebuhr, like the psychoanalytic theorists, finds this self-divisiveness to have both a conscious and an unconscious dimension. In other words, it is not only that the self is divided in terms of its conscious conflicting loyalties to different centers of meaning and value in the present, it is that aspects of the self and of its history must be cut off and denied to consciousness because the person lacks the means to hold them within a unified history of a meaningful self. He says of this, "When we use insufficient and evil images of the personal or social self we drop out of our consciousness or suppress those memories which do not fit in with the picture of the self we cherish. . .to remember all that is in our past and so in our present is to achieve unity of the self" (Niebuhr, 1941, pp. 83, 86).

The political and the psychological or intrapsychic accounts of the dilemma of self construction are not competing theories of the self, but rather two vantages on a single life process. The political locates the action of self dividedness outside of the individual or at least in "the between" of person and impinging world where life maps are made and unmade. The intrapsychic by contrast locates the activity of self formation in the conscious and unconscious structuring of the psyche; though here too it is the case that this structuring takes place in direct consequence of the interaction of the individual and significant other persons.

29

The Goal of Development: Integrated Selfhood

If the problem of the unification of the self is the dilemma that launches human faith, what is the goal towards which faith is aimed? This is our other question: what are we to hope for? What is the vision of wholeness towards which we are to aspire? Niebuhr's answer drives to his distinction between God and the gods, or between radical monotheism and either henotheism or polytheism. [4] For Niebuhr it is only in so far as individuals and communities come to repose confidence, loyalty and value in that which is ultimately trustworthy, powerful and unfailingly benevolent that they can achieve integrated selfhood. That reality which as the object of final devotion and value decisively conquers fear, mistrust and disunity is what Niebuhr calls God. In his monograph, Radical Monotheism and Western Culture, Niebuhr identifies the God of radical faith as "the principle of being" when it is perceived that "the principle of being, the source of all things and the power by which they exist if good, as good for them and good to them" (Niebuhr, 1960a, p. 38). The life of faith lived towards God as opposed to gods is the life of radical monotheism. A longer selection from Niebuhr offers a better flavor of this rare mode of faith (Ibid., p. 32):

> For radical monotheism the value-center is neither closed society nor the principle of such a society but the principle of being itself; its reference is not on one reality among the many, but to the One beyond all the many, whence all the many derive their being, and by participation in which they exist. As faith, it is reliance on the source of all being for the significance of the self and of all that exists. It is the assurance that because I am, I am valued, and because you are, you are beloved, and because whatever is has being, therefore it is worthy of love. It is the confidence that whatever is, is good, because it exists as one thing among the many which all have their origin and being in the One - the principle of being which is also the principle of value.

Niebuhr's description of radical faith, faith in God as opposed to faith in the gods, is more prescriptive than descriptive, for this kind of faith exists "more as hope than as datum, more perhaps as a possibility than as an actuality" (Niebuhr, 1960a, p .31). Yet just for that reason it is a goal for human development and an answer to the "towards what" question of human existence. "From whence" does human life begin, or what is the basic conundrum of human living? Niebuhr's answer: the problem of becoming a self over against

30

all that works against that possibility and that drives us instead towards personal and social fragmentation. "Towards what" does human growth and development aim, or what shall we hope for in life? Niebuhr's answer: to live lives of radical faith, or - using a parallel psychological language - to live personal and corporate lives of integrated selfhood.

Political and Psychological Dimensions of the Unified Self

What are the features of this integrated selfhood that Niebuhr holds up as the psychological statement of the life of radical faith or faith in God? Here, as before in his accounts of the processes of personal manyness, Niebuhr's descriptions have both a political and a psychological dimension. Politically the integrated self is the self which because of "Being's loyalty to all beings" has made a "decisive choice of God's universal cause" (Ibid, p. 44). Practically this is reflected in an expanding sense of universal community, an awareness of one's solidarity with and responsibility to the "commonwealth of being" that is history long and world wide.

For Niebuhr this sense of communion is not a private, subjective sentiment nor simply a change in cognition. It is manifested behaviorally "by the self in all its roles and relations, or (it) is not expressed at all" (Ibid., p. 48). The unified self of radical faith is not a self that thinks differently about the world in the sense of representing an advance in reasoning ability, so much as a self that acts differently by reason of seeing and being encouraged to respond to the claims of wider and wider reality. Thus when Niebuhr speaks as he does of the "unified reasoning of faith" he emphasizes that he is primarily speaking of "practical reason," the "effort to understand on the part of selves who are deciding how to act in response to action upon them, not for the sake of surviving, not for the sake of maintaining some particular cause but as loyal to the inclusive cause." The reasoning of faith, in other words, does not involve "depersonalized speculative explanations of events that call for no practical decision" (Ibid., p. 48).

Integrated selfhood also has an intrapsychic dimension though Niebuhr has less directly to say about it. The assurance that "because I am, I am valued, and because you are, you are beloved" must make a considerable difference in terms of a person's need to deny, project, repress or otherwise disown undesirable or contradictory aspects of the self. There is a new possibility for a unified history for a person or a people that no longer must expend energy in burying the truth of its past in order to maintain at all costs a sense of the

31

present as good. Presumably, too, the integrated self is now available for relationships with other selves that are characterized by spontaneity and surprise precisely because (my terms) there has been a withdrawal of the projections which have distorted the reality of the other. [5]

For the unified self of radical faith others are no longer the repositories of the frightened and the fearsome creations of our minds, and neither is the "unknown." Hence the person of radical faith would experience an internal freedom to explore, question and discover in all spheres of life in the confidence that one's being is upheld by One always greater than anything encountered in life or in death (Deus semper major). Niebuhr writes of the unfaith that trammels this boldness: "Resistance to new knowledge about our earthly home and the journey of life is never an indication of faith in the revealed God but almost always an indication that our sense if life's worth rests on the uncertain foundations of confidence in our humanity, our society, or some evanescent idol" (Niebuhr, 1941, p. 126).

The Means of Faith: A Revolution of Imagery

In order to finish off Niebuhr's "Protestant" contributions to a definition of faith, we must consider the sustained attention he gave to the further question, "How does this movement towards radical faith, or faith in God, occur?" Niebuhr's answer to that is found under the rubric of revelation or the revelatory event. Some of his most creative writing was done in the service of redefining for the Christian community what that familiar term means for the life of faith. In the language we have been using, revelation would be an event in the life of persons and communities in terms of which they are enabled to radically trust and rely upon the power that gives every man and woman their life and the power that takes that life away. This act of trust endows all aspects of life with new meaning and allows their inclusion in a comprehensive sense of one's life. "Revelation," Niebuhr writes, "means the intelligible event which makes all other events intelligible" (Ibid., p. 69). These "other events" are not events in the world of historical phenomena which are being dispassionately analyzed. They are not facts that can be approached with the tools of discursive reason. Rather they are those events about which we "reason with the heart." They are the hurts and betrayals, triumphs and longings that are the real "inner history," as Niebuhr called it, of an individual and of a community. Revelation does not add a new or a more adequate concept by which to figure out what is going on in history. Revelation addresses itself to the level of the images by which the heart makes its own sense of impinging reality. This insight, that at a most fundamental level the self orients itself to the environing world by means of images and the imagination, is a central contribution that Niebuhr makes to the analysis of human faith. Yet, we need to say just a few more things about the character of these images in order to appreciate Niebuhr's intuition.

"The heart must reason," Niebuhr insisted, "the participating self cannot escape the necessity of looking for pattern and meaning in its life and relations. . . .It cannot make a choice between reason and imagination but only between reasoning on the basis of adequate images and thinking with the aid of evil imaginations" (Ibid., p. 79). Recalling what we have said earlier of the personal character of the objects of faith and the social construction of the self, it should not be surprising that Niebuhr further insists that with respect to the life of faith the images that inform us are inevitably "personal images." "The question which is relevant for the life of the self among selves is not whether personal images should be employed but only what personal images are right and adequate and which are evil imaginations of the heart" [emphasis added] (Ibid.,p.72).

"Personal" for Niebuhr, it is important to remember, is not only a term describing the image itself but gathers together as well the nature of the individual's relationship to that image. Thus the experience of revelation is not just an event that leaves in its wake corrected personal images by which to interpret the whole of the rest of our experience, it is in its essence an experience which evokes from us so personal a response of commitment, confidence and trust that it can only be adequately described as an encounter with infinite person. [6] In the event of revelation there is an experience of being radically known rather than simply of knowing radically. "Revelation means that we find ourselves to be valued rather than valuing, and that all our values are transvalued by the activity of a universal valuer" (Ibid., p. 112). For Niebuhr, of course, the universal valuer is the God of radical monotheism but the encounter with that valuer is decisively mediated in the meeting with the images in Christian revelation of Jesus the Christ. It is Jesus who discloses in the parable of his life, death and resurrection the trustworthiness and enduring faithfulness of the One he calls Father.

When later we bring the psychoanalytic discussion of internalized object representations into dialogue with our definition of faith I believe we shall appreciate how Niebuhr's insight into the necessary relationship between the personal images and the self-constituting action of faith receives validation from the vantage of the psychological.

Summary

It is now possible to summarize some of the principal features of Niebuhr's understanding of faith with our eye towards incorporating these themes into a composite definition and analysis of faith.

(1) Faith is a universal human process. That is, all persons have faith in so far as all persons find meaning for their existence by placing their trust and loyalty in some center(s) of devotion and value that represents for them that which is sustaining, reliable and dependable.

(2) The "meaning" which is relevant for faith is more than cognitive sense-making. It is the meaning relevant to the creation and the maintenance of the life of an integrated self. Thus it involves a sense of who I am in relationship, how I am able to value and to be valued, and all that against the limiting horizon of finitude and death.

(3) Radical faith, or faith in God, is manifest in the total integration of the self by its relationship of trust and fidelity to the ultimate ground of all existence which is experienced as utterly trustworthy and finally benevolent.

(4) Faith involves the progressive creation, elaboration, destruction, and recreation of increasingly more adequate images of self and Others(s) in terms of which the self is constituted in relationship to all that is, was and will be.

III. The Operationalization of a Definition of Faith
     The Contributions of James Fowler

The Niebuhr Legacy

Some theologians leave behind as their life's work massive, completed theological systems which later laborers in the field may inhabit, dismantle, or redesign, but in any event must deal with as a finished work. Other theologians are more programatic than systematic; they gather new materials, model new ways of working with these resources, and then leave behind agendas which are compelling enough to stimulate a next generation of Christian thinkers to exercise their own creativity. H. Richard Niebuhr seems to have been this last sort of theologian. This has probably been most evident in his influence on James Gustafson, James Laney, and a whole generation of Christian ethicists whose productions were seeded by Niebuhr's work. It is also true with respect to his formulations on faith.

In a few last works like the Cole Lectures in Vanderbilt in 1960 and in an essay entitled "On the Nature of Faith" (Niebuhr, 1961), Niebuhr sounds an altar call for an investigation of faith that would involve both theology and the social sciences. He does this in the form of a number of provocative questions. He wonders in writing, for example, what the relationship might be between "religious faith" and "faith in the common life" and says that he suspects a careful study would find them more contiguous than we usually recognize or allow. Then Niebuhr asks, "What are the sources and meanings of those large symbolic patterns in human minds representing the sense of 'being in the world' which are the background and ultimate assumptions (though unanalyzed) of their reasonings and apprehensions?" (Niebuhr, 1961, p. 101) He suggests that a question like this invites one to consider not only the faith of religious believers but the faith of all persons everywhere. Finally, Niebuhr invites theology to investigate the relationship between "interpersonal faith" ("the givenness of personal existence in trust-loyalty relationships") and "noetic faith" or the faith that is found in the inferences that are made about the largest environing world. He presages the findings of subsequent researchers when he anticipates that we will likely find the influences running in both directions between these two modes of coming to trust. Niebuhr's work, both published and unpublished, is replete with these sorts of eminently suggestive questions and equally intriguing hints at what some of the answers might be. [7] What it would take to move into the theological territory he surveys is a strategy for theological inquiry that takes seriously but critically the tools of the human sciences.

Taking up the Task: The Faith Development Model

James Fowler, who did his doctoral dissertation (1974a) on the doctrine of faith in H. Richard Niebuhr, was certainly in an appropriate position to hear Niebuhr's summons to this sort of research, but then so were many other working theologians influenced by Niebuhr's thought. Fowler's own decision to take up the kind of empirical research that ground Niebuhr's theory of faith seems to have been a result of the convergence of several influences. One was Fowler's experience at a resource and retreat center for clergy where he became practiced in listening to the recurrent patterns and themes that emerge as many persons tell their own life stories (Fowler, 1976a, p. 74). Another relevant event was the encounter with the moral development research of Lawrence Kohlberg of the Harvard University Graduate School of Education who has utilized the structural developmental theory of Jean Piaget to investigate the logic of moral reasoning over the course of a life. Piaget's research with its formalist concern for the structures of reasoning as opposed to the content of thought articulates well with a similar tendency in H. Richard Niebuhr to look at the how of faith as a universal phenomenon as opposed to the what of faith in terms of particular dogmatic contents. Structural-developmental theory and the Piagetian semi-clinical interview have provided Fowler with both a congruent psychological theory of development and an adaptable research method for investigating faith along the lines of Niebuhr's unanswered questions. The result has been the accumulation of an impressive body of interview data now entering into a longitudinal phase and the progressive elaboration of a stage theory of faith development that has begun to attract considerable attention, particularly among religious educators (Fowler, 1974a, 1974b, 1976a, 1976b, 1977, 1978, 1981).

As one of the most ambitious and systematic efforts to date to operationalize and empirically study human faith, the work of Professor Fowler will necessarily be in dialogue with this and any other psychological investigation of the topic. Because his work is conducted with the conceptual apparatus of structural-developmental thought it also provides a useful contrast with psychoanalytic object relations theory that will surface some of the issues around the functional-substantive dichotomy in the study of religion. We will not be concerned to conduct a thorough-going critique of the theory or method of Fowler's faith development research. Where its limitations become apparent it will help illumine the potential contributions of a psychoanalytic object relations perspective. As its strengths become evident it will make the point that object relations theory by itself cannot carry an adequate analysis of so complex a reality as human faith. Finally what is required for these two perspectives to be brought into fruitful partnership is the theoretical synthesis of structural developmental theory with contemporary psychoanalysis. This is a separate and considerable task that is slowly underway (Friedman, 1978a, 1978b; Klein, 1976; Shands, 1963; Wolff, 1960; Meissner, 1975).

One contribution of this book may be to demonstrate that our understanding of the dynamics of faith will require the resources of this synthesis. For now, however, what is of immediate significance to us in the Fowler project is the definition of faith that has emerged from the study. Though broadly indebted to the initiatives of H. Richard Niebuhr, it is an original formulation that should offer something towards our own operating definition of faith, even though we will pursue that definition within a different theoretical framework. In the rest of this section then, we will only examine enough of the Fowler research to become clear on the dimensions of his definition of faith that can contribute to our project.

Fowler's Definition(s) of Faith

Every essay that Fowler has written on his research wrestles afresh with the problem of how to get said what human faith is at base about. The result is that running though his writing of the last seven years there is a provocative accumulation of statements which develop or emphasize now one and now another aspect of Niebuhr's idea that faith is a universal activity. One way of trying to express that idea has been for Fowler to assert that faith properly understood is a verb rather than a noun. "Faithing" rather than faith comes closer to capturing the dynamic character of the action that is the target of our inquiry. Yet elsewhere Fowler strains at the limits of even that metaphor. The activity that he desires to describe can be viewed under so many aspects and is so comprehensively organizing that he can also call it a "felt sense" or if he speaks of it as a verb, the verb becomes "to be." Hence faith is defined at one point as "a mode of knowing and being in which we shape our lives in relation to more or less comprehensive convictional assumptions about the limiting conditions of our lives" (Fowler, 1977).

The problem behind the plethora of definitions is not only the limitations of language, and the subtlety and complexity of the object of description, it is the limitations of the psychological theory that Fowler desires to apply but not be trapped by. Fowler, like H. Richard Niebuhr, wants to be able to talk about faith as an activity constitutive of the self, but the theory which he employs was constructed to deal with the development of moral logic or the forms of reason, and not, strictly speaking, with the dynamics of self-esteem maintenance and identity formation which we might assume to be central to the life of a self. Hence Fowler wants to insist that when dealing with faith what is at stake is not simply the rational but also, borrowing Willian James' term, the "passional." Thus Fowler's work may also be viewed as an effort indirectly to enlarge the work of Piaget in the direction first of incorporating the affective dimension of knowing,and second of linking the knowing process with the dynamics of identity formation. [8] It is a difficult endeavor and it accounts for

37

the need to make secondary and even tertiary qualifications. So, for example, Fowler will write that faith involves the "making, maintenance and transformation of human meaning," but must follow this with a stiff reminder that the "meaning" that matters for human faith is not simply "making sense" or logical coherence of something, but has to do with answering such profoundly affective and intimate questions as "with whom or what am I ultimately in relationship?" and, "what is the character and intention of that reality with which I am in relationship?"

A highly abstract definition of faith which exhibits the effort to hold together the heritage of H. Richard Niebuhr (and Mead, Buber and Royce) with the vantage of Piaget and Kohlberg is the following (Fowler, 1977):

Faith (is)
-the process of constitutive knowing,
-underlying a person's composition and maintenance of a comprehensive frame (or frames) of meaning.
-generated from the person's attachments or commitments to centers of superordiante value which have power to unify his or her experience of the world,
thereby endowing the relationships, contexts and patterns of everyday life - past and future - with significance.

In order to be able to appropriate from this and other definitions of faith some of the genuinely guiding insights that are there, it is necessary to show something of how this definition serves to direct concrete inquiry into the faith of ordinary men and women.

The Research Project

Fowler's investigation of faith, as we have observed, is shaped by two functional perspectives: the tacit functionalism of H. Richard Niebuhr and the explicit functionalism of Piagetian structural-developmental thinking with its careful attention to the "implicit rules underlying consciousness" rather than the specific contents of consciousness as such (Fowler, 1978, p. 34). From the Piaget-Kohlberg tradition Fowler also adopted and adapted a research method that has been singularly productive, the Piagetian semi-clinical interview (Piaget, 1929; Elkind, 1964). [9] This involves an extended interview in which the interviewer so far as possible attempts to listen for the spontaneous emergence of the subject's way of making meaning out of the moral and existential limit situations of their life. Specific questions can be asked about God but the clear preference is for the unsolicited emergence of religious materials in the course of a conversation that touches on the individual's responses to death, loss, suffering, moments of joy or ecstacy, intimacy, vulnerability, beliefs, rituals and values. An interview is then analyzed with the intention of trying to discern "formally describable patterns or structures of thought, of value, of constitutive knowing." [10] The gold that is sought by the alchemy of genetic or developmental analysis is "stages," the precipitation of these patterns into structured wholes which can be found to occur universally and in the same invarient sequence. Fowler has identified six such stages of faith development that parallel, not surprisingly, the six stages of Kohlberg's moral development model. These stages with approximate average age at which one would expect to see their consolidation are as follow (Fowler, 1976a):

Stage One: Intuitive-Projective Faith (age 4 - 7)

Stage Two: Mythic-Literal Faith (age 6½ - 11)

Stage Three: Synthetic-Conventional Faith (age 12 - adulthood)

Stage Four: Individuating-Reflexive Faith (age 18 - adulthood)

Stage Five: Paradoxical-Consolidative Faith (minimum, around 30)

Stage Six: Universalizing Faith (minimum, around 40)

Fowler says in general description of these stages that they are "tentative efforts to 'model' a sequence of certain wholistic patterns of feeling, valuing, thinking and committing." Evidence not only of the tentative character of the stage descriptions, but also of the genuinely scientific character of this research is found in the efforts Fowler and his colleagues have made to elaborate and refine the stage descriptions in order to accommodate new data and insights. One example of this is the identification of several discrete aspects of each stage which might be traced as separate developmental strands. The idea of organizing a developmental model in this fashion is strongly suggestive of similar strategies in psychoanalytic model building, in particular Anna Freud's notion of the "developmental line" (A. Freud, 1965). This concept has also been used by Gedo and Goldberg (1973) to construct a comprehensive model of psychological development. A parallel presentation of these lines of development as described by Fowler in two separate works exhibits how the system has attempted to become more precise

39

and discriminating in its identification of the components of faith.

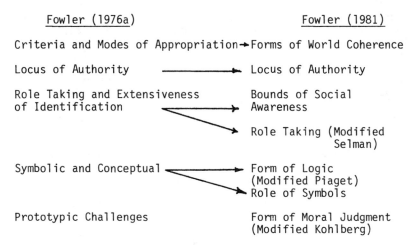

Fowler (1976a)   Fowler (1981)

Criteria and Modes of Appropriation→Forms of World Coherence

Locus of Authority   ────────→ Locus of Authority

Role Taking and Extensiveness   Bounds of Social
of Identification   ──────────→ Awareness

                                            Role Taking (Modified
                                                        Selman)

Symbolic and Conceptual ──────────→ Form of Logic
                                            (Modified Piaget)
                                            Role of Symbols

Prototypic Challenges   Form of Moral Judgment
                                            (Modified Kohlberg)

Note: The suggestion in the graphic that the descriptive contents of certain categories in the earlier list are differentiated in the later formulation is my own surmise rather than Fowler's. Nevertheless, I believe it is largely accurate without wanting to claim that the later categories have only the content of the first set of descriptions.

"From Where" and "Towards What" in Faith Development Theory

It is now possible to interrogate Fowler's formulations on faith in the same way we approached the theological and psychological reflections of H. Richard Niebuhr. First, underlying the discussion of faith, what assumption is being made about the beginning point of human development, the foundational life dilemma or challenge which initiates the process of growth ("from where")? Second, what assumption is being made about the horizon of possibility or trajectory of human development ("towards what")?

Given the inheritance of Niebuhr's analysis, we might assume that it is the problematic of the self's cohesive maintenance that is the life issue that grounds Fowler's concept of the "from where" of faith development. But this is never as explicitly stated in Fowler's work as it is in

40

Niebuhr's and hence it is harder to find in Fowler a concise answer to the "from whence" question. Here again it would seem to be the influence of the structural-developmental model with its characteristic avoidance of depth psychology's preoccupation with pathology that is behind Fowler's relatively slender discussion of the vicissitudes of human development. Thus though Fowler sets out in a 1976 version of the model a set of "prototypical challenges" with which faith has to deal at each stage of development, these are deleted in a 1978 formulation of the model. This reluctance to describe faith in terms of a life trauma or injury that must be overcome or a challenge that must be mastered seems to be the influence of the more ameliorative bent of structural developmental thought. For a developmental or stage model to avoid the charge of being elitist or hierarchical, it must maintain that while later stages may be described as "higher" that must be interpreted with reference to some life task as "more adequate" and not "better." The language of developmental fixation, immaturity or repression is never evoked because of its presumed invidious connotations. As an example, Fowler does not explore the phenomenon of "inner manyness" that so engaged Niebuhr in his description of the foundations of faith. Similarly, while he includes a protostage of "primal faith" and asserts eloquently that "the quality of mutuality and the strength of trust, autonomy, hope and courage developed in this phase underlie (or undermine) all that comes later in faith development" (Fowler, 1977), he does not suggest the psychic processes by which this undermining might take place or call much attention to it in discussion of subsequent faith development.

It would be truer to Fowler's own developmental preferences not to assume that his answer to the "from whence" of faith is coextensive with that of H. Richard Niebuhr. Rather, we might more accurately summarize Fowler's position like this: every human person is faced with the same problem, to find their way through this world in the appropriate way demanded by their age and life situation. [11] For that task everyone comes adequately equipped with a basically unflawed cognitive apparatus that functions to make emotional and intellectual sense of the widest context of human living and dying ("the ultimate environment"). What is the human person "up against" in the developmental process? Fowler's reply might very well be: the demand to find a livable and enduring answer to the question, "what are we finally up against?"

It is as one moves into the six stages proper that the value presuppositions of the faith development model begin to emerge and the "to where" vision of the telos of human development comes into focus. In part the major aspects of this vision derive from formulations about the trajectory of growth described by structural developmental theory. For example, three lines of faith development are taken over directly from Piaget, Kohlberg and Selman. With respect to "form of logic" in faith, attainment of Piagetian formal operational thinking is necessary but not sufficient condition for the highest faith development (Fowler, 1977, p. 23). The "form of moral judgment" aspect of faith follows Kohlberg's stages of moral reasoning so that the drift of development is towards principled thinking. The person of faith is at his/her furthest development something of a Kantian moralist with a belief in "the validity of universal moral principles and a sense of personal commitment to them" (Fowler, 1978, P. 32). [12]

Under the aspect of "role taking" Fowler's faith development schemata follows Robert Selman's formulations on stages of natural role taking (Selman, 1974). However Selman's constructions only carry the description up to stage three of Fowler's faith development model at which point an individual is capable of adopting a mutual interpersonal perspective. Beyond that the direction of the development of role taking, like other features of higher development in the faith development model, seems to be most indebted to those liberal Christian theological commitments and values which Fowler essentially shares with H. Richard Niebuhr. Thus faith moves in this aspect towards wider and more inclusive capacities for empathy and solidarity until in its furthest reaches it evolves a mutuality with the "commonwealth of being."

In the aspect of faith designated "locus of authority" the developmental process is marked by a progressive assumption by the individual him/herself of responsibility for critically evaluating on the basis of internal experience the authority of significant others, valued groups, ideological communities, and principled arguments. The end point of this line of development is not a solipsistic self-validation, however. At the rarely observed stage of universalized faith, authority inheres "in a heart and mind purified of egoistic striving and attentive to the requirements of Being" (Fowler,1978, p. 89).

In the hierarchy of development sketched out in Fowler's well nuanced phenomenology of faith, the capacity to tolerate complexity, paradox and conflict is valued over dichotomizing thinking that simplifies at the cost of accurate perception. The faith that is the goal of development is modest, tentative, non-imperializing, and yet also capable of genuine commitment even at the price of radical self-sacrifice. With respect to its use of symbols faith passed through the disenchantment of primary naivete, comprehends what is "really" going on in symbolization and yet comes out on the other side with a post-critical capacity to reshape and reground symbolic life in the individual's own intuitions of transcendent reality (Ricouer's secondary naivete).

As I have observed earlier, Fowler has tried to be authentically scientific at least in so far as he has worked to include within his account of faith development the full range of phenomena which his investigation has persuaded him are important. Hence one observes in the successive descriptions of the faith development stages some effort to find a place for the unconscious in the faith process. In the description of "individuative faith" (stage four), for example, the individual is said to attend "minimally to unconscious factors influencing its judgments and behavior." At the next higher stage, "conjunctive" faith, there is a heightened receptivity to "the ambiguous hidden mystery of the self and other selves" (Fowler, 1977). Perhaps the one area which is most distinctively in the ascendancy in the faith development model is the topic of imagery and the imagination. [See especially Parks, 1980] It is also the issue which poses most clearly the question of the adequacy of a purely functional account of human faith.

The mandate to explore the role of images and image-making in the life of faith is one that comes from the seminal initiatives of H. Richard Niebuhr. As noted, for Niebuhr the images that were most relevant for the life of faith were those which were both configured as personal and responded to from a depth of the faithful individual that was also uniquely personal. There is a sense then in which Niebuhr, while proposing a functional definition of faith, is not strictly a functionalist. Niebuhr, like James, would want to say that for the man or woman of faith there is "something there" towards which faith is oriented, and that something is, by the very nature of the developmental process, more adequately known as a "who" or a "thou" than as an "ultimate environment." Certainly Niebuhr would insist that for the person brought to radical faith through the Christian revelation there is the personal mediation of the figure of Jesus pointing beyond himself to a God whose presence tracks the sparrows in their flight and who hears the protests of the widow. Even for the person who construes his or her faith outside of the Christian tradition, the locus of faith, while not a "person" is nevertheless unmistakably "personal" in Niebuhr's use of that term. There is real question, however, whether a structural developmental model which attends strictly to the formal character of the faith constructive activity can give full play and proper weight to all that it is being asked to contain.

The role of personal images of the transcendent is the most important element that seems neglected in Fowler's faith development model, but there are other aspects of faith that are slighted or left out entirely. We have already mentioned a lack of attention to the place of intrapsychic processes in faith, particularly to those changes in self and object representation which occur in and through the development of faith. It is indeed the whole relational dimension that is insufficiently recognized in the faith development model to date. Hence the Fowler faith development model gives considerable attention to the development of the capacity to tolerate paradox yet does not address the capacity to tolerate ambivalence, i.e., the coexistence of powerful and opposing emotions towards oneself and others. What too of the relationship between faith and the capacity to sustain interpersonal intimacy and to contract particular commitments?

Summary

The significant contribution of the faith development research of Fowler and his colleagues has been to assemble among the most comprehensive and detailed descriptions of patterns of Western faith that are anywhere available. Controversy arises at the point of articulating a theory of interpretation and classification that makes sense of the data. It is my own judgment that the structural developmental model that enables Fowler to see so much also screens out other aspects of faith which we would want to insist with Niebuhr are important to acknowledge. Prominent among these features of faith are the influence of unconscious elements in the constellation of any given faith position, the mediating role of personal images of the transcendent in the reasoning of faith, and the interaction between significant personal relationships, past and present, and the structure of faith. At the same time what Fowler's work does offer towards our own study of faith is considerable:

(1) The strategy to approach faith as a multi-dimensional process that may be profitably studied by fretting out its distinct though related aspects, each of which has its own discrete line of development.

(2) The insight that faith involves a process that is "both rational and passional," cognitive and affective.

(3) The notion of faith as a process of map-making or way-finding, an original formulation that should take on added meaning when applied in the context of psychoanalytic object relations theory.

The theological reflections of H. Richard Niebuhr and their appropriation to a psychological analysis by James Fowler represents what I have chosen to call a "Protestant" perspective on faith. There is, however, another tradition of reflection which I have typed the "Catholic." Historically it has been seen as contrasting and even contradictory to the Protestant approach to faith. While in our own time these traditions are increasingly convergent, the Catholic vantage does retain its own distinctive style and emphases, something of which we shall want to incorporate in our own definition and analysis of faith.

IV. The Catholic Vantage on Faith: Development and Distinctiveness The "Fides Qua" and "Fides Quae" Distinction

A traditional approach of Catholic theologians to the analysis of faith has been to distinguish between fides quae creditur, faith as knowledge of revealed truth (i.e., believing that God reveals himself in Christ), and fides qua creditur, faith as personal encounter with and trusting obedience to that God that is revealed (i.e., believing in God). In the years immediately preceding the Second Vatican Council there is little doubt that it was the first definition of faith, the identification of faith in terms of epistemology, that had pride of place in Catholic thinking on the subject.[13] Though the second meaning of faith was clearly recognized, to emphasize it overmuch was felt to lead to the errors identified with the Protestant position of Luther, the formulations of the theological existentialists like Kierkegaard, or the condemned opinions of fideism. The 1967 edition of the Catholic Encyclopedia asserted, for example (Buescher, 1967, p. 798):

> A purely subjective explanation of the nature of
> faith based on a psychological analysis and
> phenomenological description of the act of believing
> is likely to lead, if the method is exclusive, to
> antidogmatic positions. . . Catholic tradition
> recognizes these subjective aspects of the theology
> of faith and of believing, although it attaches no
> more than a secondary and derivative importance to
> them. Its concept of faith is more objective,
> looking more to who and what is believed.

This emphasis upon faith as a species of real, albeit supernatural, knowledge promoted the sort of metaphysical speculation which H. Richard Niebuhr likely had in mind when he contrasted with the Catholic approach to faith his own more existential and hence more "Protestant" vantage on faith. With the Second Vatican Council, however, the ground of theological discourse has shifted dramatically so that it is now no longer possible to draw so sharp a distinction between Protestant and Catholic perspectives on faith. I would have to agree with the speaker quoted earlier who maintained that "the Protestants have won this one." To the extent that the conversation on faith within Catholic theological circles has relocated itself in the arena of the existential, the Protestant approach to the problem of faith has indeed become ascendent. The lived experience of persons of faith has become the general starting place for reflecting upon faith. With greater frequency we find Catholic writers concerning themselves with the activity of faith or "believing," preferring the notion of faith as a verb to the older idea of faith as a noun (Kennedy, 1973). Yet in examining some of the forces behind this shift in approach we will discover that the Catholic tradition still brings to the consideration of faith its own distinct set of emphases and concerns. Some of these have particular relevance for our own emerging definition of faith.

The Second Vatican Council and the Problem of Faith

Beyond a doubt it was the theological groundswell of the Second Vatican Council that re-aligned the Church's discourse on faith. Gregory Baum holds that the key shift was in the Council's interpretation of the character of revelation which had the effect of expanding the understanding of faith in two dimensions, the universal and the personal, or, as I shall prefer to call them, the horizontal and the vertical (Baum, 1969). [14] The change in the dimension of the universal or the horizontal was a movement away from a concept of revelation as a fixed body of set truths which entered human history at a certain point and towards a view of revelation as "an ongoing reality in history. . .completed in Jesus Christ" (Ibid., p. 5). Karl Rahner, whose writings so broadly influenced the Council Fathers, sets out perhaps the clearest statement of the basis for this enlarged understanding of faith (Rahner, 1968, p. 310):

> As a result of God's universal salvific will and the
> offer of the supernatural grace of faith as an
> abiding feature of man's mode of existence as a
> person, every human being, even previous to the
> explicit preaching of the Christian message, is
> always potentially a believer and already in
> possession, in the grace that is prior to his
> freedom, of what he is to believe (i.e., freely
> accept): God's direct self-communication in Christ.

Faith is extended horizontally as a universal human reality that is not restricted within the boundaries of

46

specific historical communities of belief. The task of Christian evangelism consequently must be reconceived. The missionary function of the Church is not to impart a body of knowledge alien to the history and experience of the particular culture, but rather to "endeavor to develop the already existing faith into its full Christological and ecclestical, explicit, social, consciously professed form" (Ibid., emphasis author's).

The universalizing or horizontal expansion of the definition of faith also implies a vertical extension of faith in the realm of the personal, an extension in depth. Faith is a reality developmentally prior to its explicit formulation in terms of a particular symbolic system. The roots of faith go down to the very sources of human personality and draw upon that which constitutes the human being as a unique self. Hence the theologian of faith is invited to look for faith not only outside of his environing community of belief, but in his own life is directed to interrogate his earliest and his most interior experience in order to find the ground of that faith. As Rahner writes, "to lead to faith (or rather, its further explicit stage), is always to assist understanding of what has already been experienced in the depth of human reality as grace" (Ibid.).

The Second Vatican Council's renewal of a theology of faith in many respects simply reaffirms and remandates that perennial Catholic concern to understand proto-religious experience, or how it is that grace perfects nature, gratia perficit naturam. What is new is that this project is now recognized as absolutely central to the task of fundamental theology. Contemporary Catholic theology seems to have decided as it were that our answer to the "from whence" question of theological anthropology must be the basis for the whole structure of Christian doctrine. What sort of answers have begun to appear?

The Point of Beginning: The Quest for the Real

For Karl Rahner the answer to the "from whence" of the human condition is itself a question, or, more accurately, it is the human person as questioner. What is given as the starting point of faith is the character of the human as one who interrogates being. It is Rahner's conviction that, properly understood, "the whole 'system' of doctrines of faith would appear as the one complete answer to the inescapable primordial question of human existence regarding the relationship between the absolute mystery (called God) which forms its ground and the existence itself" (Ibid., p. 311). It would be instructive to compare such a "Catholic" formulation of this "inescapable primordial question of human existence" with what we have taken to represent for us as a "Protestant" statement of the foundational life problem facing faith.

H. Richard Niebuhr might have said that the question that launches the project of human faith is something like, "how shall I be a whole self?" or, as that question is experientially known, "whom shall I trust?" The question receives its great power in Protestant theology because it arises from a total and persuasive vision of human existence as haunted by mistrust, brokenness, and alienation. I believe it would not be far off the mark to state that underlying this vision is a deficit model of human functioning in which faith must strive to overcome the burden of a flawed beginning and make up for some deep seated injuries to the integrity of the self or human wholeness. There is a certain congruity then between this theological anthropology and the fundamental pessimism of classical psychoanalytic metapsychology that has not been lost to observers standing on the boundary of theology and psychology. [15]

By contrast, Catholic statements about the human roots of faith typically are more concerned with how it is that the human person is positively impelled, persuaded, beckoned to reach out towards the yet more that is God. Rather than a deficit model of human functioning, there operates a sense of faith as proceeding from a plenum, a fullness of life which of its very nature is always pointing beyond itself to the "life more abundant" of which Jesus spoke (John 10:10). Interestingly, it is here that the perduring Catholic concern for the epistemological character of faith has reasserted itself in a fresh and fascinating fashion. Faith, the argument goes, is indeed describable as a species of human knowing, but knowing that is not detached of "merely intellectual" activity. As used by Rahner, knowing carries with it the full biblical sense of a total human activity in which one enters into a relationship which participates in the reality of that which we desire to know. What we long to know is reality, that which is real, enduring, ultimately true. The primal human question which is the beginning of faith might then be best put, "What is real?"

Jesuit theologian Michael Buckley in a superb essay, "Transcendence, Truth and Faith," makes the point that this intention towards the real which is the whole dynamism of the mind does not proceed from a lack of reality or a deficiency in knowing except in a relative way. Rather from the very beginning our life long yearning to know already assumes a horizon of intelligibility that holds out for us a promise that this quest even if never completed will never ultimately be frustrated (Buckley, 1978, p. 645):

The drive of the mind is towards the real. The drive of the intellectual search is for more inclusive contexts in which the real, either understood or simply encountered, exists. Even the drive for meaning is not for abstract formulae which bear no relationship to existence, whether possible or actual, but towards those which provide an understanding of and a context for everything affirmed as real. Human inquiry takes place within a primordial grasp of the real and is an effort to deepen and extend that grasp. The real is found - or, rather, speaks to me - right from the beginnings of rationality.

The further move of the argument of course is to analyze this "endlessly intelligible or infinitely rational" horizon of all knowing as the Absolute or the Infinite and that as finally, paradoxically, incomprehensible or sheer mystery. It is perhaps the difference between conceiving of mystery as a wall which one runs into and must acknowledge as limiting and thinking of it as the endless inexhaustible source of solvable problems. It is this absolute mystery "present to consciousness as the asymptotic horizon of its transcendence" that Buckley identifies as the experience of God. He is quick to acknowledge as he does this that God is not present thematically to consciousness at the level of our ordinary knowing and yet is there anonymously as the direction or horizon of our consciousness.

There seems to me to be something of great value and wisdom in the Catholic association of faith with a fundamental hunger to know what is "really real" and to view that drive as the developmental inheritance of "a primordial grasp of the real and. . .an effort to deepen and extend the grasp." Anticipating a later discussion, I would suggest that this intuition which has taken shape within contemporary Catholic thinking about faith converges with a theme that has also come to prominence within the psychoanalytic study of child development. In its own way psychoanalytic object relations theory has concerned itself with just such a drive but "from the inside," that is, from the subjective experience of feeling oneself, or failing to feel oneself to be real and to be in contact as an agential self with a world that is itself real. It is a significant discovery of the psychoanalytic clinicians and theorists with whom we shall be dealing that there is a human grasping to know, i.e., to be in relationship to the real

49

which is as fundamental as the need for breath or bread. This conviction is derived from the analysis of persons who may be functioning in the world but whose presenting plaint is that they feel dead inside, unreal, insubstantial.

From the reconstruction in analysis of the developmental histories of such persons, as well as from the direct observation of parent-child interaction, psychoanalysis has attempted to understand how the growing human person is gifted with that "primordial grasp of the real" which makes the adult sense of reality an achievement most persons are fortunate enough to take for granted. In charting the complex developmental history of the human sense of being real and being in relationship to the real, psychoanalytic theory has begun to offer a psychological foundation for this traditional Catholic concern for the epistemological dimension of human faith. We shall return and consider this at greater length when we locate this aspect of faith within our own compound definition.

The Goal of Development: The Overcoming of Concupiscence

To recapitulate: the origin or "from whence" of faith from the perspective we are calling "Catholic" is in the human being's natural conatus or intention towards Reality Itself, that is, towards God. Yet this drive to involve oneself fully in the fullness of life is itself known more in its weakened and flawed character than in its potency and completeness. [16]

The parallel to H. Richard Niebuhr's argument that we know faith more under the conditions of unfaith immediately suggests itself. Indeed, a Catholic analogue to Niebuhr's notion of the inner manyness of the human self might be found in Karl Rahner's discussion of concupiscence: "The impossibility of being able to commit oneself totally at every moment - the impossibility of a total making--of-oneself in every moment what one wants to be" (Rahner, 1967a, p. 21). [17] In other words, the human person is unable to fully enter into any of his or her moral actions, including and especially those acts by which one intends a relationship to the mystery of God.

In all our movements towards knowing there is that in us which does not want to know. In all our efforts to meet and be met by that which is real and lasting, at some level of our being something is reserved from that meeting, some part of ourselves holds back in fear, in doubt, in the sheer inertia of old ways of knowing and relating which however unsatisfying are at least familiar and hence seem safer than the unknown and untried. The "from whence" of faith by this analysis is not only the conatus towards Divine reality, it is also the

50

resistence to that pull which Rahner terms "concupiscence." But such an analysis also implies the goal or direction of faith's development in terms which have a visible psychodynamic aspect. Faith operates against the grade of human concupiscence to gradually increase the "radical existential depth" of the person's actions, to intensify "man's capacity for an ever more total self-commitment by ever deeper personal acts" (Ibid., p. 21).

Rahner's account of the goal, or what we have called the "to where" of faith, certainly resonates with H. Richard Niebuhr's vision of the life of integrated selfhood that is the subjective face of faith in the God of radical monotheism. Similarly Rahner would find himself in strong agreement with fellow Jesuit theologian Avery Dulles that "faith is not the addition of new truths to the human intellect; faith is, rather, a transformation of human consciousness" (Dulles, 1971, p. 14). Yet just as strongly would Rahner insist that this transformation of human consciousness, while it may involve processes of psychic integration leading to a deeper discovery of one's own personality, is inadequately described simply by an account of those processes. The new consciousness of faith is not comprehensible apart from the positive content of what faith grasps, "the acceptance of God's self-communication in Christ."

Following Rahner, the descriptions of the fullness of faith that are found in contemporary Catholic theology and devotional literature have a texture and richness that is not found in the more psychological and yet oddly bloodless notion of "integrated selfhood" or its equivalents. They are accounts of how one lives individually and in community when one has grown by grace to recognize that one's own most personal and most profound longings are at their depth co- existent with what it is that God wants for us - a life of fellowship with God and with all creation patterned on the intimacy of Christ with the Father. In consequence one finds that phenomenologies of the goal or telos of faith return again and again to the language of "self-commitment" (Rahner), self-donation and self-dedication (Wright, 1978), and courage which "as the courage of Christ means sharing the form of his life and interpreting one's own life accordingly" (O'Donovan, 1978, p. 383).

To be fair, while it is less explicit in claiming its Christological paradigm, H. Richard Niebuhr's rendering of the maturity of faith as citizenship in the commonwealth of being is certainly congruent with these portraits of the person of faith. Nevertheless, what these Catholic descriptions of the goal of faith tend to emphasize (and what we have found

51

understated in the writings of both Niebuhr and Fowler) is the notion that the telos of faith has something to do with love - with the character and quality of life lived among others on behalf of others. [18] It is this aspect of the "to where" of faith which I would hope would find a place in any fully adequate definition of faith.

We have seen how the work of theologian H. Richard Niebuhr was influential on James Fowler in his operationalization of faith as a category for psychological investigation. Both writers were chosen not only for being in some important sense representative of their tradition but also with a frank eye towards their potential contributions to a definition of faith that serves the purposes of this present dialogue with contemporary psychoanalytic thought. Our reading of the Catholic tradition on faith has been selective and for the same reason. To parallel our treatment of the Protestant vantage on the definition of faith, I would now like to consider how a Catholic psychologist of faith approaches the psychodynamics of faith. The debt that W.W. Meissner may owe to his tradition, and particularly to any one exemplar of that tradition, is in no way as explicit as Fowler's relationship to Niebuhr. Nevertheless we can discern a set of concerns within Meissner's work on faith which are distinctively "Catholic." Perhaps it is equally instructive to observe with Meissner, as we did with Fowler, that the system of psychological theorizing which one chooses to think with can be every bit as influential on how one approaches faith as any specifically religious loyalties.

V.   William W. Meissner: A Psychoanalyst Looks at Faith
       Deciding on Terms - Grace or Faith?

       The contributions of Jesuit psychoanalyst William Meissner to the psychology of faith have been made in a number of suggestive essays on faith written over the last ten years. While his approach has been neither systematic nor empirical, he has identified the major issues that face a revised psychoanalytic investigation of religious faith and begun to interrogate faith selectively using for that purpose the conceptual resources of object relations theory (Meissner, 1964, 1966, 1969, 1977a, 1977b, 1978a). More to the immediate point of this chapter, Meissner's essays present a composite definition of faith that contains important features that cannot be neglected in framing our own understanding of faith processes. As succinctly as possible I will lay out that definition of faith, locating it both in the context of Meissner's general psychoanalytic approach and in terms of what one might presume are some of his value loyalties as a Catholic Christian.

It is significant, I believe, that Meissner first enters print on the subject of religious development not with an examination of faith but rather with a preliminary study of the psychology of grace (Meissner, 1964, 1966). Grace is the tradition's term for the way in which God shares God's nature with human persons, not in such a way as to annihilate or cancel out human personality but rather to fulfill and transform it. [19]

Again the scholastic dictum, gratia perficit naturam, grace perfects nature, offers the warrant to look for the continuities between human developmental processes, understood using the best resources of the human sciences, and the transforming activity of God in our lives, interpreted in the light of revelation and the Church's faithful reflection upon that experience of the transcendent (i.e., tradition). [20] But grace proves an awkward term to which to attach a - "psychology of." In traditional usage grace refers to the "God-ward" side of a spiritual reality - the mysterious, gratuitous activity of the divine in human life. Needed is the "human-ward" face of that reality where the action of grace can be traced in the actual processes of life. "Faith" is the chosen term for Meissner to refer to the "psychological impact of the action of grace" (Meissner, 1969, p. 73).

Something is lost and something gained in shifting the category of analysis from grace to faith. Gained is the permission for psychological pursuit appropriate for a term which fits more nearly on the boundary of the psychological and the theological. Missing, or liable to be missed, is the awareness that cannot be avoided with the term "grace," namely, that we are considering a reality which while it can be examined psychologically is finally not reducible to psychological processes or predictable by the analysis of genetic origins. There is that of faith which is sheer gift, superogatory, breaking through and confounding all over categories and calculations, that is - simply - graced.

Faith: From Primal Trauma to Ego Integration

In any event, having turned to consider the psychodynamics of human faith, Meissner must take up those two persistent questions of a theological anthropology: the "from whence?" and the "towards what?" of human development. Here it is primarily the psychoanalyst that asserts himself; and here, too, we observe a touch of irony. If we found Fowler, by virtue of his structural developmentalist psychology, more optimistic and

53

ameliorative about human origins than H. Richard Niebuhr and the "Protestant" position, Meissner, under the influence of Freudian psychoanalysis, appears at first more pessimistic and severe in his assessment of human possibilities than might be predicted by what we have just typified as a "Catholic" viewpoint. [21] The "from whence" of human faith for Meissner is a situation of trauma, specifically the injury to the primary narcissism of the child occasioned by the more or less severe experience of loss and separation that is an inevitable concomitant of growing up. He writes in description of the origins of faith (Meissner, 1969, p. 60):

> I think that the exigency of faith is rooted in narcissism. It answers in a very profound sense to man's most basic needs. The loss of personal meaning and the threat of meaninglessness of existence lie at the heart of that dread that is rooted in existence. It is to this that faith answers primarily, but its answer reverberates at many levels of man's existence. It touches also the unconscious and infantile dread of loss and fear of abandonment that is rooted in narcissism in the purest sense. At this level, then, faith is more surely and most distinctively a wish-fulfillment - or better, wish fulfillments. As Erikson writes, man 'forgets that he achieved the capacity for <u>faith</u> by learning to overcome feelings of utter abandonment and mistrust.

For Meissner the enduring truth of Freud's reflections on religion is that religion represents "illusions, fulfillments of the oldest, strongest and most urgent wishes of mankind" (Freud, 1927/1961, p. 30). Of course, as should already be evident in the above quote, Meissner, like the object relations theorists we shall be discussing, significantly reinterprets the nature and scope of those "most urgent wishes" and reassesses their place in the overall economy of the human psyche. Nevertheless he remains clear that one powerful motivating force for faith is to be found in the progressive overcoming of these psychic splits and fractures in functioning which occur as a consequence of the vicissitudes of development. In a fashion that recalls H. Richard Niebuhr's discussion of faith's healing of "inner manyness," Meissner identifies the processes of faith with an activity of psychological integration or unification. "Faith," he suggests, is "a disposition in the human psyche. . .an organized sequence of acts that derives from various levels of the mind and integrates the diverse functions of these various structures into a unified and organized whole" (Meissner, 1969, pp. 49-50).

The above definition of faith appears highly abstract, even formal, yet Meissner does proceed to flesh out what this integrating activity might look like and in so doing fills in his proposed answer to the "to where" of faith development, the goal of faith at least in so far as it might be psychologically described (Ibid., pp. 70-71):

> . . .faith is a transforming process that touches all parts of the psychic structure and reorganizes them into a pattern that is different and integrates them into a more mature and effective level of function. Faith has therefore an integrative function in the psychic economy. True faith is thereby restorative, recuperative, and effectively maturing.

> . . .To the extent that the integrative function of faith is realized, it enlarges and intensifies the sense of personal identity that is the hallmark of mature psychological adjustment. In faith, man realizes more fully his psychological potentiality - and this in turn enlarges his capacity for autonomous, conflict-free function, for spontaneity, and for freedom from impulsive gratifications and for freedom from impulsive gratifications and restrictive compulsions.

In Meissner's descriptions of the integrative effect of faith as an enlargement of the capacity for a spontaneous, conflict-free investment of ego energies, one hears a distinct echo of Rahner's discussion of the effect of grace as the overcoming of concupiscence, i.e., the progressive deepening and intensification of the individual's capacity to be whole-heartedly present in his or her actions.

The Double Paradox of Faith

The language of "autonomous, conflict-free function" in the above description has its debt to the discussion of deneutralized instinctual energies and independent ego energies found in the work of Hartmann (1970) and White (1963). Yet the full significance of Meissner's account of the dynamic processes of faith is missed if this "effectively maturing" development is read as a straightforward matter of leaving behind "the things of a child" as St. Paul put it. Quite the contrary. Faith, as Meissner presents it for our inspection, is a process that involves what I would term a double paradox.

The first part of the paradox is that faith is a process which involves a return to the resources of an earlier stage in life precisely for the purposes of a higher degree of psychic integration. Faith is the one step backward which is the condition for the two steps forward; or to employ a more descriptive direction, it is the movement downward that becomes the possibility for climbing further. More technically expressed, Meissner has identified in the faith process what Ernest Kris has referred to as "regression in the service of the ego" (Kris, 1971). Specifically, the "place" of return is the disposition towards basic trust, as Erikson termed it, which in varying degrees is the developmental heritage of the child's earliest experience of being adequately loved and recognized by the parenting ones. It is Erikson who has most eloquently defended this process which flies in the face of the conventional psychoanalytic judgment that religion is the persistent residue of infantile or historically primitive illusion and must needs be outgrown for real maturity to be achieved both by individuals and by human society (Erikson, 1958, p. 255):

> But must we call it regression if man thus seeks
> again the earliest encounters of his trustful past in
> his efforts to reach a hoped for and eternal future?
> Or do religions partake of man's ability, even as he
> regresses, to recover creatively? At their creative
> best, religions retrace our earliest inner
> experiences giving tangible form to vague evils, and
> reaching back to the earliest individual sources of
> trust; at the same time, they keep alive the common
> symbols of integrity, distilled by the generations.
> It is this partial regression, it is a regression
> which, in retracing firmly established pathways,
> returns to the present amplified and clarified.

The general pattern of Meissner's analysis is to try and demonstrate how certain psychological processes which may originally have had a defensive function in the psychic economy, under the right life circumstances, can come to serve adaptive ends. As a serious theorist of human development, Meissner has himself been involved in the revision of psychoanalytic theory which has brought into sharp relief just this paradoxical pattern in human development: that the very psychic mechanisms which are involved in the costly defense of neurosis or psychosis are also the very condition and possibility for the kind of creativity which we would regard as the finest flowering of the human spirit. [22]

This is in many respects an appropriate summary of a central pattern emerging in psychoanalytic object relations theory, and indeed Meissner explicitly links his analysis with this broad current in contemporary psychoanalytic thinking (see especially Meissner, 19//). In my subsequent presentation of object relations theory I shall hope to illustrate more clearly the way in which this revision involves the recognition of paradoxical movement. But I have stated earlier that Meissner finds in the processes of faith a double paradox and so far I have described only one part - the part which is comprehended by theoretical advancements at the growing edge of psychoanalytic theory and practice. The other paradox of faith is perhaps beyond the competence of depth psychology altogether. In the presence of this second paradox of faith Meissner's chosen interpreter is not Klein, Kohut, Winnicott, or any other psychoanalyst, but rather that chronically confounding psychologist of the spirit-depths, Kierkegaard.

In his 1969 essay, "Notes on a Psychology of Faith," Meissner identifies his description of the full development of faith with the movement of infinite resignation described by Kierkegaard. In this movement of the soul one strips oneself of all finite consolations and wish fulfillments in order to enter into a relationship with the absolute that is God, the sole warrant for one's hope and the ground of one's existence:

Thus faith is not precisely because it requires resignation. It is not an instinct of the heart, but a paradox of life and existence. . . The paradox is rooted in the antithesis of God and man. It is a submission to God that required ethical maturity and the capacity for resignation, which leaves man with no recourse but the impossible. At this point the absurd begins. And the paradox is that man, by reaching through the veil of dread into the emptiness of the absurd, finds a relationship to God that is stripped of all the trappings of the finite and in which man finds the highest realization of himself.
(Meissner, 1969, pp. 51-52)

Faith does not complete itself with the recovery of the psychic resources of basic trust, as though the provision of "good enough mothering" (Winnicott) either originally or in subsequent therapeutic intervention were in itself adequate to address the ultimate problem of death and separation. The double paradox Meissner wants his readers to grasp is that while faith, psychologically examined, involves a reaching back to reappropriate the unconscious origins of interpersonal trust, mature faith according to Meissner moves beyond these resources and possesses them for the sake of resigning them, or as he puts it, "It returns to trust to go beyond it" (Meissner, 1969, p. 65):

> Thus Kierkegaard is partially correct in his insistence on the infinite resignation. Faith must effectively resign infantile wish-fulfillments before true faith becomes possible. Yet is is part of the paradox of faith that in its progression beyond finitude it simultaneously regresses to the most primitive levels of that finitude. In resigning all wish fulfillments, it revives and refreshes the most fundamental wishes and finds their fulfillment by virtue of faith. (Ibid., p. 57)

We shall want to return at a later point to consider this double paradox of faith as Meissner and others propose it, particularly to ask whether or not psychoanalytic object relations theory as it stands can allow for this movement of negation which enters the analysis of faith primarily from the side of the theological witnesses as opposed to the psychoanalytic commentators.

A Proposed Methodology for the Study of Religious Experience

The last comment I would make regarding Meissner's study of faith concerns the methodology for analyzing religion which he has proposed in the essay, "Psychoanalytic Aspects of Religious Experience" (Meissner, 1978a). In this essay he has again underscored his commitment to a developmental perspective in approaching human religiousness. In this he is loyal to the original intent of Freud's own analysis of religion. Where he clearly moves beyond Freud is in adopting a revised and extended psychoanalytic perspective based on the work of Heinz Kohut, D.W. Winnicott and others which permits him to view religious phenomena as something other than a simple repetition of "primitive" or "infantile" patterns of behavior. "Thus primitive and archaic symbols undergo a transformation of function and significance, which allows us to identify the originating context and relevance of the archaic symbol and its more evolved and symbolically differentiated and enriched context, without reducing this connection to one of identity and without resorting to the developmentally obtuse formula of repetition" (Meissner,1978a, p. 127).

Meissner structures his analysis using the developmental schema proposed by Gedo and Goldberg (1973), a decision which parallels Fowler's decision to trace the discrete but interrelated "dimensions of faith." Because we shall want to contrast some of Meissner's decisions in this area with our own it is useful to observe that in this essay he identifies three discrete lines of development which constellate not around faith as a category of analysis, but around "religious experience." Faith is regarded as one dimension of religious experience, the other two are the developmental lines of narcissism and dependency. The actual model Meissner uses is an epigenetic chart similar to the staircase model made famous by Erikson.

With a consideration of Meissner our examination of the theological vantage on faith through the Protestant and Catholic is completed. Selective and highly condensed though it has been, it presents the major influences from the perspective of the theological with which we shall be in dialogue and introduces as well the pioneering work of two colleagues which is to date the most significant psychological operationalization of these two tradition's views of faith.

FOOTNOTES CHAPTER TWO

1.   It should not be thought that because Niebuhr's definitions of faith find a strong resonance in personality theory that this is the source of definition. On the contrary, Niebuhr's understanding of faith originates in an explicitly biblical theology. Niebuhr's decision to link faith with trust as a decision for what he calls at one place a "Hebrew," as opposed to a "Greek," understanding of faith (Niebuhr, 1961, p. 98). The latter he associated with the word "belief." Faith under that understanding is something like knowledge but different. It could mean variously something accepted on the reliability of others, a commitment to an unproven first postulate, or a total assent to a dogmatic content. The Hebrew understanding of faith, by contrast, has its roots in Old Testament usage. There faith is a term that describes a

relationship. The Hebrew word batah, rendered as faith, means to feel secure, to rely upon or to trust (DT 28:52; Is 31:1). Abraham's confident waiting upon the trustworthiness of God (GN 15:6) is the paradigm for this meaning of faith. For the Hebrew people faith is a statement of their whole relationship to One who has demonstrated and continually demonstrates constancy, fidelity, and mercy, in spite of their own repeated unfaithfulness (Is 14:1; 30:18-19; Micah 7:19-20).

This relational meaning of faith carries over into the New Testament as well where to believe also frequently carries the sense of to rely upon or to trust (Mk 13:21; Jn 4:21; Acts 27:25; Rom 4:17). An important usage of faith in the Pauline epistles is its application in description of the conviction of Christians that God has been and always will be faithful to the promises He is all-powerful to fulfill, preeminently the promise that we, like Jesus, will be raised to the glory of God (Rom 3:25; 4:3-25; 2 Cor 1:9).

Though Niebuhr acknowledges the value and legitimacy of the various meanings of faith that congregate around "belief" as its equivalent, his preferred emphasis is on faith as a fiduciary term. Faith is a virtue, meaning by that a quality or characteristic of persons in relationship. It is associated for him with notions of faithfulness as loyalty, reliability, the capacity to "keep faith" with another, the disposition to believe in (as opposed to "believing that").

2.   The notion that the life of faith, or the faithful life of the religious being, can be fruitfully understood by analogy with political life has been imaginatively developed in Richard R. Niebuhr's book, Experiential Religion (R.N. Niebuhr, 1972, p. 35): "What is religion, then? It is a quality of man that is unique. But what is it like? It is like politics, for the man who practices the art of politics must know how to balance friend against foe, enforce covenants, exploit the physical situation of his city, promote the health of its citizenry, and plan perspectives leading the eye to the horizon's immensity. He must deal with the entire environing world as a world of power."

3.   The important difference between Miller and Niebuhr is that Miller actually sees the condition he describes as normative if not optimal. Under the sway of the Jungian revisionism of James Hillman (Revision in Psychology, 1975), Miller holds that a quest for "wholeness" or the integration of the self in terms of a single focus of transcendent value is misplaced and self-defeating. Instead he opts for a "sequential monotheism" or even better a "new polytheism" (appropriately the title of his book). A similar though more

ambivalent stance towards the phenomenon of diverse and shifting self-commitments is found in Robert Jay Lifton's discussion of "protean man." As a modern character type, Lifton's protean individual is a product of the massive social disequilibrium, proliferation of ideology, attrition of central communal values, and pervasive mistrust which Niebuhr too finds at the base of "personal and social manifoldness." Lifton, however, appears to affirm the individual capable of flexibility in style and commitment as adaptive to a pluralistic age, even as he laments the circumstances that make it necessary (Lifton, 1967).

4.   "Henotheism" Niebuhr defines as loyalty to one god among many, but a god that is less than the God of radical monotheism. "Polytheism" is a simultaneous fidelity to many gods or many centers of meaning and value.

5.   In a passage of characteristic psychological perceptiveness, Niebuhr observes that it is not only that we must become selves in order to genuinely encounter the other self, but that it is precisely as we encounter a fully self-disclosing other we are enabled to claim our own being: "A meeting with an incarnate self is an event of different character from all our isolated surmises, fears, dreamings and wishes about ideal companions or enemies; after such meetings we can never again return to the self knowledge which was ours before the meeting" (Niebuhr, 1941, p. 107).

6.   "Revelation as the self-disclosure of the infinite person is realized in us only through the faith which is a personal act of commitment, of confidence and trust, not a belief about the nature of things." (Niebuhr, 1941, p. 112).

7.   In the Cole Lectures in 1960, only a few years before Niebuhr's death, he developed a few of these questions a bit further and began himself to enlist the resources of a developing ego psychology as a companion in thought:

"Further, I believe that emotional relations to otherness, to objective being, are prior in meaningfulness to intellectual relations. Trust in parents or distrust of them is prior in time and probably personally prior to all identification of parents. So also it may be that love of God or enmity to God, hate of God, is prior to all articulation of our idea of who God is. And so with all our relations to his creatures. I am thinking here in part of what Erikson says in Childhood and Society about the place of basic trust in child life and in the life of the parents. (Niebuhr, 1960b)

61

In the same lecture series H. Richard Niebuhr set out the hypothesis in which he said he wished he had another career to explore: "that they (the emotions) put us into touch with what is firm, reliable, real, enduring in ways that are inaccessible to the conceptual and spectator reason." Niebuhr, looking out from the mountain top of his own life into the theological task ahead expressed the conviction that "the next steps must be into the frontier lands of men's feelings." This book might be seen as an effort to take a few of those steps into human affectivity in the company of some contemporary pioneers .

8. See Robert Kegan's <u>The Evolving Self: Problem and Process in Human Development</u> (Harvard University Press, 1982), for a stimulating and systematic attempt to have the Piagetian paradigm carry the entire burden of accounting for affective development. Kegan seems clearly to be pointing in a direction in which the field should thoughtfully move.

9. Structural-developmental models and the semi-clinical interview have been used by other researchers to study religious development but for the most part these studies differ strikingly from Fowler's work in the fairly narrow identification of their subject as "religious concepts" and their definition of the problem of religious development as one of cognitive readiness to handle the concept of God. Two influential examples of this research strategy are David Elkind's "The Origin of Religion in the Child," (Elkind, 1970; see also Elkind, 1971), and Ronald Goldman's <u>Religious Thinking from Childhood to Adolescence</u> (Goldman, 1964). Adaptation of these approaches are illustrated by Fleck, Ballard and Reilly (1975), Pitts (1976) and Williams (1971). Fowler alone of researchers adopting a Piagetian viewpoint has been thorough-going in applying a functionalist approach to both the designation of subject and material and the method of research and analysis.

10. There are statements Fowler makes about prizing the "richness, individuality and concreteness" of the individual content of each person's faith (Fowler,1976a, p.179). While such comments are undoubtedly sincere, such content is finally beside the point in an analysis that aims to get at what is "less variable, and more constant and capable of comparison between persons and communities" - namely structure. This is, of course, fully consistent with the structural developmental paradigm and congruent as well with one theme in Niebuhr, the desire to find faith a universal human process.

11. See John Bowker's discussion of the religious task as finding a "life way" through the "compounds of limitation" that confront us (Bowker, 1976).

12. The most complete discussion of the Kantian character of higher stage development is found in Kohlberg's essay, "From Is to Ought: How to Commit the Naturalistic Fallacy and Get Away with It" (Kohlberg, 1971). There is an on-going debate about the relationship of the moral development stages to faith development. Do the latter depend upon the attainment of the former or are they more comprehensive developmental movements which contain moral development but do not necessarily wait upon it. For a review of the arguments in both directions, see Kohlberg (1974) and Fowler (1976a, pp. 207-211).

13. This pre-Vatican II discussion of faith was conducted under the sway of the definition of faith promulgated by the First Vatican Council: ". . .Faith, which is 'the beginning of salvation,' the Catholic Church holds to be a supernatural virtue. By it, with the inspiration and help of God's grace, we believe that what he has revealed is true, not because of its intrinsic truth, seen by the natural light of reason, but because of the authority of God revealing it, who can neither deceive nor be deceived" (Denzinger, 3008).

14. See also Gregory Baum, "Vatican II's Constitution on Revelation: History and Interpretation," Theological Studies 28, 1966, 51-75.

15. For other statements of this perception see Reinhold Niebuhr, "Human Creativity and Self-Concern in Freud's Thought" in Freud and the Twentieth Century, Benjamin Nelson (ed.), New York: Meridian Books, 1957, and Philip Rieff, Freud: The Mind of the Moralist, New York: Doubleday, 1959, pp. 297-306.

16. Within Catholic theology this discussion is traditionally conducted under the rubric of "original sin." I have chosen Rahner as a spokesman for one influential Catholic position, but as Fr. Brian McDermott's excellent review of the doctrine shows, Rahner represents only one of a number of different approaches to understanding original sin that are currently being put forward in Catholic theological circles. Brian McDermott, "Original Sin: Recent Developments," Theological Studies 38, 1977, pp. 478-512.

17. See also Rahner, 1960, p. 347-283.

18. It might be thought that the Catholic emphasis on the epistemological aspect of faith would shape a different statement of the goal of faith development. Indeed Rahner in an essay entitled "Reflections on the Problem of the Gradual Ascent to Christian Perfection" (Rahner, 1967b) does point out how Catholic Christian spirituality, historically dominated by the gnostic bent of early Church Fathers like Clement of

Alexandria, Origen and Evagrius, has tended to conflate mystical ascent with the process of faith development. Rahner holds, however, for distinguishing the two. When freed of its neoplatonic associations, the concept of faith as a mode of knowing or a hungering for participation in the real, aims to re-invest the individual in the flux and action of the world which is now seen as the arena of God's saving activity. Knowing and doing, action and contemplation, are distinct but complementary modes of being in this understanding. Hence the person of faith is not one who must withdraw from involvement in the world in order to "know" the reality of God, but rather one who encounters and realizes that reality precisely in the following of the one who "emptied himself taking the form of a slave" (Philippians 2:7-8).

19. "The Christian believer, in and despite his creatureliness, and although he recognizes that he is a sinner both of himself and by his origin, must understand that he is (the) one who has been historically summoned by God and the efficacious Word of God's free, absolute self- disclosure to enter God's own intimate life. The vital point here is that God. . .allows him to participate in the divine nature itself, to be joint heir with the Son, called to eternal life face to face with God in the intuitive beatific vision of God" (Rahner, Theological Dictionary, New York: Herder & Herder, 1965, p. 193).

20. This conviction, that God uses the forms and structures of human personality for the process of sanctification, is foundational for both Catholic and Orthodox Christians, however much they may disagree about the actual nature of those personality givens. Roman Catholic psychologist Eugene Kennedy gives popular expression to this notion when he writes concerning the activity of believing: ". . .believing is subject to the approximately understood laws of development that regulate all the other aspects of human growth. Believing does not live above and beyond the growing personality; it does not possess a fully mature mode of being independent of the individual's general personal development" (Kennedy, 1974, p. 38).

21. I emphasize "appears at first" because one finds through Meissner's essays on faith, particularly when read in company with his other papers on aspects of psychoanalytic theory and practice, that his thinking moves in the direction of a revised psychoanalysis with its own much debated mitigation of some of Freud's judgments on the human prospect. Nevertheless, Meissner might be regarded as a basically conservative theoretician if by that we mean he attempts to retain as much as possible of Freud's genetic, economic and

structural models for the operation of the psyche (see especially Meissner, 1974, 1975, 1976a).

22. Meissner's most systematic engagement of one dimension of this paradox is his recent book, The Paranoid Process (Meissner, 1978b) which illustrates the ubiquity of paranoid or projective mechanisms throughout the life cycle, not only in illness but also in health.

CHAPTER THREE

FAITH: A THEORETICAL ANALYSIS

I.   Working on the Boundary. . . . . p. 67

II. The From Whence of Faith . . . . p. 72

     Faith is involved in the
     development of the sense of being real. . . . . . .p. 76

     Faith is involved in the growth of a sense of being
     in relationship to a real and meaningful world. . .p. 78

     Faith is integrally related to the
     development of the capacity to be alone . . . . . p. 81

     Faith is to be found in the processes involved in the
     development of the capacity to tolerate dependency p. 83

III. The To Where of Faith . . . . p. 87

     Faith is involved in the development
     of the capacity to tolerate ambivalence . . . . . p. 92

     Faith undergirds the sense of oneself
     as available for loving self-donation . . . . . . p. 96

CHAPTER THREE

FAITH: A THEORETICAL ANALYSIS

I. Working on the Boundary

The creative efforts of James Fowler and William Meissner to use faith as a category for psychological investigation demonstrate more clearly than one could state simply the complex and difficult methodological issues which attend an interdisciplinary project such as theirs. Both researchers are working on the boundary between theology and psychology. However different their parent theological traditions or their chosen psychological systems, the work of both individuals displays the subtle and rarely systematic interaction of those two influences. Before laying out our own analysis of faith from a psychoanalytic object relations perspective, I would like to call attention to some of the relevant methodological issues as these writers make us aware of them.

Both Protestant and Catholic Christian traditions seem to be agreed that whatever else may be the phenomenon pointed to with the word-symbol "faith," it is a reality that comes close to the heart of how human begins are when they are most truly themselves, or at least when they are themselves as God intends them to be. As a human reality, then, faith should be in some measure describable by the terms and the tools generally available to us to render an account of human growth and development. If faith is indeed a "universal, dynamic process" then it also follows that no single community or discipline can presume to exercise control over that term or function as its sole interpreter. Moreover, the concerns with which faith deals are held to be of potential interest to anyone who cares to understand human beings in depth. Together all of this gives the psychologist of faith permission to draw on the common resources of the human sciences to service his or her project of understanding. Having said this, however, we must turn and again recognize that faith is not a word proper to the secular sciences. It is a word that is embedded within an historical community's experience of relationship to transcendent reality. Inevitably, therefore, the conversation about the psychology of faith is one that in all its parts is likely going to be of greatest concern to the religious community or to persons of good will who are interested in admitting into their consideration of the human the dimension of the transcendent.

It is natural then that those of us who are involved in studying the psychology of faith will bring to that inquiry two sets of resources. First, we have those intuitions, sensitivities, beliefs and value judgments which are the heritage of the particular religious format on and experience that for us made the phenomenon of faith lively, compelling, and often problematic. Second, we carry with us the analytical tools, conceptual models and often the implicit value orientations of the particular psychological perspective within which we have chosen to work. [1]

In the definitions of faith and in the methods of inquiry adopted by Fowler and Meissner one can discern something of the way in which these loyalties to a religious perspective and parallel loyalties to a psychological analysis mutually influence and inform one another. Sometimes we observe the guiding influence of a psychological mentor, other times the sway of a religious teacher. Most often the synthesis of theological insight and psychological knowledge is more subtly managed and it is difficult to gauge where the one leaves off and the other begins. Does Fowler's emphasis upon the universalizing dimension of mature faith derive from convictions he shares with H. Richard Niebuhr about the character of radical monotheism, or is it something he is primed to see by the particular psychological frame of reference he employs? Does the one make him more receptive to the other? Evidence suggests that the tide of influence rips in both directions.

Similarly, Meissner's training and background as a psychoanalyst clearly inclines him to locate the origins of faith in the vicissitudes of early infantile narcissism. What is it, however, that compels him to think his way past the reductionism of Freud's interpretation of religion to a position that holds out for the possibility of an integrative and mature religious life? Again, we see a certain complementarity or convergence of theological and psychological reasoning. From the side of Meissner's informing religious tradition comes a warrant to inspect the ways of human development for evidence of its openness to the transformative activity of grace. Congruently, as an analyst he has been influenced by and indeed contributed to just such revisions of psychoanalytic theory as posit a constructive basis for adult development in the processes of internalization and projection characteristic of religious origins (Meissner, 1978). Both Fowler and Meissner have conducted their inquiry without explicit reference to the methodology which governs their use of both psychology and theology. Before proceeding further, therefore, it would be instructive to make explicit the model for interdisciplinary dialogue which informs this project.

William R. Rogers has suggested a typology with illustrative diagrams which usefully describes the variety of ways in which the interdisciplinary dialogue between psychology and theology has been carried on (Rogers,1980). It is Rogers' "constructive-relational" model which both Meissner and Fowler, at their best, are employing in their use of psychology and theology. It is this same model which has guided these present efforts to discourse between psychology and theology on the matter of faith. [See figure 1.]

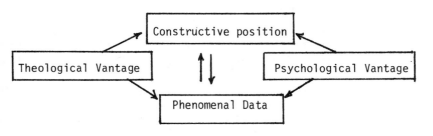

Figure 1.

For a constructive-relational model of interdisciplinary study, the object of inquiry is some common data of human experience which can be addressed both from the vantage of the psychological as well as the theological. This is what is referred to in the diagram as the "phenomenal data." For the purposes of this study I shall be looking at those inter and intra-psychic processes by which, in the course of the life cycle, the human person creates and maintains a sense of integrated selfhood, available for relationships of love, service, and self-commitment. There can be no doubt that there is something "out there" begging to be understood. Children are born into a network of relationships, do undergo a species-exceptional period of external dependence, and somehow do emerge with a composite of psychic strengths and wounds - all of which they may bequeath and/or inflict on an emerging generation. Yet why look at just this body of data and not some other, and why the decision to link it to faith? That decision is the consequence of the convergence of insights from these two chosen vantages or perspectives, the theological and the psychological, as they survey the human developmental process.

These two positions enter into a dialogue of mutual criticism and correction the outcome of which is a constructive

69

position. A constructive position does not subsume the theological to the psychological or vice versa, but so far as possible allows them their own voice and valence. The arrows in the illustrative diagram suggest how, when this process is pursued in a protracted fashion, the constructive position is always accountable to the the data itself, to the actual life experience being studied. One is always, in this model, refering back to the phenomena which was the original ground for both the psychological and theological formulations.

Obviously a constructive position is only really possible when one begins from a theological point of view and a psychological approach which do not a priori dismiss the potential contributions of the other. Rather when placed in dialogue with one another the two perspectives convergently validate a number of critical insights. This for me has been the case with psychoanalytic object relations theory and the theological vantages on faith discussed in the previous chapter. A combination of selected Christian perspectives inclines me to view faith less as the graced assent to a revealed body of truth and more as a reality in human life pointed to the transcendent but historically and developmentally antecedent to the actual encounter with revelation. Furthermore, as we saw, the composite influence of these theological positions directs attention to specific aspects of human life as crucial for faith, among them: the dynamic of trust and fidelity, the sense of subjective and objective reality, the development of the integrated self needed for the risk of radical love. When I turn to the side of psychological inquiry I find that these are also the aspects of human development that have been chiefly explored and illumined by that growing edge within psychoanalytic theory that has most engaged my own interest and imagination: object relations theory.

The analysis of faith which follows displays the general influence of a psychoanalytic perspective on human development, particularly in its assumption of the genetic point of view, the view that early life experience lays down the patterns which influence the shape of later development. More particularly, aspects of this definition of faith reflect the adventures of post-Freudian psychoanalytic theory in its discovery that the early life experiences which are most critical for development are those involving the pre-oedipal relationship of parent and child. At the same time there should be visible in the course of this book the counterweight of insights derived from a theological reflection upon faith. Such insights have not only guided my selection of materials from the analytic literature, but, additionally, function in a critical fashion to judge the adequacy of a psychoanalytic account of faith.

In a sense this analysis of faith is also the hypothesis of the book. We are proposing a body of human data and its theoretical explication which offers a basis in human development for much of what the religious tradition has wanted to say about faith. The testing of the hypothesis is in the adequacy and coherence of the account of faith which psychoanalytic object relations theory makes possible. What is given to our understanding by employing its perspective, and what is neglected or left unaddressed? Where do we find ourselves at the limits of the theoretical vantage itself and must look ahead to a yet-to-be-drawn integration with other investigative models: systems theory, cognitive psychology, structural developmental theory? Similarly, where do we see these limits as the limits of human science itself and recognition must be made of that which can only be expressed, however inadequately, by theological speech?

The beginning point of our own constructive position on faith is to state my agreement with both Fowler and Meissner that faith has a developmental character. Faith means different things at different times in the course of a human life. It takes on different configurations, deals with different life tasks. Faith has a beginning and it has an ending, like any narrative, indeed like the human life story itself from which it is inextricable. It was in recognition of this developmental character that I suggested earlier that every serious discussion of faith would involve more or less explicit answers to two questions: (1) "From whence does human life proceed?" or "What is the constitutive condition for human growth and becoming?" and (2) "Towards what does human life develop?" or "What is the horizon possibility of human living, the full life, the completed existence?" These two questions are the warp and the weft of the analysis of faith that follows.

In brief, the position which will be developed in the rest of this chapter is this:

Faith is that human dynamic of trusting, relying upon, and reposing confidence in, which (1) is foundational to the life-long process of becoming a self, and (2) is fulfilled in the progressively enlarged capacity of that self for love and self-commitment.

II. The "From Whence" of Faith

I would argue that the condition of the human person which is the beginning point for the processes of faith is contained in what Freud described as "an immensely important biological fact and a fateful psychological one: namely the human child's lone dependence on its parents and the oedipus complex" (Freud, 1933, p. 66). It is the distinguishing characteristic of great minds that they observe the significance of facts so commonplace that most of us usually take them for granted. Retrospectively viewed, Freud's momentous step was to ask, in effect, two questions. First, what does it mean that compared with the entirety of other animate life we human beings are born "prematurely," born without the guidance of those instincts which enable lower forms of life to separate from their mothers in a matter of hours or days? Secondly, what does it mean for human development that this long-dependent child is born into the matrix of power relationships to which in his or her helplessness and need he or she must somehow begin to adapt? This I take to be the enduring meaning of the "oedipus complex" in its broadest sense, that the growing child is possessed of yearning and desires and a sheer energy for activity which confronts the invincible authority and physical supremacy of those more powerful persons on whom the child is dependent not only for the physical necessities of life but more importantly, for the love and the recognition that is life itself for the human child (Becker, 1962, pp. 54-64).

The consequence of this "immensely important biological fact and fateful psychological one" has been articulated most eloquently by Margaret Mahler, a child analyst who has taken psychoanalytic ideas to guide a systematic clinical study of early childhood development. The conclusion of Mahler and her colleagues is that we human beings must undergo two birth processes: the first is parturition, the actual event of physical separation from the mother; the second, no less dramatic and fraught with its own sorts of dangers, is "the psychological birth of the human infant," the process whereby the child becomes a self distinct from the self of the mother (Mahler, Pine and Bergman, 1975).

Mahler's concern to investigate this second birth began with her study of childhood psychosis which she came to see as a response to trauma in the process of becoming a self (Mahler, Ross & DeFries, 1949). What she observed were children suspended "half in and half out" in the process of self-becoming, oscillating painfully "between the longing to merge blissfully with the good object representation, with the erstwhile (in one's fantasy at least) 'all good' symbiotic mother, and the defense against reengulfment by her, which could cause loss of autonomous self-identity" (Mahler, Pine and Bergman, 1975, p. 230). From her initial study of infantile psychotic conditions Mahler went on to conduct her research with a normal population. Her conclusions are convergent with those of other investigators who also have done observations of normal infants and with psychoanalytic researchers who have been involved in the therapy of persons formerly regarded as "unanalyzable," adult schizophrenics and so-called "borderline personalities" (Kernberg, 1967; Balint, 1968; Fraiberg, 1959).

What emerges from this research is a theory of human development with implications for more than just cases of pathology. It is this theory which I have broadly referred to as psychoanalytic object relations theory. One of its central relevant insights is that the formation and maintenance of a sense of self is a life achievement that takes place in the complex interaction between the human child and the interpersonal environment into which he or she is born. Furthermore, this is not a once and for all time event. Although the critical experience of separation and the process of individuation presumably takes place in the first three years of life, throughout the life cycle the human person faces challenges to the cohesiveness and coherence of his or her sense of self. At various times and under various circumstances the human person re-encounters in new and different ways the tensions that characterized the beginning of life: the tension between oneness, affiliation, community, closeness and separateness, individuality, uniqueness, difference. Mahler writes of the polarity of this never-wholly-completed life task:

> For the more or less normal adult, the experience of being both fully "in" and at the same time separate from "the world out there" is among the givens of life that are taken for granted. Consciousness of self and absorption without awareness of self are the two polarities between which we move with varying degrees of alternation or simultaneously. . . As is the case with any intrapsychic process, this one reverberates throughout the life cycle. It is never finished; it can always become reactivated; new phases of the life cycle witness new derivatives of the earliest processes still at work. (Mahler, 1972, p. 333)

Between these two polar possibilities then is the problem of being a self: the problem of claiming the integrity of one's own experience and knowing and power while also remaining a beloved part of a greater whole.

The weight of this psychodynamic material offers validation from the side of psychology for what we first observed to be the thesis of H. Richard Niebuhr, namely, that faith is a fundamental human process intimately involved in the life-long task of becoming a self. From the very beginning of life, the human person, as Niebuhr so perceptively observed, is a responder (Niebuhr, 1963). The world, and first and primally the interpersonal world of the parenting other(s), comes at the fledgling self as a reality that communicates in a myriad of spoken and unspoken ways its valuation of that newly emerged human being. The individual in turn responds with others but by extension towards the totality of that which is. The subsequent process then of the development of the self, the negotiation of oneness and separateness, is at every point founded upon and conditioned by this interpretation of the whole as good or evil, trustworthy or untrustworthy, deserving of loyalty or requiring a constant vigilance. Niebuhr consequently defines faith as "the attitude of the self in its existence towards all the existences that surround it, as beings to be relied upon or to be suspected. . .that attitude that appears in all the wariness and confidence of life as it moves among the living. . . fundamentally trust or mistrust in being itself" (Ibid., p. 118).

This last statement suggests how the transcendent, or faith in God, is defined for Niebuhr and will be for us in this project. It is as the individual in the process of self-becoming responds to the single creative and generative reality, "the One in the many," as ultimately good, valuing and valuable, that one can be said to have faith in God. [2] In point of fact we seldom explicitly, intentionally or self-consciously place ourselves in relationship before that single "alien and inscrutable power that elects us and all things into existence" (Ibid., p. 82). What is more visible more often in the conduct of our lives is the distribution of our loyalties and the location of our sense of what is to be trusted and relied upon among a number of centers of penultimate meaning and value. Even where we can discern behind these fragmented and divided objects of our faith the shadowy outline of our relationship to the one creative Source of all our comings and goings, that relationship is apt to be equivocal, characterized as much by mistrust as by trust. The One beyond the many becomes, again in Niebuhr's words, "the enemy, the creative source whence comes destruction" (Ibid., p. 140). The movement in the development of faith can therefore be understood as the movement from "God the enemy" to "God the companion" (Whitehead, 1926/1960).

Later in this chapter we shall be argue that there is a dynamism comprehended sheerly within the psychology of self-becoming that impells the human person to address the transcendent referent of faith, that which the tradition calls God. We shall want to approach that matter obliquely, however, by moving first through the question of the relationship of faith to the object representational process in self-becoming. The ultimate aim of course is to link up this analysis of faith in God with faith in "God" as an explicitly thematized mental mode by which an individual handles the issues of psychic integrity in the process of self-becoming. The first step, then, is to examine how faith, simply considered as fundamental trust, is implicated in the psychodynamic process by which human persons establish and maintain a sense of self.

There are two points that must be stressed in approaching the study of self-becoming. The first is that such a study must be developmental, that is, it must see its object as an ongoing process that is never static and never completed. The pressures upon the wholeness and integrity of the self change as the individual enters upon new areas of personal development and social relationship. The ideological demands of adolescence, the invitation to intimacy and commitment of young adulthood, the vision of the completed life that is the gift and the final challenge of old age - all present to one degree or another "normative crises" that permit an individual to rework and modify the psychic structures and patterns which were developed in early life to manage the maintenance of the loving and beloved self. It is a developmental process which I believe is most usefully seen as linear, that is moving by incremental changes, rather than phasic, progression by identifiable stages.

The second point is that the creation of the self is no "one thing." It is not a single discrete process. The concept of the self is a fairly subtle and still elusive notion within psychoanalytic thinking (Kohut, 1971; Levin, 1969; Lifton, 1976; Schafer, 1976). What seems agreed upon by those who admit it as a category in the study of personality is that self-becoming is best observed obliquely, that is, by looking at an individual negotiating certain basic problems of living, developing certain capacities, achieving a sense of him- or herself in ways that can be testified to or observed. In sum, becoming a self is a multi-dimensional process. Some of those dimensions must be directly relevant to the phenomenon of faith if, as I have proposed, faith is described in its "from whence" by the problems of becoming a self. In the discussion that immediately follows I have selected four of these dimensions of self development and by placing them aspect by aspect on a graphic have constructed a composite picture that conveys the inter-related character of these life tasks. My debt to the methodology of Professor Fowler should be evident here though it is also clear that the decisions as to what "strands of development" are relevant for faith is informed by a different psychological perspective (i.e., psychoanalytic object relations theory). In reading this section I invite the reader to remember that this is not yet a longitudinal model. The various areas of self development described below have significance throughout the human life cycle but will emerge as critical developmental issues at different times.

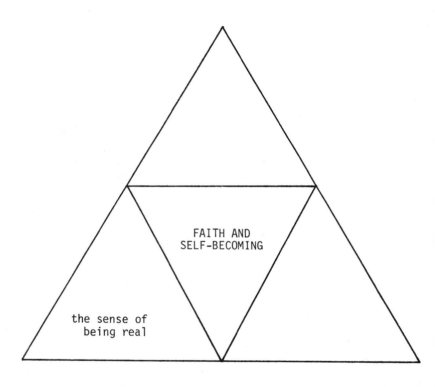

figure 2.

Faith is involved in the development of a sense of being real.

In our discussion of the Catholic perspective on faith we highlighted the concern, prominent in that tradition, to see faith as an expression of the human being's fundamental hungering after the real. In the light of contemporary

76

psychoanalytic theory we would now propose that this yearning for reality has two aspects: a subjective and an objective face. Let us first consider the former.

The subjective face of this quest for the real is the profound and indefatigable desire to be real oneself, to feel that one's historical existence has an "actuality" (Erikson, 1964). A sense of "being" is something that most persons take for granted except perhaps in those odd moments of disassociation which occur in life. Therapists who have related to clients whose presenting complaint is of a nagging sense of unreality, of being detached and unconnected, have proposed that "an absence, non-realization, or dissociation of the experience of 'being' and of the possibility of it, and along with that an incapacity for healthy natural spontaneous 'doing' is the most radical clinical phenomenon in analysis" (Guntrip, 1969, p. 255).

The sense of "ego-relatedness" is a developmental achievement that proceeds from the relationship of the growing child to his/her interpersonal world (Sandler and Jaffe, 1968; Lichtenstein, 1974; Chessick, 1977, pp. 405-426). It is also "the beginning and the basis for the realization of the potentialities in our raw human nature for developing as a 'person' in personal relationships" (Guntrip, 1969, p. 255). Faith is engaged not only in that formative process but is potentially there in later life as well, supporting the drive for a sense of personal reality which may have been compromised or lost in the processes of the development of the self. Faith is also there enhancing and sustaining the human quest to deepen and extend that sense of a lively participation in being.

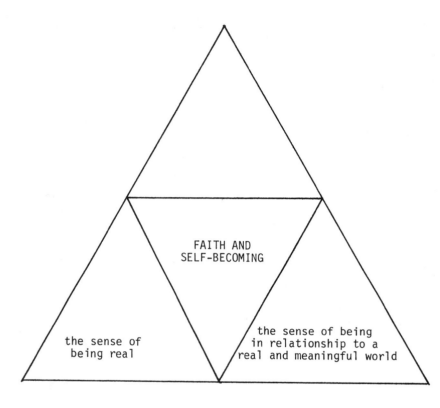

figure 3.

Faith is involved as well in the growth of a sense of being in relationship to a real and meaningful world.

The other side, the "objective side," of the human need to have a sense of "being" is the need to be related to and vitally engaged with "what is." The development of a reality sense tends to carry with it the positivist shadings of Freud's important use of the concept (Freud, 1924a). When considered in terms of Freud's discussion of the "reality principle," the acquisition of the sense of reality can appear to be a sad gift or at least an ironic one since it represents the compromise which must be made between the demands of the pleasure principle and the intransigence of a world that will not cooperate in the immediate gratification of the infant's instinctual needs (Freud, 1911, pp. 220-223). Hartmann (1964) attempted to mitigate this reading of the reality sense as the

78

"natural opponent" of the human desire for pleasure. He did this by pointing out that behavior under the control of the reality principle "... is aimed at gaining, in a new way, assured pleasure at a later stage, while giving up momentary pleasure" (Hartmann, 1964, pp. 244-245). Furthermore, he observed, we must appreciate "the pleasurable potentialities of sublimated activities" in their own right. This may seem a small concession, and one still wed to the assumptions of an instinctual gratification model of the psyche. It was, however, a first step towards recognizing what has become increasingly apparent in the study of the growing person, namely, the intrinsic interest and enjoyment which human beings have in the exploration and manipulation of their real environments.

That a sense of reality, of the way things are "out there," is an essential part of the human maturational process with survival value cannot be denied. Nevertheless the motivational model for the development of that reality sense that is most adequate to the nature of the human would see the human infant not as the cautious and calculating negotiator of a hostile territory who tries to make the best trades and least costly bargains with the natives, even less as the fledgling scientific utilitarian, but rather as the fledgling lover. [3] In other words, our first efforts at science, at finding out how things are, are an aspect of what Phyllis Greenacre called the child's "love affair with the world" (Greenacre, 1957). The child's first universe is an interpersonal one. It is the space between the child and the initially undifferentiated caretaker/parent whose responsiveness to the needs of the child assuages anxiety and convinces the child that the world is indeed a place in which he or she is welcome and that it rewards the investigations of the child with new delights and fresh wonders. When the upright toddler makes the first foray of discovery into this world it is with the belief/fantasy, to evoke Michael Balint's poetry "that the whole world - apart from a few accidental hazards - is a kind of loving mother, holding her child safely in her arms, or phylogenetically, the structureless sea offering the same friendly environment in limitless expanse" (Balint, 1959, p. 85).

The child soon enough suffers some disillusionments in this love affair. The exhilaration and elation of mastery runs up against the limits of the child's competence and power and a rougher reality forces itself upon the child. The development of cognitive skills and the capacity for conceptualization make the world more and more available for the growing child, but the will to make that inquiry and hence the capacity for a creative and imaginative engagement with "reality" depends in large measure on the continued renewal in age adequate ways of that fundamental faith which sponsored the first voyage of exploration. The sense of being in relationship to a real and meaningful world is dependent then on the faith resources which provide answers to the urgent and usually unconscious questions: "Can I trust that my knowing will not undo my sense of self?" "Do I have a place within this world of action, or, where do I fit in?" "Is the unknown the dark harbor of my fears and badness, or is it the potential source of wonderful surprises?" What I am suggesting is that at a level of development prior to clear conceptual expression and in many ways prior even to consciousness, for every human being "metaphysics" precedes "physics."

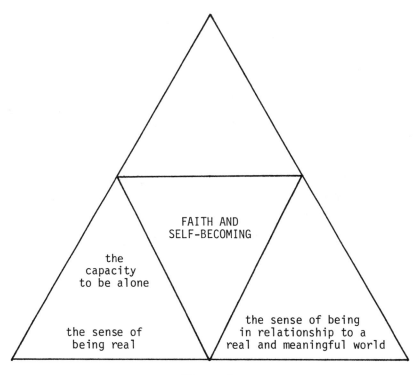

figure 4.

Faith is integrally related to the development of the capacity
to be alone.

"Religion," proposed Alfred North Whitehead, "is what the
individual does with his solitariness" (Whitehead, 1926/1960).
The question of what a human being does with his or her
solitariness, indeed how solitude can come to be tolerated at
all, is a matter that has also engaged the imaginations of
those psychoanalytic theorists who have taken for their study
the development of the self. It may seem ironic when the main
burden of adult neurotic suffering is the problem of being with
others or failures in the capacity for intimacy that the
capacity to be alone should be landmarked as a major developmental achievement. As we shall shortly see when we consider
the work of the object relations theorists, and in particular
that of D.W. Winnicott, after the child's intense symbiotic
bonding with the mother the ability to tolerate separation and

81

aloneness is a complex accomplishment. It represents the successful internalization and subsequent evocation of the object representations that sustain a sense of self-in-relation (Winnicott, 1953). The ability to endure, let alone to value, separateness actually becomes a factor then in the later capability of the person to pursue intimate relationships or make commitments to other persons, causes, or ideals without the trammeling fear of devastating abandonment. When we speak of faith in the context of this dimension of self-becoming we are referring to the quality of trust and reliance that colors the processes of internalization which create the inner representational world sustaining the ability to be alone.

Although the development of what I am calling the capacity to be alone occurs in its most basic form in the first three years of life, it is a developmental achievement that is at risk periodically throughout the life cycle. In the context of the ultimate aloneness that must finally be faced by every last person, the question "who are you with when you're alone?" (Perry, 1979) pushes to the depths of what we mean by faith.

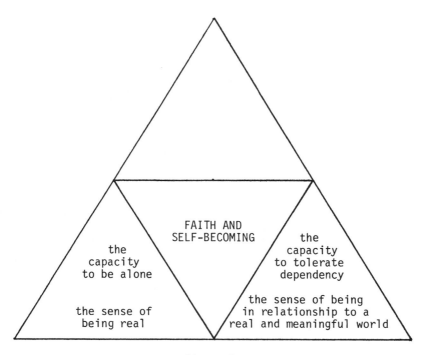

figure 5.

Faith is to be found in the processes involved in the developed
capacity to tolerate dependency.

It is an influence from our Freudian culture, amplified
perhaps in this society by the cult of rugged individualism and
self-reliance, that the term "dependent" applied in description
of an individual is clearly invidious. Freud's penetrating
dissection of the relationship between neurosis and dependency
has been so broadly persuasive that "it has generated a climate
in which all subsequent forms of dependency appear suspect,
especially those forms that have either theological sanctions
or the ritual affirmations of religious justification" (Rogers,
1974, p. 171). [4]
The climate of opinion on the matter of dependency has
also begun to affect our religious judgments as well. Christian theologians from Augustine to Schliermacher have variously
made the awareness of our absolute creaturely dependence a
central aspect of the human being as homo religiosus. Now,
however, we are more inclined to think of the human person as

83

"come of age" and maturity, religious and otherwise, as consisting in the assertion of our responsibility and self-determination. There is a legitimate recognition in this that religion has been complicit in maintaining individuals and whole social classes submissive to authority in a way that cut the nerve of creativity and self-expression and thwarted that growth that only happens under the risk of independent living. But that analysis is at best one-sided. As we come to understand more about the processes of self-becoming, instructed in part by the insights of object relations theory in psychoanalysis, the problem of dependency is cast in a different light.

The study of early childhood development, and the correlative ethological studies of mother-infant attachment among the higher primates (Ainsworth, 1969; Bowlby, 1958, 1960; Harlow, 1961) have resulted in a growing recognition of the "fact of normative dependence" (Saul and Parens, 1971, p. 6). By this we mean that the extended period of parental care required by the human infant by virtue of its immature state at birth makes the child utterly dependent on the ministrations of parental others not only for the provision of physical needs but also and as crucially for the organization of psychic structure. As Mahler expresses this point, the child "is at first absolutely, and remains later on - even 'unto the grave' - relatively dependent on a mother" (Mahler, 1972, p. 333). Dependence then is perhaps better defined, using the language of psychoanalysis, as "the need each human has, whether child, adolescent, or adult, for a libidinal object relation in order to insure his optimal psychic functioning" (Ibid., p. 9).

This definition of dependence is useful as far as it goes, but it requires an important extension. This way of describing normative dependence obscures the important insight that our dependence in the adult present is not only on actual persons potentially available to us as friends, lovers or familiars, but as crucially on the total experience of past significant relationships which, leaving behind an internal constellation of self and object representations,preserves a sense of "inner sustainment" (Parens, 1970; Saul, 1970). It is this inner sustainment that enables us to accept the fact of our perpetual indebtedness to help that must come from beyond us and of our enduring need for the love and acceptance of another. The "libidinal object relation(s)" upon which we are dependent then are not confined to concrete individuals in the here and now but include our on-going relationship with past individuals as we hold them alive psychically and even our relationship with objects that never drew breath as mortal beings. Faith is essentially related to this inner sustainment which makes possible a mature dependency (Fairbairn, 1952).

84

Here it would be helpful to make something of a digression and distinguish dependency in the sense we are employing it from the concept as it has generally appeared in the psychological literature and from a related notion, "attachment." "Dependency" was a higher level concept that early organized the research of American learning theorists with a non-clinical interest in psychoanalytic theory. Dependency was defined in the work of Robert Sears, John Whiting and their colleagues as a "learned motivational system, the manifestations of which are help-seeking, approval-seeking, and proximity-seeking behaviors" (Sears, 1972, p. 15) [5]

The attachment researchers, later historically, were by contrast largely British clinicians with a psychoanalytic background (Ainsworth, 1969; Bowlby, 1969). Attachment as used by these investigators refers to an emotionally intense tie or bond between the child - or infant primate in the case of the ethological studies - and the mother or other significant adult figure. This emotional linkage is one that is uniquely motivating and psychologically central in the development of the individual. Since the relatively recent encounter of these two literatures and research approaches there has been a sustained effort to determine where the two concepts refer in fact to two different processes and if so how they might be equivalently analyzed (for example in terms of behavioral systems) and how they might also be related developmentally (Gerwitz, 1972). Ainsworth has argued that for research purposes attachment should be the preferred concept because it serves the primary explanatory function of the dependency concept with none of its limitations (Ainsworth, 1969, 1972). Key among those limitations is the fact that dependency seems in popular usage not to admit levels of maturity. She is calling attention to the same attitude towards dependency which we have just described.

> To describe an adult as dependent implies an
> undesirable trait; to identify him as
> independent is to praise him. Attachments, in
> contrast, do not necessarily imply the
> immaturity and helplessness that dependency
> connotes. The describe an adult as attached to
> one or a few other persons implies a normal
> state of affairs; to characterize him as
> incapable of attachment connotes pathology."
> (Ainsworth, 1972, p. 101)

I want to agree with Ainsworth that attachment, i.e., the focused "enduring and pervasively influential" relationship to significant others, is the crucial concept directing our attention to the most important factor in human development.

Nevertheless, in abandoning the category of dependence to the social-learning theorists, Ainsworth overlooks a very important sense in which "dependence" and "dependency" is a term directly relevant to attachment issues. As Saul and Parens (1971) have pointed out, human beings are dependent upon their objects of attachment for the maintenance of psychic life. We can view human beings then in two distinct though clearly related ways: (1) in terms of the quality of their attachments, and (2) in terms of the character of their dependence upon those attachments.

Considered from this position we do not have a polarity of dependence/independence but rather a continuum of age and condition-appropriate dependence. A child up to a certain age is dependent on the actual physical presence of the parent, indeed "proximity-seeking" and "contact-maintaining" behavior is regarded by Ainsworth and others as the hallmark of attachment behaviors in both human beings and higher primates (Ainsworth, 1972, pp. 115-117). But on a schedule very much contingent on the security or insecurity of the child's attachment to these significant adults, a process of internalization occurs in the child whereby the child is able to maintain the sense of well-being and relatedness even in the absence of the parent. This is the process which Winnicott has brilliantly examined under the rubric of transitional object phenomena (Winnicott, 1953). We would say of a child who past a certain age still becomes anxious and upset when the mother or father is out of their sight that he or she displays an immature dependence. A more precise way of putting it, however, would be to say that there is evidence in the behavior that dependence on the visible and available parental figure has not shifted to a dependence on the internalized representation of the parent or some representation ("proto-symbolized" in the transitional object) which holds for the child that sense of the reliability of goodness - the child's own goodness and that of the world (Winnicott, 1965, pp. 83-92)

What must be emphasized is that this new vantage on the dynamics of dependence has consequences for how we see maturity, and in particular the maturity of faith. Until recently we have been accustomed to seeing the failure of development in the fearfulness about being "as a self,' that is, in a clinging and persistent neediness manifested as the conscious or unconscious conviction that one can not be adequate by oneself.[6] But missteps in that elaborate choreography of separation and individuation can have opposite consequences. Without a fundamental sense of trust in the reliability and the availability of love and care, without the processes of faith that renew and sustain that sense, one can be left with an intolerable sense of weakness and vulnerability in which the self is constantly at risk. "People who need people," so a popular song goes, "are the luckiest people in the world." In some respects this song speaks to the inner experience of those persons whose faith in the possibility of a rewarding attachment to another has been early compromised. It expresses the poignant situation of one who looks out from the prison of that betrayed faith into a world of relationship that may be attractive to contemplate but too fearful to enter. The "schizoid" defense against the sense of vulnerability that dependence induces involves in part the assumption of an attitude of self-reliance and self-containment that denies one's natural human dependence for love and support on those who (that which?) is beyond us (Guntrip, 1969, p. 43).

We are witness to a convergence of what the religious tradition in the West at its best has always known and what the psychoanalytic community has begun to suspect over the last decade. Behind the stubborn assertions of independence and adequacy of the self-made individual, as well as the implacable generosity of the relentless altruist who never seems to need or ask anything for him/herself, there may lie a quality of unfaith that regards the world as hostile and threatening to that side of themselves which would acknowledge need and seek relationship. The admission of dependence would be an invitation to reexperience disappointment and betrayal. To push the matter to its most radical point, perhaps to admit an ultimate need, one that exceeds the resources of any finite source of love and strength, would be to risk ultimate frustration.

III. The "To Where" of Faith

We have taken the position that the foundational problem with which faith has to deal is the life-long project of becoming a self. This is not given with birth, it is not an unquestioned or unconditional endowment. Rather, the creation and maintenance of a cohesive and coherent sense of self begins in the complex interaction of the child's innate readiness to respond and the concurrence of an "average expectable environment" which in the human situation means an interpersonal environment, the matrix of relationship with parents made "uniquely adaptive by reason of love" (Winnicott, 1965). It is within this interpersonal universe that is the child's first world that the foundations of faith are laid which will have to support the construction of those aspects of self-becoming which we have singled out for particular attention: the sense of being fully alive, real and vitally engaged in a world that is itself real, nuanced, expanding and responding; the capacity to be alone; and the capacity to accept that dependency which is simply given with our existence as human beings.

The process of becoming a self begins in the family circle, and preeminently in the mother-child dyad, but it does not end there. It is carried on in the ceaseless interaction of the inner world of the individual and an ever expanding arena of interpersonal interactions. To say that faith must be regarded developmentally is only to acknowledge that at every bend and turn in the course of a life the confluence of circumstance, social factors and the maturation and declination of one's personal capacities, faculties and talents presents a new claim on one's sense of self. It is as though life says, "Here, can you accommodate this piece of reality?" Can you enlarge your map of the world (i.e., your map of yourself in the world) to include the fact of your sexuality, the mystery and design of the sexuality and personality of another person, this loss and that gain, the awareness of your own finitude, the intrusive face of your own death? At the advent of each of these crises - these dangerous opportunities and opportune dangers - there is an assent that must be summoned from the depths of those psychic resources which constitute us as selves. John Dunne writes of this assent:

> A Yes is required of one, it seems, at every
> stage of life. There is a task at each stage
> which begins with a consciousness and ends with
> a consent. The world emerges into
> consciousness, then sexuality, then morality,
> then spirit. At each stage, one's task is
> accomplished when one makes one's way through to
> consent. If one does not reach that point the
> task remains unfinished and carries into the
> next stage of life. If one does succeed in
> consenting, then the thing that has emerged into
> consciousness becomes something human. It loses
> its divine and uncanny quality and becomes part
> of one's humanity. (Dunne, 1973, p. 81)

Underwriting this capacity for consent at every point is that organization of psychic energies we call faith. Its program is the movement through these life situations which progressively extend consciousness and solicit consent. The consequence, as Dunne proposes, is an enlargement and an enrichment of our humanity. We might very well ask here, however, whether we do not feel a need to say more about this process and its direction. Do we not want to ask, looking at the developmental history of faith, "What is the objective of this assent, where does it lead, what is the end of it all?" In the words we have chosen to organize the multiple aspects of an anthropology of faith: What is the goal of human self-becoming? What is the "to where" of faith development?

Here it must be acknowledged that while psychoanalytic theory in its present state of development shows itself fairly proficient at identifying the failures and fixations in the development of the self, particularly as these display themselves in the hazardous crossing of later life crises, it has been less able to render a convincing account of normative, let alone optimal, self-development. Perhaps Freud's laconic statement of the goal of successful analysis as the achievement of the capacity to love and to work - leben und arbeiten - is as adequate a rendering of the goal of human development as a secular human science should aspire to. But is this as much as we would want to say of the process of faith in human life? I think not, or at least not without some crucial qualifications. However, to claim a direction for our growth in faith and to begin to develop a psychological description of what that "fullness of faith" might involve, I believe that we must turn first to the theological for guidance. Within the wealth of that reflective tradition we do not want for descriptions of the life of faith towards which all our efforts are bent. We have already seen a number of such accounts in Chapter Two.

H. Richard Niebuhr identified the "to where" of faith development as the life of "integrated selfhood," a peculiarly psychological sounding term for a theologian but one which he richly amplified by reference to the idea of participation in the kingdom of God, or, as he otherwise described it, "the commonwealth of being." The integration of split-off and fragmented aspects of the self by a trusting loyalty to the Principle of Being enables a kind of whole-seeing that moves the individual beyond lesser allegiances and conflicting commitments and towards a vision of the whole as God might see it. But observe, faith as whole-seeing for Niebuhr finally only finds its significance in the whole-acting which it enables. This order of faith-knowing derives its final significance from the life of dedicated responsibility which it enables.

The Catholic writers we examined drove more directly for this last stage as a statement of the telos of faith. Faith exists for charity. We do not see the mature man or woman of faith directly. What we see are lives of courageous self-donation; lives lived on-behalf-of; lives that replicate or incarnate the sacramental presence of the living Christ. [see Chapter 2, part IV]. There is a sense in which at least the Catholic perspective on faith that we have looked at, and likely the Protestant as well, would give their own equivalent to Freud's answer when asked the question, "What is the developmental goal of the faith which sustains self-becoming?" Their reply might also be "to love and to work": to love - where that love has as its horizon and final paradigm the inclusive, justicing and compassionate love modeled in the life of Christ; to work - when the ultimate theatre of labor regardless of the particular vocation is seen to be the comprehensive caring of the kingdom of God. [7]

If we were now to return from these sorts of statements to the universe of psychological discourse, for what portion of this picture might we find description within the psychoanalytic interpretation of self-becoming? We know as we do this that our descriptions will never nearly exhaust the whole of the meaning of the full life of faith, but that has never been our presumption. Our question remains, what is offered to our understanding of the processes of faith by the vantage which modern psychoanalytic theory gives us on human development? We have described the "from whence" of faith development as the problem of the formation and maintenance of the self, and within that we have identified four aspects which have correlates within traditional religious descriptions of the activity of faith. Let us now do the same for the "to where" of faith development. Having taken our first cues from the side of the theological we look for the parallel discussion on the side of the psychological.

It appears to me, translating the foregoing theological discourse on mature faith into the language of psychodynamics, that the fullness of faith development is most adequately reflected in the human capacity for love and self-commitment. Now in the first instance the love and intimacy I am referring to is nothing more esoteric, and yet, nothing less remarkable, than the relationship that may happen any time in the course of a life from the child's first love affair with the mother, to the onset of chumship, from the encounter with the beloved stranger that is husband, wife or lover, to the love extended to friend and neighbor. When we appreciate the often precarious problem of self-becoming, set within the context of inevitable human limitations and finitude, then we appreciate with Ernest Becker why "the ability to stand open to love is a sort of heroism" (Becker, 1962, p. 84).

The venture of love requires the same inner sustainment that makes it possible to bear aloneness and to accept dependence, for in loving someone, anyone, we make ourselves vulnerable to the first and gravest threat to the integrity of the self - being abandoned, bereft or disappointed by the loved one(s). It is for this reason that George Goethals observes that to love is to put oneself "in harm's way." To love is to risk the coherence and wholeness of the self by admitting one's reliance upon another and by putting their happiness and interest on a par with and even before one's own (Goethals, 1978). Every such experience through to the end of life may potentially re-evoke the trauma associated with earlier experiences of loving and leaving or loving and losing. At the same time every summons to the engagement of love draws upon the psychic resources constituted in earlier experience of life which encourage the individual to risk self in acts of sharing and radical caring.

Love is related to self-becoming then as both the goal of the life of the self and as a source or beginning of the development which eventuates in a human being capable of giving and receiving love. Awareness of this should give us a fresh appreciation of the psychological profundity of St. Augustine's comment, "Qui amasti me, fecistime amabilem" - "because Thou has loved me first, Thou hast made me lovable." It is because we are "loved first," received from the beginning as creatures loved for ourselves, that we know ourselves as lovable, worthy to receive the love of others, and love-able, capable of loving others in return. The faith that is present at the beginning in the trust which enables an individual to reach towards the single other is on a line of development with the faith that undergirds the love that crosses boundaries of race, class and caste; the love that creates communion and discovers intimacy with the stranger and the alien; and finally the love that takes the Mystery itself to be known by no better name than love (1 John 4:8).

Just as we broke the notion of self-becoming down into four discrete though related aspects, so too it would be helpful here to analyze the capacity for love as we have been discussing it in terms of two component parts chosen because of their relevance to faith as a dynamic process: 1) the development of the capacity to tolerate ambivalence, and 2) the development of the sense of oneself as available for loving and self-donation.

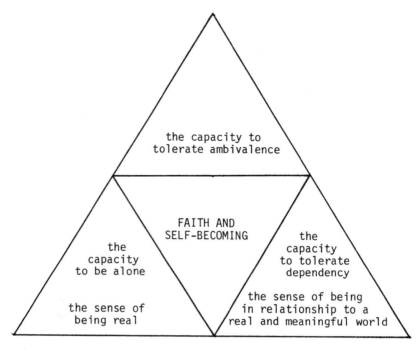

figure 6.

Faith is involved in the development of the capacity to tolerate ambivalence

    C.S. Lewis was fond of quoting a brief prayer which to his mind captured the heart of what the relationship of prayer was all about: "May it be the real Thou that I speak to; may it be the real me that speaks." This same wish might very well be taken to express the dual aspects under which we assess the maturity of any human relationship, whether that relationship is with God or with another person. We want to know whether the individual is relating to the whole indistorted reality of the other or only to a part perception. We also want to know whether that relationship fully engages the whole self or whether for some reason the self is reserved from the relationship, the "real" or true self hiding behind some sort of persona of which the individual may not even be fully aware. The latter aspect of this twin problem in relationships we have begun discussing under the general rubric of the challenge to become a whole self which we have claimed is, in its broadest sense, the fons et origo of the problem of faith. The former aspect of the problem of loving "wholly" is also intimately related to the processes of self-becoming. This aspect we shall discuss using the category of "ambivalence."

Freud used the term ambivalence (Ambitendenz) in his 1913 monograph Totem and Taboo to refer to a phenomenon he had observed earlier in his correspondence with Fliess (1892-1909). The decisive characteristic of this phenomenon was "the simultaneous existence of love and hatred towards the same object" (Freud, 1913, p. 157). It was a normal occurrence, he held, "but a high degree of it is certainly a special particularity of neurotic people" (Freud, 1912, p. 106). Freud's own thinking about the possible origins of these powerful conflicting emotions went through a number of developments that follow the major phases of his theoretical evolution (Holder, 1975). In the end he proposed a dual instinct theory that counterpoised innate aggressive and libidinal energies (Freud, 1920, 1923). Yet even after this he seems to have left room for the decisive effect of early experience in the generation of the conflict between love and hate as emotions directed toward the same significant other.

> A powerful tendency to aggressiveness is always present beside a powerful love, and the more passionately a child loves its object the more sensitive does it become to disappointments and frustrations from that object; and in the end the love must succumb to the accumulative hostility.
> (Freud, 1933, p. 124)

Discussion on the role of ambivalence in the process of human development has turned on just this issue of whether it reflects an innate conflict or one that has its origins in the universal experience of infancy. Analysts have also been divided on whether the discussion of ambivalence appropriately refers only to an affect resident in the individual, or whether attention must also be given to the effect of this conflict on perceptions of the interpersonal world. In other words, is ambivalence a quality of objects as well as an experience of subjects? In this dissertation I opt for the latter, following a line of study that begins with Karl Abraham's formulation of a developmental schema for ambivalence (Abraham, 1924) and passing through the work of Melanie Klein to influence the work of object relations theorists such as W.R. D. Fairbairn, Margaret Mahler and D.W. Winnicott.

In the process of this passage the notion of an innate source of aggression drops away in favor of a concept of aggression as a response to the vicissitudes of the interaction between parent and child and the almost inevitable frustrations which to a greater or lesser extent are built into that relationship. The child, it is held, experiences both an intense, almost "devouring" need for the parent and at the same time a tremendous anger or rage over failures in parenting, frustrations in the need for attachment which are a consequence of the limitations of the parents and to a certain degree are a necessary part of the slow weaning of the child. The infantile dilemma is what to do with these intolerably conflicting affects. The solution, it is hypothesized, is in the twin processes of projection whereby the developing child locates in the external world those undesirable emotions, and the processes of introjection whereby the child "takes in" those aspects of the interpersonal universe associated with what is good and satisfying and dependable. Thus in order to preserve the goodness and reliability of the parent, the child in projecting both hatred and love, goodness and badness, is utilizing the defense of splitting. Almost as though there were two separate and unconnected figures in the universe, the child identifies as good the parental representations associated with the memory of the satisfaction of the need for closeness, acceptance, nurturance and the alleviation of anxiety; and as bad those representations linked to the tension of unfulfilled needs.

As children get older and under the optimal conditions of parenting they slowly come to perceive the parent as a "whole object" capable both of satisfying and frustrating. At the same time the child is arriving at a more unified and more realistic sense of being a whole person as well, a person possessed of the capacity for both love and hate, injury and pardon. Entering what Melanie Klein called the "depressive position" the child comes to have a need to make reparation for the injury which his or her anger is perceived as capable of in the life of the parent. Here begins the dynamic origin of the capacity for mutual role taking and for the experience of empathy, or as Winnicott preferred to call it, for "ruth" (Winnicott, 1963).

We have moved very quickly over a tremendously complicated, still imperfectly understood and much controverted developmental process, but the general structure of my argument should be visible. The human dilemma, succinctly put, is that we desire to regard ourselves as loving and beloved creatures intimate with a universe that is itself disposed kindly towards us and welcoming of our initiatives. But what we encounter early on is the problematic character of reality and the conflicting nature of our own feelings. Even before it is layered over with our own projected negative emotions, the impinging environment comes to us as both welcoming and

94

forbidding, gracious and hostile, satisfying and frustrating. The various ego defenses which we have alluded to are a means, often ingenious, of maintaining a perception of a world that is still hopeful and, so far as possible, of ourselves as worthy of love.[8]   The cost of these strategies unfortunately is a paring down and diminishment both of ourselves and our world. Faith, I would argue, is related to love as the power of trust and reliance which enables us to see clearly and assent wholly to the genuine condition of ourselves as would-be lovers and of the would-be objects of our love.   Though the crisis of ambivalence is initially focused in the first three years of life, the problem of accepting the coexistence of love and hate in ourselves and good and evil in the world remains with us throughout life.

In order to genuinely love the world we must first find it, and that is no small accomplishment. Faith, as Fowler observed, is involved in the process of constructing a "life map" by which we can find our way through the "compounds of limitation" (Bowker) which ring us around and to the others that are given us to love and serve. The accuracy of this life map, which I shall shortly relate to "the representational world" (Sandler and Rosenblatt, 1962) is not determined on positivistic grounds. It is not about the withdrawal of all projections. This would be an undesirable prospect even if it were possible.   What we can move towards is the mitigation of those defenses against ambivalence which require us, in the interest of preserving a beloved self and a loving world, to distort both ourselves and the world in the direction of polarization.

Faith then is set against what William Lynch called "the absolutizing imagination," the imagination bereft of a sense of irony which goes about dividing the world into camps and categories of radical good and radical evil, saints and sinners, sick and well (Lynch, 1965).   The faith that overcomes ambivalence and enables mature love and genuine intimacy is the faith that supports a whole-seeing.   It is a trust that endures the realization that most objects of my attachment are at their best less than my idealizations would have them and at their worst better than my severe judgments upon them.   It is also a trust in my fundamental worth and lovableness in spite of the fact that I show up invariably less than my lofty expectations for myself and yet more adequate than my worst fears.   Faith describes an underlying assurance of goodness and possibility that supports an awareness that the world as the object of my love and attention is imperfect, fallible, frustrating and yet confounding of all my efforts to divide it into good and bad, acceptable and unacceptable, us and them, mine and yours.

95

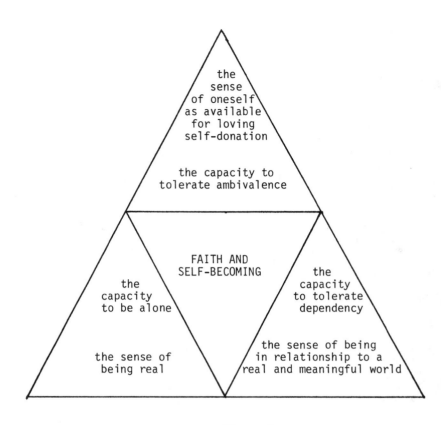

figure 7.

Faith undergirds the sense of oneself as available for loving
self-donation.

By this statement I mean to state only more explicitly and
with more precision what we have been considering all along:
the way in which faith supports the human self-becoming which
is begun and fulfilled in love. That the human person is made
for communion - and made by communion - is a truth which the
Christian and Jewish traditions have understood well before the
work of George Herbert Mead, Martin Buber or Harry Stack
Sullivan gave us the language of the social self to express
this elemental fact of our lives. "The self is a will to
belong," Daniel Day Williams puts it (Williams, 1968, p. 205).
And yet every invitation to communion simultaneously involves
an activity of self-giving and hence is potentially experienced

96

as a threat to the self as we know it. What is our assurance that what we are giving away will be returned or renewed? How are we about to change and can what we trust that that change will not undo us? Williams accurately catches the sense of this inner and largely unconscious debate which strikes us on the threshold of sharing:

> The objective self at a given moment is largely the deposit of experience as shaped by our self-understanding. This given self bears its freight of hurt and hope, its creativity and anxiety, its self-seeking, and its groping for love. We cling to this self as it is. We fear it is all we have. Even its sufferings are familiar and we clutch them because their very familiarity is comforting and saves us from facing the deeper suffering hidden underneath.
>
> (Ibid., p. 207)

The move towards self-donation of the sort that builds true community between two people, among many people, requires faith. It requires an enduring trust that such an action, perhaps against all evidence to the contrary, will author life and not death, a fuller, larger self and not the self's final impoverishment. In penultimate but relevant ways we know about the need for faith from the study of the psychodynamics of human intimacy. Intimacy, of which sexual intimacy is a privileged though not exclusive paradigm, involves a significant risk and vulnerability. It requires a capacity to forget oneself in the desire to give to another while at the same time allowing oneself the openness to receive what is sheer gift. In intimacy ego boundaries become uncertain and the fantasy of merger is a psychic possibility which may either be tremendously gratifying or utterly terrifing (Kernberg, 1976, pp. 183-213). Does identity precede intimacy (Erikson), or intimacy precede identity (Sullivan)? The debate exposes a complex dialectic of human development. Some measure of identity, some relatively cohesive sense of self appears requisite to risking the self-giving of intimacy, and yet it is equally true that it is largely in and through such sharing that the human person comes to know him- or herself as a self capable of love (Goethals, 1973).

An analysis of interpersonal intimacy still only offers us an analogue to the self-giving and self-sacrifice which is announced in the Gospel as the way of life. All that psychologists have begun to understand of the ways of interpersonal intimacy does not gut the paradox or dull the offense of Christ's words that "He who would save his life shall lose it, and he who would lose his life for my sake shall save it" (Luke

97

9:24), and "No greater love has any man than that he lay down his life for his friends" (John 15:13). Still, our examination of the dynamics of human communion does offer us some clue towards comprehending what must finally remain a mystery of grace. The desire we have for communion, for a mode of sharing in which our capacity for self-giving is fully realized, is as immense as those forces which seem set against that ever being a reality - our own finitude, the unreliability and limitations of our natures, the entropy of human passion. The stubborn persistence of this desire to belong, to find a place with, and to give of oneself is evidence perhaps of the goal of that drive. Williams again:

> For every particular love contains an implicit question of which we become gradually aware, and which may come into sharp focus only in crisis: "Where is the absolute and trustworthy fulfillment of the self's will to belong?" The will to belong cannot stop short of an absolute that fulfills it. . .man seeks community with the source of his being. . .The self craves the completely trustworthy fulfillment of the will to belong. Only to whatever fulfills our being can we give ourselves without despair.
> (Williams, 1968, p. 209)

The Christian revelation names that which can receive in complete trustworthiness all that we have to give "the God relationship." Properly speaking the discernment of where and how this relationship begins to invite commitment is the domain of theology. What we can legitimately ask in an investigation of the psychology of faith is what is the "humanward" side of the process by which an individual is brought to the capacity for this order of radical love. In line with what we have said till now of the psychodynamics of faith, it would be reasonable to expect that the same conditions which cause an individual to hold back from the risk of interpersonal intimacy and self-donation are at work in the fear and mistrust which resists the transforming reception of God's agape. The matter is this: our sense of ourselves as available for communion or what I have called "loving self-donation" never proceeds from a deprivation or an inner emptiness but rather from a taste of the satisfaction in sharing which creates a hunger and a capacity for more comprehensive and more profound sharing. Without that basic inner sustainment of which the psychoanalysts have tried to speak, the person is not wholly available for self-donation. Some part of the energies of the self for relationship remain reserved in a kind of holding action that is a never-to-be-relaxed guard against the

98

potential disappointment which could be an attack upon a fragile sense of self. There is a paradox here, and it is the one captured in the scripture, "To the one who has more shall be given him, and to the one who has little even that little shall be taken away" (Matthew 25:29). The literature of Christian aescetical theology is, to be sure, full of the language of the individual's absolute neediness and impoverishment before the plenum of God. But, psychologically speaking, the awareness of that abundance, and even more the faith that risks leaving a familiar position, however much a desert, would seem to proceed from some prior foundational sense of the trustworthiness and goodness of the object of faith.

In saying this I am in effect proposing an answer, or the beginning of an answer, to a persistent question for the psychology of faith which H. Richard Niebuhr posed as the problem of "whether the self is led more to trust in the ultimate because it finds all the finite beings about it unreliable, or more because it is led by stages from trust in the near-at-hand to trust in the ultimate. . .is it because all finite powers on which we have relied for value have failed us that we turn to the ultimate, or because we have seen traces of the structure of faith in the whole realm of being that we are led to confidence in Being simply considered?" (H.R. Niebuhr, 1963, p. 120). Both options, so sharply counterposed to one another, have a sort of intuitive sensibleness. Almost like William James' portrayals of the healthy-minded and the sick soul which these two alternatives so closely resemble, we can imagine with little difficulty what exemplars of these two ways of faith might look like. The one we might picture as the person who moves from one defeat and disappointment to another and in the process is driven to reliance on the infinite from the depths of a life which feels like a downward spiral. The other by contrast would be one of those persons we have all encountered who seem to bound from one graced relationship to another like spiritual mountain goats and who when they reach the top of the mountain simply keep climbing.

There is always something appealing about the economy of dualistic distinctions, and almost always something untrue about them if we look more closely at the actual data of human lives. In this case I would argue that both processes Niebuhr identifies are at play in the faith life of most people. The spirit of argument which we have been pursuing would tend to emphasize the continuity between the structures of faith in ordinary life and faith that is directed towards the infinite, but this continuity is often there in a foundational way making it possible for an individual to negotiate the experiences which birth a more radical form of faith. In other terms, some form of fundamental trust, laid down in the concreteness of our actual experience of trustworthy and available others, creates the conditions whereby we might remain enough intact in the face of the failure of the finite to be empowered and motivated to reach beyond it.

FOOTNOTES CHAPTER THREE

1. For an instructive discussion of how two theoretical positions within psychoanalysis can exhibit divergent world views, see J.O. Wisdom, "Freud and Melanie Klein: Psychology, Ontology and Weltanshauung." In C. Hanley and M. Lazarowitz (eds.), Psychoanalysis and Philosophy, New York: International Universities Press, 1970.

2. It should be observed that H. Richard Niebuhr here and elsewhere takes radical monotheism to be theologically normative and, correspondingly, "wholeness" or integration of the psyche to be psychologically primary. As noted earlier, the latter is contested by certain psychologists who argue that a plurality of psychic roles is truer to human experience and optimal for human functioning (Hillman, 1975; Lifton, 1967). The former draws fire from theologians who urge a return to a recognition of a plurality of "gods" to which we are sequentially devoted but no one of which can be regarded as ultimate (Miller, 1974). Presumably there could be as well objections raised against Niebuhr's assumptions from the position of non-Western religious traditions where the ideal of oneness or unity in the divine receives little recognition. In this book I have chosen to side with the psychological position which regards psychic cohesiveness and integration as a prized, if seldom fully realized, aim of the developmental process. Similarly I have identified myself with Niebuhr's radical monotheism wanting only to point out in its defense that even on its own terms it requires us to acknowledge the cultural boundedness and limitations of all ideas of God, even presumably the ideal of monotheism in so far as it is a cultural artifact.

3. See also the work of Gardner Murphy on the interaction of human consciousness, creativity and the active construction of reality (Murphy, 1958; Murphy and Spohn, 1968).

4. "We must therefore not forget to include the influence of civilization among the determinants of neurosis. . .Since the demands of civilization are represented by family upbringing, we must bear in mind the part played by this biological

characteristic of the human species - the prolonged period of
its childhood dependence - in the etiology of the neuroses"
(Freud, 1940, p. 185).

5. The authoritative review of this social learning concept
of dependency is Maccoby and Masters (1979).

6. I am using the idea of fearfulness about being "as a self"
in Tillich's sense where it is contrasted with the fear of
being "as a part." The courage "to be as oneself" and "to be
as a part" parallels the tension we have observed between the
dynamics of separateness and oneness, the need for
individuality and uniqueness, and the need for community and
affiliation. (Tillick, 1952).

7. The other contemporary theological work which is highly
relevant here is Daniel Day William's The Spirit and the Forms
of Love (Williams, 1968). Williams makes some important
distinctions which offer direction for our discussion. First,
he confirms the point that the meaning and destiny of biblical
faith is found in love, and more particularly the love which
has as its goal communion, "experiences of joyful ecstacy,
delightful companionship and reconciliation" (Williams, 1968,
p. 14). But secular humanists have offered to say about as
much about human life and the art of loving and without reference to the transcendent dimension. The problem for Williams
as a Christian theologian is how to describe the relationship
between human loves (eros) such as the love of mother and
child, husband and wife, lover and beloved, and God's love for
creation, the agape of the New Testament. Notice that the
distinction is not drawn between our love of human others and
our love of God as though that was the radical and primary
division to be made. The first distinction is between the love
we are naturally, capable of, all human loves including the
love we have for God, and God's love for us. As Williams puts
it, "the important question is how and where the human loves
discover that they cannot fulfill themselves, yet are fulfilled
beyond themselves" (Williams, 1968, p. 13).

The assumption guiding William's inquiry into the relation
of the divine and human loves is the same as guides our
interrogation of faith, and that is that it has a developmental
history which is inextricable from the dynamic processes of
human growth as a self. Williams offers this assumption thus:

> . . .that all the loves work within the history of
> the self's becoming. No love, whether it be the
> ethical love of neighbor, or the love in the sexual
> life, or the love of God for man, is a "thing," a
> static pattern or form. It is a spirit at work in

101

life and taking form in the process of becoming. Therefore we have to understand love as history, and we are concerned with its origins, development and fruition.

(Williams, 1968, p. 13)(emphasis added)

To adopt and adapt a phrase from William's quote, we are concerned to understand faith as history and are discovering that the history of faith is very much bound up with the history of those loves. Indeed, it might be fair to say that it is the inextricable character of those two histories that is the burden of this project.

8. What we know clinically is that persons will sacrifice a sense of themselves as good in order to retain a sense of contact or relationship with another. At least where there is a relationship, however persecutory and unrewarding, there is the confirmed sense of self. As Harry Stack Sullivan wrote, it is better to be a "bad-me" than a "not-me" (Sullivan, 1953, p. 161). W.R.D. Fairbairn described this particular strategy for maintaining the self as the defense of guilt. His particular metaphor for the process, though he did not seem to appreciate it, is a literal description of the use of a particular form of God and self-representation for the maintenance of a sense of self-in-relation: "It is better to be a sinner in a world ruled by God than to live in a world ruled by the Devil. A sinner in a world ruled by Goid may be bad, but there is always a certain sense of security to be derived from the fact that the world around is good. . . ." (Fairbairn, 1952, pp. 66-67).

CHAPTER FOUR

HOW DOES FAITH FUNCTION? ENTER THE MATTER OF CONTENT

I.   The Questions in the Margin. . . . . p. 104

II. From Personal Images to the Transcendent . . . . p. 105

III. From the Transcendent to "God" . . . . p. 114

IV. Object Representations Revisited . . . . p. 117

V.   The Object Representation of God
     and the Conceptualization of God . . . . p. 124

VI. Summary . . . . p. 133

CHAPTER FOUR

HOW DOES FAITH FUNCTION? ENTER THE MATTER OF CONTENT

I.   The Questions in the Margin

In his book The Rock and the River, Anglican theologian
Martin Thornton describes his experience of reading the later
writings of Bonhoffer in which Bonhoffer proposes a
"religionless Christianity" and describes the state of faith
beyond religion. As Thornton read he says he found himself
constantly scribbling in the margins of the test the short-hand
query, "Y.B.H.?" which he translates, "Yes, but how?"
(Thornton, 1965). The reader of a functional analysis of faith
such as presented in the preceding chapter may very likely be
making the same marginalia. The accounts of the beginning and
end points of faith development may be persuasive and even
compelling, but we come upon ourselves asking, "How,
concretely, does the faith which sustains self-becoming
establish itself?" What is the medium or vehicle or effective
presencing of that fundamental trust which undergirds the sense
of one's own reality and that of the world, that supports the
capacity to be alone and to tolerate the necessary dependence
we have on others, that sponsors a life of love and commitment
in a world of paradox and irony? How even do we observe these
processes in action? We might think we know what to look for
in assessing the quality of interpersonal communion in everyday
life (though that is a harder task than it might appear), but
where do we look to observe a person in relationship to "Being
simply considered?" As we have done before, I suggest that we
find our way into a psychological answer by way of the
intuitions of a theologian.

H. Richard Niebuhr in discussing just this problem of how
an individual comes to faith links the process of faith with
what he terms "the reasoning of the heart," that activity
whereby the human person makes personal sense of the cumulative
weight of the past, the total impinging reality of the present
moment, and the lure or terror of the future (H.R. Niebuhr,
1941, pp. 71-100). The reasoning of the heart is not the
objective, discursive and dispassionate operation of the mind,
though it is a cognitive operation and by no means
anti-rational. It is the affective act of interpretation of
our total experience. Its medium is not abstract concepts that
can be cooly and critically manipulated. Its material is
images, the living products of the human imagination. Niebuhr
sadly recognizes that we know this reasoning of faith more
often in its broken form in which it involves "the evil
imaginations of the heart," the distorted images of self and

104

others that is at the root of our mistrust and fearfulness and envy before the prospect of community.

> We meet each one with an imagination whereby we supply what is lacking in the immediate datum and are enabled to respond, rightly or wrongly, to a whole of reality of which this affection is for us a symbol and a part. In this realm all our images seem to be personal. We cannot think here with the aid of impersonal ideas; we cannot use machines as our models or mathematical formulae as our patterns. . . The question which is relevant for the life of the self among selves is not whether personal images should be employed but only what personal images are right and adequate and which are evil imaginations of the heart. (Ibid., p. 72)

The need for adequate images to reason with is not confined to the area of interpersonal relationships. When the individual person or when a community of persons is pressed to reflect upon the totality of the existence in which it is immersed and to take a relationship to that totality, then there is a compelling need for images that can bear the weight of that reality and interpret it to the heart. Here, too, Niebuhr suggests it is "personal images" which arise as the most adequate and the most appropriate. By personal images Niebuhr does not necessarily mean images of a person, but he does mean nothing less than those images which we encounter and which encounter us with the power and the address of the personal. He means images which are adequate for a heart that asks not "What is the nature of the universe?" but more primally, "Who is finally there for me?"

II. From Personal Images to the Transcendent

If we shift now from Niebuhr to recall the preceding discussion of self-becoming we can discern the convergence of a remarkably similar intuition. It is a central tenet of object relations theory that the human being's first universe is an interpersonal one, that dyadic and subsequently the triadic relationship with the parenting other(s). To secure a footing for the fragile but growing sense of being a separate self, the human child is absolutely dependent upon the reception he or she receives from birth in this interpersonal world. The sense of being loved as oneself, or loved for being someone else, or not loved at all, is known by the processes of internalization. That is, it is known by the formation of representations of the loving, ambivalent or rejecting other and of oneself in relationship to that other. The child may deal with these representations in so far as they are threatening to the integrity of the emerging self by projection, denial, "splitting" or some other defensive process - all of which have implications for the evolving self and object representations. These become the foundation and active referent for the individual's sense of value and meaning, the sense of one's own life as valued and possessed of meaning and the world at large as a reality to be prized and trusted. We might think of the creation of an inner world which functions as "mental model," a "working" model in every sense, by which to assess what is to be valued and what is to be avoided, what enhances the sense of our selves as good and worthy and what threatens that sense (Sandler, 1960).

Faith, as that fundamental trust and reliance basic to self-becoming, always is anchored in some center of meaning and value (Fowler, 1974). Psychoanalytic object relations theory reveals that such centers have their developmental origins in these processes of self and object representation. It is because of this history that we find upon investigation that the "images" by which persons make emotional sense of their lives, of their existence as selves, are profoundly personal. We would expect to find this true even when the secondary process elaboration of these images appears highly abstract or conceptual. Behind even these apparently impersonal images is the shadow of the personal relationship whose history made these particular images potent for the self.

If we are to connect this analysis to the concerns which are basic to the theological enterprise, a crucial point must be made about these "centers of meaning and value" which are the locus of faith. The point is that the representational constructions which secure and hold our faith, however tenuously, are not constant through the course of a single life. Rather, they must be constantly re-elaborated and reworked if they are to accommodate new challenges to the integrity of the self. Failing that they are abandoned and new centers of value must be constructed in the complex interplay of the self and object representations which are the psychic inheritance of an individual's relational past, the symbolic resources available in the environment, the ongoing interaction with others in the present, and - most elusive, and yet most crucial - the individual's living encounter and response to the limit of human existence (Kaufman, 1969) - the mystery of finitude and fullness which addresses the individual at the boundary and in the very midst of human living.

As it has evolved, psychoanalytic theory has come to understand in some detail the beginning stages of this developmental process the way in which basic trust is related to the elaboration of a libidinally cathected internal mother image (Sandler, 1960). To the imago of the mother is joined that of the father, if the father is a psychological presence in the life of the child, and together their multiple memories may function preconsciously as a "background of safety" that sponsors the growing child's venturing out into the world. Beyond this basic start, however, the account of the fate and function of these foci of faith becomes somewhat unclear in the psychoanalytic literature. Freud saw that to the patterns set down in the parental relationships could be "linked the influences of teachers and authorities, self chosen models and publicly recognized heroes" (Freud, 1924b, p. 168). He also saw that the human person when later confronted with the fact of fate and the harshness of the universe would deal with it at a higher symbolic level, religiously or philosophically, but would draw upon the material of these earlier, personal representations. Hence we have Freud's insight that God, or Providence, or Nature, as efforts to manage the pain and privation of living, relied upon the configuration of parental representations laid down in earlier life and largely kept from consciousness (Freud, 1924b). For Freud, of course, such a means of adaptation to life was inherently deficient, based as it was on wish fulfillment and relying as it did on an infantile pattern of dependency. Yet this left open the issue of the fate of these parental introjections and the feelings which surrounded them. In so far as they survived as superego phenomena the problem through life seemed for Freud more a matter of how to disarm them or render them less punitive than how to draw them into more mature and more adequate support for the adult ego.

Subsequent analytic theorists have done better by this problem, understanding that the super-ego can be both "loving and beloved" (Schafer, 1960), can function in processes of integration and orientation (Schecter,1979) and can play a positive role in adult adaptation (Schafer, 1967). The notion of the possibility of "regression in the service of the ego" (Kris, 1935) names the intuition that a return to the foundations of our self-formation in the psychic interaction with our earliest representational world can have positive implications for our adult functioning. In all of this there has yet been little attention to the way in which the inner world of self and object representations can in fact develop in tandem with intellectual and emotional growth. We are told that the optimal fate of these earlier representational constellations is to be cleaned up of ambivalent affect, the sexual and aggressive drives which render them problematic (Meissner, 1979); and to become more complex and stable, more integrated into the self system (Loewald, 1962). Yet there is, curiously, relatively little work that follows up on Freud's sense that the fate of our early faith in the parent was to find its way into the structuring of our subsequent faiths as adults - a fate that he had admittedly negative judgments upon.

We are left with the question of where the development from the "background of safety" leads to. What is the horizon of this development? To cast the question in the terms of our present discourse, is there a dynamism which moves the processes of faith beyond finite centers of meaning and value even as it maintains its continuity with those centers?

H. Richard Niebuhr, as we have earlier seen, answers this question for the tradition of religious monotheism. The human person when endeavoring consciously or unconsciously, to respond to the single reality beyond the many that confront the self, enters into a relationship with the transcendent. That unitary reality may yet be experienced as inimical to the life of the self (God the enemy). In so far, however, as it can be related to as benevolent, as a trustworthy reservoir of meaning "qualitatively different from what we normally perceive or assume" (H. Smith, 1969, p. 9), then the effect of that faith relationship is the unification of the self, the healing of the "inner manyness" that is our characteristic condition.

That there is such a reservoir of meaning and superordinate value; that there is a "One beyond the many," a relationship to which is the goal of the faith development that began with the first discovery of the miracle of the parental other, this cannot be established from the position of a purely psychological analysis of human faith. Such a claim would clearly violate the hard earned modesty of a natural theology. [1] What can be argued from the standpoint of psychoanalytic object relations theory is that there are reasons why the object representations by which faith is grounded will tend to develop in the direction of the more inclusive, the more complex, the more fully nuanced, the more accommodating of paradox and contradiction, the more ultimate, and finally the more "verily other" or transcendent.

Of the reasons that can be offered from the side of psychoanalysis for faith's drive to anchor itself in a transcendent reality, I will examine only two. The first reason involves the experience of absolute limit which inevitably confronts the integrity of the self with the threat of dissolution. The second reason for the lure of the transcendent, by contrast, derives from the human yearning for communion with more and more reality. It is an experience we might say of transcendence proceeding from the fullness of living as opposed to transcendence at the boundaries of possibility.

The first reason for the emergence of the transcendent as the object of the faith process is that the life challenges to the developing self are such as to radically call into question the adequacy of a faith that is centered on any finite or penultimate reality. This process of disillusionment, or of idol-breaking if you will, begins early. Freud describes, for example, how the young child seeks to transfer onto the father and subsequently onto God or some other such supernatural other the powers for protection and nurture when first the mother and then the father in the flesh are revealed to be themselves finite and limited beings.

In this function (of protection) the mother is soon replaced by the stronger father. . .When the growing individual finds that he is destined to remain a child forever, that he can never do without protection against strange superior powers, he lends those powers the features belonging to the figure of the father; he creates for himself the gods whom he dreads, whom he seeks to propitiate, and whom he nevertheless entrusts with his own protection. (Freud, 1928/1961, p. 24)

As Rizzuto has pointed out, Freud does not account for the fate of the indestructible, idealized God/parent imago in the life of the unbeliever, himself included (Rizzuto, 1976). Nor does he acknowledge how the persistence throughout life of the same existential conditions which caused the early location of the protective and meaning making function in a Divine Other may continue to work to engender similar solutions, shaped and formed to be sure by a developing cognitive apparatus and the complex constraints of a given cultural order. To put the matter in terms of Freud's own life, nowhere does Freud analyze the dynamic connection that may obtain between his early experience as the adored son of his mother and his later faith in those pale but powerful gods of his maturity, Logos and Ananke (Freud, 1928/1961). [2] Yet it was precisely Freud's genius to convince us that the later must be understood in terms of the earlier. The life problem of making sense of our existence, reconciling ourselves to fate and finitude, does not go away just because we may believe that we have unmasked the dynamic origins of one set of symbolic solutions. Somehow the structure of faith must be built, however stern and spare. Though it might be reorganized and reworked, the foundation for that structure in early self and object representations cannot be repudiated.

It remained for another psychoanalyst, Otto Rank and his brilliant contemporary interpreter, Ernest Becker, to make the argument that the human conditions of ultimate limitation and dependency necessitates a heroism of everyday life which requires the support of "explicit immortality ideologies and myths of heroic transcendence" (Becker, 1973, p. 285). This account of the human dilemma closely parallels the preceding discussion of human self-becoming.

For Becker the human person is caught between two compelling and conflicting ontological needs. On the one hand there is the need to separate from the other, to stand out from the mass and realize one's own uniqueness and distinctiveness and specialness. There is the need to be "apart from." On the other hand the human person also longs for the fulfillment of merger, communion, sharing and solidarity with as wide a personal reality as possible.[3] This we might speak of as the need to be " a part of." In either direction lies the possibility of the terror of death and the threat of non-being. An affirmation of one's particularity as an individual evokes the fear of abandonment and isolation, or the death of the self-in relationship. Conversely, the experience of merger threatens to overwhelm, smother, dissolve the uniqueness of the self.

It is our defense against awareness of this ontological contradiction which results in the myriad permutations of "inner manyness" of which H. Richard Niebuhr wrote. We give our loyalty over to strong leaders, or ideological causes, or intense interpersonal relationships and attempt thereby to dissolve the lonely integrity of the responsible self. Or in the opposite direction we retreat from commitment, intimacy, sharing into some variant of splendid isolation and deny our dependence and essential interconnectedness. At the furthest extremes of the schizoid posture there is an attempt to deny altogether that one is embodied and incorporated in a society, and internal manifoldness becomes a private world (Guntrip, 1976, pp. 79-85).

The taming of this twofold terror requires "transference," the alliance with a source of power and stability which one presumes to find beyond oneself. Transference phenomenon then is not simply the prerogative of the neurotic who cannot stand to face life relying on his or her own resources. The fact of the matter is that no one of us has on our own the power to face the contradictions of our situation. The unavoidable reality of the limitedness and powerlessness of the human being in the world makes some form of transference a necessity if we are to function at all. In place of the word "transference" in Becker's discussion and in the quote that follows we could substitute without significant qualification what we have called faith and particularly faith as it is grounded in some center of meaning and value with dynamic origins in processes of self and object representation.

> If transference represents the natural heroic
> striving for a "beyond" that gives self-validation
> and if people need this validation in order to live,
> than the psychoanalytic view of transference as
> simply unreal projection is destroyed. Projection is
> necessary and desirable for self-fulfillment.
> Otherwise man is overwhelmed by his loneliness and
> separation and negated by the very burden of his own
> life. (Becker, 1973, p. 158)

The first locus of transference, or as I have chosen to call it, the first object of the dynamic of faith, is derived from the interaction with the powerful protective figures of childhood. The task of maturation, however, is not the elimination of such internalizations in favor of stoicly "going it alone." If Freud is right about the "immortality" of the object such an elimination would be in any event psychically impossible (Freud, 1917; Schafer, 1968). If Becker is correct about the nature of the life project it would also be existentially impossible. The real question is what self/object representations sustaining of faith are creative and life enhancing and which are, as Niebuhr put it, "evil imaginations of the heart" that testify more to our fearfulness and desire to flee our freedom? What projections are supportive of human freedom and dignity and do not "lie about life, death and reality"? (Becker, 1973, p. 202). The conclusion of Rank, certainly seconded by Becker, is that only a transference to absolute transcendence finally meets this criterion. Strictly in psychological terms, then, the human person is a "theological being" and the religious solution to the human dilemma - i.e., faith that takes as its object transcendent reality - is also the most humane, worthy and workable life way (Ibid., p. 175). With this insight Becker holds that psychoanalysis has achieved closure on the theological vision of Kierkegaard and Tillich. His conclusions deserve to be quoted at length:

> Religion, then, gives the possibility of heroic
> victory in freedom and solves the problem of human
> dignity at its highest level. The two ontological
> motives of the human condition are both met: the need
> to surrender oneself in full to the rest of nature,
> to become a part of it by laying down one's whole
> existence to some higher heroic personality. Finally
> religion alone gives hope because it holds open the
> dimensions of the unknown and the unknowable, the
> fantastic mystery of creation that the human mind

111

cannot even begin to approach, the possibility of a multidimensionality of spheres of existence, of heavens and possible embodiments that make a mockery of earthly logic - and in so doing, it relieves the absurdity of earthly life, all the impossible limitations and frustrations of earthly matters. (Ibid., pp. 203-304)

The idea that the life experience which presents the necessity for the transcendent is the life-long need to deal with limitation, restriction, and "hemmed-in-ness" has a strong and respectable tradition in Christian thought and has been a central theme in the work of a number of modern theologians (Bultman, 1955; Kaufman, 1969; Tillich, 1967). Though such a vantage has its own power, and one enhanced as we have seen by its congruence with key insights in modern psychoanalytic thinking, as the single statement of the relationship of the transcendent to human nature it has serious limits. Franz Josef van Beeck in his recent book Christ Proclaimed (van Beeck, 1979) has pointed out that an approach to understanding God or God in Christ that begins in human experience but elevates the theme of againstness and limitation to central importance risks either defining God in terms of the diminishment of the human person, or setting God apart from the positive, real functioning of human wants and desires.

The theological alternative to this approach would be something on the order of Karl Rahner's transcendental Christology which begins the inquiry into the nature of God by examining the character of the human person as questioner. From this line of analysis Rahner derives his understanding of the human person as a potentia obedientalis, a creature characterized by a radical openness to the incomprehensible mystery of God (Rahner, 1961). It is this openness to the absolute which finds expression in all human activity but most particularly in the human being's address to others. In so far as the human permits herself to live into this yearning for the more, this tacit awareness of the inexhaustible depths of other particular existences and of reality in total, the human being gives play to the desire for the transcendent. This general theological approach to understanding human nature also finds warrant in contemporary psychoanalytic thinking.

The human person we have observed has a primary need for a relationship with the real. The most creative and most powerful energies of early childhood are invested in the process of determining what is real, the dependable, the trustworthy. As Freud himself observed, past a certain age the child listening to a fairy story will demand to know if it is "for real" and will turn away with all the dignified disdain

112

of a young philosopher when informed that it is make-believe. In a similar fashion, Freud maintained, we cannot sustain our interest in religion by the fiction of pretending that it is true once we are otherwise convinced that it is not "for real" (Freud, 1928/1961, p. 29). The very logic of Freud's observation explains, however, why human faith drives relentlessly for the transcendent. As Louis Dupre argues, evoking Eliade, it is not for nothing that philosophers and theologians have chosen to discuss God in terms of the category of Being. "More primary than the sense of the holiness or power of transcendent reality is the sense of its ontological richness - God is eminently real" (Dupre, 1972, p. 327). Accordingly, as D.W. Winnicott so brilliantly demonstrated, the child's first efforts at configuring a lasting and reliable sense of the enduring reality of the parent involves the creation of a symbolic sphere, the space of the "transitional object" (Winnicott, 1971). The successful passage of this early experience in interpersonal metaphysics was, Winnicott saw, the optimal beginning for a lifetime of creative inquiry into the more-that-is-possible. In other words, it is posited that there is a motivating hunger for the real that proceeds not from a sense of the impoverishment and limitation of life or of the failure of being to be benevolent, but precisely from the plentitude of being. [4]

To summarize, then, the discussion to this point, we may add to our earlier definition of faith the following coda:

It is of the nature of faith as self-becoming that this activity of trust and reliance always involves a sense of being in relationship to some center or centers of meaning and value, represented to the individual psychologically at multiple levels of cognition and awareness, and originating developmentally in the processes of internalization whereby an inner representational world is constructed.

This relationship must be adequate to sustain the individual as a self before the limit conditions of human existence - the fact of ultimate dependency, contingency and finitude. The relationship must also accommodate the conatus of the self towards a deeper and richer sense of the real. For both reasons the process of development is towards faith that has as its object the transcendent.

III. From the Transcendent to "God"

Faith, I have urged, involves a reasoning of the heart and that reasoning at base utilizes not abstract theological or philosophical concepts but what Niebuhr termed "personal images," or what we might now refer to psychodynamically as self and object representations. It has been further argued that there is a natural movement in human faith development towards the evolution of these representations in the direction of the transcendent. Yet it is not just any personal image which has concerned theologians of faith in the West, not just any attempted representation of a transcendent object of faith. "God" is the way the Jewish Christian West has traditionally elected to address the transcendent object of the presentational process of faith. Though we are instructed by a theologian like Niebuhr that an individual's self-proclaimed faith in "God" may on inspection be an idolatry (Niebuhr, 1943/1970); and though we are advised by Rahner and others that genuine faith may still remain dumb and inarticulate with respect to its symbolization (Rahner, 1966, pp. 165-188): nevertheless, for all of these theologians it is faith in God, faith that names the Name, which they most desire to understand, form and reform.

Yet the movement from a philosophical, or, for that matter, a psychological discussion of the transcendent possibility to a discussion of God is an immense one. This is so because, as Dupre pointed out, "The problem of God is not a metaphysical one. . .Metaphysics reaches the concept of transcendent, it does not attain the idea of God" (Dupre, 1972, p. 323). What is said of metaphysics might be taken as equally true of psychology. While we might find in the psychodynamics of faith development those suggestions of the transcendent just described, we cannot establish from the position of a purely psychoanalytic inquiry that the proper referent for the faith which intends the transcendent is what Christianity has called God. The linkage between the psychologically describable longing for a transcendent warrant for faith and "God" properly falls under the category of revelation. It is the theology of revelation which must finally deal with the difficult problem of how it is that that which is by definition utterly beyond the finite and mundane nevertheless communicates itself in history in ways accessible to the structures of the human mind.

This leads us to ask whether there is any reason, except that it is revelation's referent for the trusting of faith that a psychological inquiry into faith should give any special status to an individual's imaging of "God" per se. In other words, independent of the contribution of revelation, would we still discern some essential connection between the internalization processes integral to faith and the processes whereby an individual comes to explicitly hold that faith in terms of a set of conscious and unconscious representations of God. If we do find such a connection it would not be in itself an argument for the validity of revelation. It would, however, begin to make the case that faith, as a dynamic life process, has some contents that are uniquely "fitted" to it, and specifically that to image the center of meaning and value upon which faith is moored as a personal Other has a certain psychological appropriateness and even predictability. Discerning such a relationship would also be a contribution towards understanding how revelation "works" from the humanward side.

To spin such a connection let us entertain a line of inquiry that proceeds as follows: Suppose that we were to take seriously this pursuit of the images by which one reasons with the heart and attend not to the static pictures of God presented by religious culture, still less to the God of the philosophers. Rather, let us attend to the now changing, now fixed, now conscious, now unconscious configuration of emotions, memories, self-feelings, dreams, and evocative images which constellate around the symbol "God" for every human being who has come to consciousness in a culture such as ours which is saturated with the memory and presence of that word-symbol. It is a definition which we will have to draw tighter and explain at greater length, but for the moment let us call what we pursue the object representation of God.

Now what if it were the case that the psychic processes by which persons become selves, all the dimensions of the creation and maintenance of the self which we have just linked to the dynamic of faith, were also and simultaneously the processes involved in the formation and transformation of God? What if both the representation of God and the self as we have begun to define it had their origins in the same matrix of relationship, bore the birthmark of the same process of separation and individuation, looked to the same vexed or blessed circumstances of family and culture? Would this not have the consequence of making "God" uniquely available for the processes of faith, or that which decisively blocks faith's explicitly religious self-formulation? The development of history of faith and the history of the object representation of God would then belong together, not as the union of a universal process and an arbitrary content, but as synchronous and inter-related processes which mutually inform and influence one another.

To make this argument would not be to say that faith is necessarily or inevitably mediated by the object representation of God. Whether that representation is usable for the multiple dimensions of self-becoming depends upon the complex interplay of the many factors which bore upon its origin and development: (1) the vicissitudes of the early relationship with the adults which potentially offered the psychic "material available for the representation of God; (2) the circumstances of religious instruction and the child's first introduction to the notion of God; (3) the images of God available in the family and in the religious or popular culture at large; and (4) whether the processive elaboration, reworking, and revisioning of an individual's object representation of God has evolved simultaneously with the individual's self-representation in such a way as to make it accessible for the integrative processes of faith. Yet even where the object representation of God may not be available for the activity of faith, either because it is too terrifying, too unreliable , loaded with too ambivalent affect, or because it has remained an unevolved and undeveloped childhood companion that cannot be related to under most circumstances of adult life, even then an examination of that representation discloses much of what is central to the individual's struggle of faith. The God which an individual cannot believe in, trust in, rely upon, may often be as revealing of the vicissitudes of faith as that God which can be consciously affirmed.

In summary: the matter of a special content for faith, specifically the idea of faith as involving a personal relationship to a reality identified as God, was shown out the front door when we came upon a functional definition of faith as the trust which is foundational for the process of self-becoming. However, we turn to discover that this content may re-enter by a rear door when: (1) it is found that the formation and maintenance of the self is linked to the processes of self and object representation; and (2) the object representation of God is shown to originate in the human life cycle in such a way as to make it peculiarly available for and relevant to the integrative process of faith.

The terms "object representation" and "object representation of God" have now been introduced into the discussion of faith but with only some preliminary explanation as to their meaning. We have linked the terms to Niebuhr's discussion of the "personal images" by which the heart reasons, yet have insisted that we are not talking about static mental "pictures" or symbols. We have also suggested that while there is a reasoning or meaning-making function at stake in the processes of object representation that reasoning is not "simply" a cognitive operation but one that is profoundly affective as well. Finally, we have stated that the dynamic of object representation in general and the formation of the object representation of God in particular, is inextricably involved in the processes whereby human beings maintain themselves and develop as selves. In order to make sense of these statements, it is necessary to proceed to a more detailed consideration of the psychology of object representation.

IV. Object Representation Revisited

Before launching into a technical discussion of the meaning of an "object representation of God," we would do well simply to pause and remind ourselves of the sort of experiential data which this psychoanalytic concept, if it is to serve, must help us to understand without reductionism. My initial concern to relate the object representation of God to the problem of faith was provoked by certain phenomena which are often embarrassing to academic theologians and hence often ignored. Yet these or similar sorts of experiences persistently impress the working pastor, the spiritual director, the practicing clinician who has allowed religious language and concerns to enter the therapeutic arena, and ourselves in moments of prayer or crisis, or spontaneous religious experience. What sort of phenomena? [5]

. A young man, by no means uneducated or theologically uninformed, confides in a period of emotional turmoil that he longs to be held and rocked in the arms of God.

. middle-aged woman describes a sense of the consoling presence of God which is so constant and dependable that its sudden disappearance for a brief time in her life throws her into alarm and deep distress.

. A religious professional with a sophisticated and rigorously demythologized notion of God appropriate to his liberal theology is surprised to discover in the midst of a threatened airline crash that his spontaneous prayer leaps back over the carefully developed formulations of his adult life to address the God of his childhood.

. With anger and a weary resignation, a college woman describes her sense of being relentlessly hounded by God to make a more radical commitment of her life in service.

117

A man who says he is unable to pray or meaningfully relate to God in any sense undertakes psychotherapy in the course of which he breaks through to an awareness of deep-seated anger towards his formerly idealized father. Coincident with this development in therapy he reports that he finds he is able to evoke a new and positive sense of God for the first time.

It is these sorts of experience, coexistent with the more conceptually refined dogmatic expressions of religious belief or unbelief, which demand to be taken into account in our analysis of human faith. Yet both the very subtlety of these experiences and their apparent primitivity has often functioned to disqualify them from either psychological or theological attention. Formal beliefs are simply much cleaner and easier to catalogue and analyze. Still, an awareness of the religious significance of these phenomena has persisted even if it has been a minority position.

One psychologist who early considered accounts such as these as central to the study of religion was William James. In The Varieties of Religious Experience, James suggested that there persists "in the human consciousness a sense of reality, a feeling of objective presence, a perception of what we might call 'something there,' more deep and more General than any of the special and particular 'senses' by which the current psychology supposes existent realities to be originally revealed" (James, 1904/1958, p. 61). It is this sense of reality, often only vaguely articulated and not always thematized as God which James suggested provides the psychic foundation for our receptivity to beliefs about divinity presented at other levels of cognitive organization. [6]

With James we acknowledge that what we can say about the ontic reality of such a sense on its "further side" is the purview of theology proper. On its "nearer" side, however, such experiences of "something there" admit of at least some psychological account. Today we might usefully see this dynamic which James called "the human ontological imagination" as one manifestation of that complex process which psychoanalytic theorists have termed the process of object representation (Ibid., p. 71).

The notion of object representation has its origins in Freud's observations on the manner in which the child's interactions with the central individuals in the first interpersonal universe are memorialized in the form of memory

118

traces or "imagos" which are the enduring inheritance of early childhood (Freud, 1914, p. 243):

The nature and quality of the human child's relations to people of his own and the opposite sex have already been laid down in the first six years of his life. He may afterwards develop and transform them in certain directions but he can no longer get rid of them. The people to whom he is in this way fixed are his parents and his brothers and his sisters. All those whom he gets to know later become substitute figures for these first objects of his feelings. (He should perhaps add to his parents any other people, such as nurses, who cared for him in his infancy.) These substitute figures can be classified from his point of view according as they are derived from what we call the "imagos" of his father, his mother, his brothers and sisters, and so on. His later acquaintances are thus obliged to take over a kind of emotional heritage; they encounter sympathies and antipathies to the production of which they themselves have contributed little. All of his later choices of friendships and love follow upon the basis of the memory-traces left behind by these first prototypes. . .the imagos - no longer remembered.

This passage suggests the main features of a theory of object representation which Freud himself never fully developed: (1) that our earliest involvement with parents and family members has a lasting influence on the character of our later relationships; (2) that this influence is mediated by the "imagos" of the earlier personages which may be transformed and changed but which, (3) can never be destroyed and hence are, in a psychic sense at least, "immortal" (Schafer, 1968, p. 220).

The preceding quote reveals as well an aspect of Freud's approach to the problem of object representation which has been a source of controversy throughout the subsequent history of that concept in psychoanalysis. I refer to the tendency of the language and metaphors to imply that object representations are "things," concrete and discrete entities which can attract desires both sexual and aggressive, and in turn exert an independent power upon us.

There is a static character to the notion of object representation in Freud's work and picked up by subsequent theorists which perhaps explains why little attention has been given to now it is that object representations do in fact undergo change throughout the course of a life. Having registered this complaint, it is necessary to pay an equally strong compliment. Appropriately enough for a theory of which

119

it has been said that all its truth lies in its exaggerations, the tendency in psychoanalysis to reify object representations reflects a profound truth. Persons when they describe the actual experience of their own stream of consciousness report mental processes which are genuinely interaction with what Schafer called "primary process presences" (Ibid.). There is an important sense in which it is not untrue to speak of object representations as consoling and persecuting, comforting and confronting, provoking anxiety and demanding retribution. But the truth of these observations is phenomenological and not meta-psychological. This particular distinction is not well drawn within contemporary psychoanalysis but it is clearly emergent and even ascendent. [7] If this is so, it is precisely because analysts have allowed themselves to be impressed by the real accounts of real lives that there has grown within psychoanalysis a powerful and progressively more refined awareness of the role of the object representational process within the total economy of a human life. The substance of this awareness is that there is an essential connection between self and object representations and the formation of the self.

As the latest chapter in the history of the of psychoanalytic theory after Freud, this development has had many significant contributors. The most recent and most substantive synthesis of these convergent theoretical offerings!s to be found in the work of Ana-Maria Rizzuto. The publication in 1979 of her detailed investigation of the object representations of a diverse clinical population represents the first time that a psychoanalytic object relational perspective has been systematically applied to the study of this aspect of religion in more than a single case approach. Of equal importance to this research is the theoretical clarification Rizzuto gives to the term "object representation." The following are extracted from her formulations to identify the key components of a theory of object representation that seem to hold in the current state of the discussion.

(1) The child's interaction with the significant others in his or her life is codified to be retrieved as representations which may become available at a variety of representational levels. The representation may involve physical sensation, either the rememberance of past sensations or their actual physical enactment in the body of the individual (visceral and sensori-motor memories). The young man mentioned earlier who spoke of wanting to be held and rocked by God may very well have a constellation of preconscious God representations which have preserved the somatic memory of being held and rocked as a small child. The object representation may also take the form of a sense of

presence, visual or audial, that is not hallucinated but nevertheless experienced as quite real (perceptual and iconic memories). Or, finally, the object representation may operate at a certain level of abstraction and secondary process elaboration and survive in the association of sentiments and sensations evoked by certain ideas and words (conceptual memory) (Blatt, 1974; Blatt, Wild & Ritzler, 1976; Bruner, 1964).

(2) The experiences which are synthesized to produce the complex mental phenomena we term object representations are the actual perceptual memories of the original interpersonal experience at whatever level of cognitive development the memory was formed, but also and as crucially, the defensive and adaptive distortions and permutations of that perception which were historically needed at the time the representation was first formed, or which are active dynamic factors in the present. To illustrate, an individual's object representations of the parents might have been formed under the sway of a defensive need to idealize one and devalue the other. The persistence of such an object representation would be influenced by the continuing need for such idealization and devaluation in the historical present. Conversely the attenuation of such a defensive need in time, either with the real changes which might occur in the individual's relationship with his parents, or with the maturation of a sense of self that does not depend upon such distortions, could result in the reconstruction of an object representation of the parents which might more realistically resemble their actual character. When we go after the object representation of God it will be important to keep this principle in mind. At any time "t" our sense of the object representations of God that might be apparent in any of the variety of ways they are produced (projective tests, interview material, etc.) has the character of a motion picture stooped to examine a single frame.

(3) Always concurrent with the formation of object representations is the formation of self-representations. In other words, we form memories not only of the significant others, but, as crucially, of how we felt, sensed ourselves to be, reacted in relationship to that other. This intimate interconnection has its origins in the developmental history of the human person. The very process of the formation of self and object representations takes place in the service of the human child beginning to make the discrimination between self and other. Indeed the memories that are most relevant for the representational process are those derived from the child's interactions with the parenting other(s) (Kernberg, 1966). Throughout the life cycle these self and object representations are on continual dynamic interaction. Growth experiences which

result in changes in the one will generate a sense of conflict or incongruence that precipitates the modification or re-elaboration of the other. This process of change-conflict-change is where the action is in the maintenance of the self. As Rizzuto expresses this insight, "the richness, the complexity, the dialectical connection which object representations have with our self-representations is what gives the constantly reworked memories of our objects their paramount importance in mental life" (Rizzuto, 1979, p. 78). If faith is involved in the processes of self-becoming as I have argued, then it necessarily must have to do with the dialectic Rizzuto describes.

The preceding three points were formulated on the basis of a psychoanalytic study of the history of interaction with the actual human objects of our early environment. They are nonetheless applicable in description of the object representation of God with some crucial additions required by the singularly different status and character of our subject.

(1) The object representation of God, quite evidently, is not produced by actual encounters with a perceptual object of the concreteness of a parent of sibling. The representation of God begins to take shape later than the first formation of object representations of the parent, but it can and does draw upon the resources of those parental imagos, though not necessarily in the straightforward transposition predicted by Freud (and then exclusively of the paternal imago)(Freud, 1932, p. 163) or hypothesized by most subsequent psychoanalytic researchers (Beit-Hallahmi & Argyle, 1975).

(2) The object representation of God is an imaginative creation or active construction of the developing child conditioned by "the pre-oedipal situation, the beginning state of the oedipal complex, the characteristics of the parents, the predicaments of the child with each of his parents and siblings, the general religious, social and intellectual background of the household. . .and the circumstances of the moment in which the question of God emerges" (Rizzuto, 1979, p. 45).

(3) We shall find it appropriate, anticipating a discussion of the work of D.W. Winnicott, to conceptualize the creative process involved in the formation of the object representation of God as taking place in the space of transitional object phenomena, the "between" of primal creativity that occurs in the interaction of child and parent (Winnicott, 1953). As such the object representation of God when first formed is unchallenged as to its status. That is, it is regarded by the child neither as solely a creation of his

or her fantasy and hence under magic control, nor as wholly "outside" the self like the real mother.

Transitional objects and transitional phenomena belong to the realm of illusion which is at the basis of initiation of experience. This early stage in development is made possible by the mother's special capacity for making adaptation to the needs of her infant, thus allowing the infant the illusion that what the infant creates really exists.

This intermediate area of experience, unchallenged in respect of its belonging to inner or external (shared) reality, constitutes the greater part of the infant's experience, and throughout life is retained in the intense experiencing that belongs to the arts and to religion and to imaginative living, and to creative scientific work. (Ibid., p. 14)

(4) The child encounters the raw material for the object representation of God in the same place and in the same way as the material for super-heroes, and devils, monsters and imaginary companions. The child brings to all these the same vital agenda, the problem of becoming a self which means the problem of negotiating the terrors and traumas of achieving a sense of self that is both separate and securely related.

Bruno Bettleheim has masterfully described how the characters of classical fairy stories can be used by the developing child for the purpose of working through the assaults on his or her natural narcissism inevitably sustained in the process of growing up (Bettleheim, 1976). The object representation of God, though participating in the same psychic dynamics, is in a unique position. Although religious traditions may differ in terms of the concrete pictorial representations they may formally make available in the religious environment (Pitts, 1976), Western religions are alike in offering a host of clues - verbal, conceptual, symbolic, representational - which encourage the child from about age three on to configure God on the model of his or her own idealized and omnipotent parental or significant adult figures.

The object representation of God is also unique in that unlike the case of most of these other figures, the parents - or at least the culture at large - does not systematically disabuse the child of the reality of the representation. In devout homes the child observes that this figure is the one personal, invisible reality which seems to elicit the respect, or fear, or admiration of even the powerful parents. God may even be directly evoked by the parents as the cosmic sanction for their own authority or as omnipotent and omnipresent enforcer of the family rules (Nunn, 1964). Even in those homes where the parents may place God in the same basket of discarded transitional objects with Santa Claus and the tooth fairy, the society sustains in its very language and popular usages the rumor that this God is not just another fairy story. At the time then of the resolution of the oedipal complex, that is, when the process of internalization of parental relationships has laid down the basic structure of the individual's inner world, the object representation of God in any of its countless variations is part of the psychic furniture.

In conclusion, while it may very well be the case that some form of parental or peer permission is needed in order for most children to sustain and develop a self-conscious relationship with their object representation(s) of God, I am in agreement with Rizzuto that "no child in the Western world brought up in ordinary circumstances completes the oedipal cycle without forming at least a rudimentary God representation, which he may use for belief or not" (Rizzuto, 1979, p. 200). Our central focus in this book is upon the fate of these object representations of God, absolutely idiosyncratic for every individual even as they bear the common impress of particular religious environments. Specifically our continuing question concerns how it happens that these conscious and unconscious configurations of affect, imagery and memory formed around the complex symbol "God" and linked to patterns of self representation become available for the faith integrative process. Conversely, what circumstances of development and personal history render them unavailable for faith? Before proceeding into this besetting problem of the project, it is necessary to make one further distinction. It is a crucial though subtle one and failure to draw it has created confusion In most previous discussions of the relationship between faith and the imaging of God. I refer to the distinction between the object representation of God and the concept of God.

V.   The Object Representation of God and the Conceptualization of God

The largest context in which this issue is situated is the continuing discussion of the inter-relationship of cognitive development and the representational process (Horowitz, 1970; Piaget, 1957; Werner & Kaplan, 1963). The two processes are connected developmentally but they are also discrete. This fact has been overlooked by many investigators of the psychology of religion. As Rizzuto argues, Freud himself in a work like Moses and Monotheism jumps the discussion from a

consideration of unconscious mnemic images to the elaboration
of the monotheistic idea of divinity without recognizing that
these may be operations at very different psychic levels
(Rizzuto, 1976, p. 174).

It is understandable why this confusion might occur in a
study of religious development. One of the unfailingly
fascinating displays of human developmental processes is the
operation of the mind of the child struggling to make cognitive
sense of the world. The concept of God as an omnipotent
creator shows up at the time in the life of the child (age 2½
to 5 and 6) when questions of causality and explanation are
cognitively central. The questions of children at this age
advance from efforts at anthropomorphic understanding ("Does
God have arms and legs? "Who made God?" "Does God have to go to
the bathroom?") to their later intense engagement with the
sheer intrigue of the ideas themselves ("If God is all
powerful, could he make a building that he couldn't destroy?").
The compelling puzzle of cognitive development, as well as its
greater accessibility to systematic investigation, has led to
an emphasis among researchers on religious development as
fundamentally a matter of the child's capacity to handle
religious ideas, and preeminently the idea or concept of God
(Elkind, 1970, 1971; Fleck, Ballard & Reilly, 1975; Goldman,
1963, 1964; Pitts, 1976; Williams, 1971.)

Elkind (1970) for example relies upon Piaget, as do most
of these other above referenced writers, to construct a model
of religious development that posits the problem of
"conservation of life" as the first life issue (or "cognitive
need" in his words) that sends the two year-old child off in
search of a cognitive solution. Elkind proposes that:

> Religion to which the young person has been exposed
> offers a ready solution (to the problem of the
> conservation of life). This solution lies in the
> concept of God or Spirit which appears to be
> religion's universal answer to the conservation of
> life. God is the ultimate conservation, since He
> transcends the bounds of time, space and corporality.
> By accepting God, the young person participates in
> His immortality and hence resolves the problem of the
> conservation of life. (Elkind, 1970, pp. 31-38)

Certainly Elkind is correct that something like the
problem of the fragility and impermanence of human life is a
major motivating force behind the child's turn to God, though
this problem I have suggested is more accurately and more
precisely seen as the experienced threat to the integrity of
the developing self posed in the process of separation and

125

individuation. It is also correct that God as commonly conceived is uniquely suited for a potential alliance to deal with the terror of our condition as finite and limited creatures. Nevertheless, whether the growing child can actually use God for this purpose depends on the peculiar developmental history of the individual's unique object representation of God. Evidence abounds of children for whom God has early come to be represented as the very source and symbol of the annihilation for which Elkind posits God as the psychic solution. C.G. Jung, for example, in his autobiography Memories, Dreams and Reflections, presents just such a case from his own childhood in which an early representation of God as "the Lord Jesus" went from being a benign presence to a representation that was the locus of the terror of death and separation.[8]

> I began to distrust the Lord Jesus. He lost the aspect of a big comforting, benevolent bird and became associated with the gloomy black men in frock coats, top hats and shiny black boots who busied themselves with the black box. (Jung, 1965, p. 10)

The conceptualist problem also appears in the works of theologians, even those who have looked for guidance to psychoanalytic theory as opposed to cognitive psychology. A revealing illustration of this problem is found in an essay by theologian Gordan Kaufman entitled, "Attachment to God" (Kaufman, 1977). In a subsequent revision of this essay for his book, The Theological Imagination (Kaufman, 1981), Dr. Kaufman has in fact addressed himself to a number of the problems I am about to discuss, and by introducing the notion of "image" and "symbol" has begun to work out some of the developmental linkages missing in the earlier essay. Nevertheless the first essay, as a stronger statement of the notion that it is the "idea" of God that is the primary locus of religious attachment illustrates the problem more clearly.

In that first version of the essay, Kaufman examines with insight and appreciation the work of British ethologist John Bowlby on early mother-child attachment and then proposes that God be understood on analogy with this material as an ideal attachment object. However, it soon becomes apparent that Kaufman's use of Bowlby remains at the level of analogy and metaphor for he insists that the "ontological anxiety" of the human being and its religious solution are in no way related psychologically to the phenomenon of separation anxiety and its solution in the processes of internalization. Kaufman is so concerned here, and rightly, to make the Kantian protest that God cannot just be another object of attachment in the world of experience that he leaps over the intermediate area of transitional object phenomena and insists that we regard God solely as an "idea":

> . . .God is present to us and known by us primarily
> and fundamentally in idea rather than in person or in
> fact - if we mean by the latter the presence of a
> directly and empirically perceivable object. . .
>
> God is a very different sort of attachment-figure
> from any human being, and the transfer of attachment
> from parent, for example, to God, will involve a move
> from a concrete present finite person to the idea of
> the absolutely dependable eternal person. Attachment
> here is to an idea, not to a directly given or
> perceptible object.
>
> (Ibid., p. 267)

In the process of making point to which most Christians would likely give assent, i.e., that God is not just another person "out there," a radical disjunction is introduced between the psychological processes involved in our experience with human love objects and those involved with our relationship to God as the eternal lover. In consequence the religious fact becomes unmoored from the developmental process. The problem of dealing with the critical life issues of faith is cast as essentially an intellectual or cognitive project, a matter of the management of language and concepts: "Difficulties here [i.e., with ontological anxiety] may be affected by new and deeper understandings of who God is, i.e., by changing one's ideas" (Ibid., p. 270). The net effect is to downplay and diminish the role in religious development of the interplay between the individual's unique interpersonal and intrapersonal experience and the witness of the religious community and its tradition:

> Relationship to God is pre-eminently through the idea
> of God which has been given in language and
> tradition, not through this or that particular
> experience or sort of experience, however much
> particular experiences may deepen, intensify, vivify
> or undercut and weaken - this relationship. (Ibid.,
> p. 267)

In the subsequent revision of "Attachment to God", the disjunction between one's "idea" of God and the primal experience of self and others is not nearly so sharply drawn, although the discrimination of levels of psychic representation which would be clarifying is not fully developed. What Kaufman does end up saying is in fact a valuable contribution from the side of theology to the problem at hand: "... the image or idea

127

of God, like my image or idea of myself, has very deep roots in the self - in its primordial interpersonal experiences, and in the system of symbols by means of which the self gives fundamental order and orientation to its life." (Kaufman, 1981, p. 77-78)

It is our position that an approach to religious development as a cognitive process and to God as a concept," while it draws attention to some important features of the total phenomena of human religiousness, fails to grasp the psychological uniqueness and developmental complexity of an individual's relationship with his or her God. At base it is a failure to distinguish theoretically between the processes whereby the child handles concepts and the processes whereby the child forms and relates to significant objects. Not, to be sure, that this relationship is at all clearly understood at this time. This is precisely the subject of the dialogue that has only recently begun between cognitive psychology and psychoanalytic object relations theory (Anthony, 1976; Friedman, 1978; Kegan, 1978; Meissner, 1975). Without pursuing that particular discussion, still very much in progress and by no means conclusive, let me just briefly suggest some of the ways in which the ideas and concepts of God that an individual may encounter might affect the way in which they deal with their object representation of God. I do this for the purpose of making the point that while these processes may be related there is something crucial given to our analysis by continuing to regard them as psychodynamically distinct.

Sometimes it is the case that the sheer intellectual contradiction of certain notions of God makes it impossible for an individual to use their object representation of God for the activity of faith. In such a situation the individual neither represses nor necessarily explicitly rejects their object representation of God, they simply set it aside - rather like the outgrown teddy bear of earlier years. The representation persists preconsciously and at the time of later life crises may be re-evoked and re-examined. However, unless the conditions are right for reworking it into congruence with the cognitive and affective loyalties and identifications of adult life, it is sent back again to the place where abandoned but not necessarily lost objects reside. If we look again more closely at the original circumstances which resulted in the dismissal of the God representation we might find that it is not so neatly described as a "cognitive conflict." Often it is a case of a contradiction between an individual's self representation and the self representation which would be forced upon him or her by an assent to particular concepts of God. Though on the surface the problem may be cast, even to the individual himself, as "that idea makes no sense to me," from another vantage it is a matter of "I can not hold my sense of myself as a self with intellectual integrity and independence and continue to relate to that representation of God," or "Scientific moderns don't think that way and if I am going to identify myself with the particular community I cannot hold these ideas."

The important point is that an individual's apparent acceptance or rejection of certain ideas about God is not in any simple sense a cognitive problem but rather one that involves the complex interaction between those ideas and the God and self representations which the individual brings along to the confrontation with those ideas. It is too seldom appreciated that even prior to the formal exposure to religious indoctrination, or a religious indoctrination as the case may be, children have been their own theologians and have constructed for themselves a sense of the One with whom religion has to do. The future possibility of the availability of the representation of God for the activity of faith may be decisively affected by the outcomes of that first confrontation between the primary creativity of the child and the constructions of the tradition. Rizzuto writes of this event:

> But the child brings his own God, the one he has himself put together, to this official encounter. Now the God of religion and the God of the child-hero face each other. Reshaping, rethinking, and endless rumination, fantasies and defensive maneuvers will come to help the child in his difficult task. This second birth of God may decide the conscious religious future of the child. . .No child arrives at the "house of God" without his pet God under his arm. (Rizzuto, 1979, p. 8)

What is crucial to remember is that in this encounter between the private representation of God and the cultural representation the issue is still one of faith. What representation will support the process of self-becoming at that stage in the individual's life? Because the issue is one of faith we must be open to seeing that one possible outcome might be the growing child's rejection of the formal notions of God presented by the religious/family culture because they are perceived as unworthy of the object representations which the child already has or which the child knows in a profoundly intuitive way are necessary for faith development. This outcome presents the paradox of a conscious rejection of the concept of God and the subsequent abandonment of interaction with the object representation of God out of a deeper loyalty to the career of faith. This could occur at any point in the developmental process though it is often seen to happen with great storm and stress, in the period of adolescence and in the college years. When it can be observed in its quieter and more subtle form in very early childhood it displays this dynamic with particular poignancy. Jean Paul Sartre, in his autobiography The Words, exhibits just this pattern (Sartre, 1964).

Sartre describes being raised as the adulated and spoiled child of a bourgeois tri-generational family in which, bereft of a father from birth, his own childhood grandiosity never encountered the security of the limitations and constraint of a serious standard. Hence he suffered the confusion of self produced by always being on display, always seduced to conformity by love, or worse, by the narcissistic needs of both a widowed, infantilized mother and an inflated but death-haunted grandfather (Kohut, 1972). The God offered young Sartre came in the train of bourgeois authorities who solicited a polite deference but made no genuine demands and commanded no real respect. The young Sartre's rejection of this God appears to have been a protest made in loyalty to an earlier representation of God grasped almost more in potential, a representation that might have supported faith.

> Raised in the Catholic faith, I learned that the
> Almighty had made me for his glory. That was more
> than I dared dream. But later I did not recognize in
> the fashionable God in whom I was taught to believe
> the one whom my soul was awaiting. I needed a
> Creator, I was given a Big Boss . . .Good Society
> believed in God in order not to speak of Him. How
> tolerant religion seemed! How comfortable it
> was. . . In our circle, in my family, faith was
> merely a high sounding name for sweet French freedom.

> At bottom the whole business bored me. I was led to
> disbelief not by the conflict of dogmas, but by my
> grandparent's indifference. Nevertheless, I
> believed. In my nightshirt, kneeling on my bed, with
> my hands together, I said my prayers every day. But
> I thought of God less and less often. (Sartre, 1964,
> pp. 97-99)

When Sartre the adult looks back upon the process what he mourns is not the loss of particular beliefs but the abortion of an object relationship by its failure to be confirmed in beliefs worthy of faith.

> I have just related the story of a mixed vocation: I
> needed God, He was given to me, I received Him
> without realizing that I was seeking Him. Failing to

take root in my heart, He vegetated in me for a while and then He died. Whenever anyone speaks to me about Him today, I say, with the easy amusement of an old beau who meets a former belle: "Fifty years ago had it not been for that misunderstanding, that mistake, the accident that separated us, there might have been something between us. (Ibid., pp. 102-103)

Sartre is resigned to the loss of this relationship and for himself seems to see no possibility that an encounter with a different concept of God from the God of "sweet French freedom" might manage a reconciliation of that early affair of the heart. Yet that is a possibility, if not for Sartre, then for other persons who took leave of their relationship to God over comparable faith issues. An engagement in later life with a new set of ideas about God might awaken the possibility of a renewed relationship with one's object representation(s) of God and sponsor a process of reworking those representations so that they are once more available for faith (Rizzuto, 1979, p. 202).

Examples of this phenomenon are not difficult to come by. One that has impressed me is the way in which Process Theology, a Christian theology constructed on the metaphysics of Alfred North Whitehead and Charles Hartshorne, has been uniquely powerful in provoking a dynamic reconstruction of the God representation of persons who have encountered that theology - particularly on the other side of a period of personal estrangement from formal religious belief and spiritual aridity. Judging from the accounts given me, this permission seems to be operative at several levels. By presenting a contemporary, intellectually credible metaphysics, it has re-engaged persons who could not find their experience reflected in more traditional metaphysical systems. At the same time, in offering an image of God as vulnerable, suffering and compassionate with creation, the theology offers a resource for correcting an object representation of God that was remote, uninvolved and untouched by human pathos, the Prime Mover of Thomistic theology for example.

But note that we are not here fronting an argument for a process of "ideas" correcting "ideas." Where a later life encounter with a new set of conceptions of God has re-evoked a relationship with the object representation of God in a way potent for faith, two things must have occurred. First, the power of alternative notions of God is found only in so far as they do in fact engage the conscious and unconscious object representations of God. Unless that engagement takes place no amount of argument at the level of intellectual discourse would be sufficient to effect the radical change of heart that might

131

be expressed in a conversion to belief. Second, this correction, or con version, or transformation of the object representation of God and the relevant self representations only occurs as these new ideas allow for the reorganization of alternative memorialized experiences. Rizzuto puts it thusly:

> Even someone who believes intellectually that there must be a God may feel no inclination to accept Him unless images of previous interpersonal experience have fleshed out that concept with multiple images that now coalesce in a representation that he accepts emotionally.
>
> (Rizzuto, 1979, p. 48)

Another way of saying this is that no amount of talk about a God who is in solidarity and compassionate union with creation can make any affective sense at all, least of all the sense that catalyzes psychic reorganization, if the individual hearing that talk has no available referents for the experience of being loved in that way. Put more simply still, "God is love" can make no saving sense to a human being who has never known what it feels like to be loved, however inadequately. This distinction between the set of ideas or notions about God which we may hold at any given time ("the God of the philosophers") and a core experience which is the deep source and referent for our sense of God ("the God of Abraham, Isaac and Jacob") is obviously one that antedates this psychoanalytic statement of the difference. William James was drawing just this distinction when he wrote:

> The truth is that in the metaphysical and religious sphere, articulate reasons are cogent for us only when our inarticulate feelings of reality have already been impressed in favor of the same conclusion. . .Our impulsive belief is here always which sets us the original body of trust, and our articulately verbalized philosophy is but its shadowy translation into formulas. The reasoned argument is but a surface exhibition. Instinct leads, intelligence does but follow. If a person feels the presence of a living God after the fashion shown in my quotations, your critical arguments, be they never so superior, will vainly set themselves to change his faith. (James, 1904/1958, p. 73)

We might also say that where there is no available foundation in the individual's inner representational world with which a belief in God can make articulation, arguments for belief "be they never so superior" would be similarly futile.

VI. Summary

In the previous chapter we laid out in a schematic way the various psychological dimensions of faith as a complex structure that underlies the processes of the formation of the self, particularly as that self-becoming relates to an individual's capacity to love and to accept love. In this chapter, by pursuing the "yes, but how?" question of faith we were led to consider the function for faith of "personal images," first as that category was suggested by a theologian, H. Richard Niebuhr, but subsequently as it points to the role in the creation of the self in the object representational process examined by contemporary psychoanalytic researchers. From there we explored two related arguments from a psychological and a theological position for why those "centers of meaning and value" represented by the individual as the locus of faith, would tend to develop in the direction of a representation of the transcendent. Our argument utilizing Becker and Rahner respectively concerned the condition of the human person as a creature with a yearning for endless expansion and communion hard against the limitations of human finitude, and a creature with openness to progressively greater participation in the real. We observed that the psychological comprehensibility of transcendence does not in itself give special status to the object representation of God per se. The relevance of "God" for faith becomes evident psychologically only as we begin to bring to mind the central significance of the representational process in the formation of the self and then attend to the crucial role which the object representation of God can play by virtue of the unique circumstances of its appearance in the course of the life cycle. The last section of this chapter was devoted to a clarification of the meaning of object representation in general and the object representation of God in particular, with care to distinguish the latter from concepts or ideas about God.

With this last distinction between concepts of God and object representation of God, the work of this chapter is at an end. We are in a position to see how James' "presence of a living God" on its humanward side is related to an individual's lively commerce with his or her object representation(s) of God and how this representational process may relate to the many facets of faith as self-becoming: the capacity to be alone and the capacity to tolerate dependency, the sense of being real and the sense of being in relationship to a real world, the capacity to tolerate ambivalence and the sense of oneself as available for loving self-donation. The task now is to take the analysis of faith which has been built upon the resources of psychoanalytic object relations theory and apply it to the data of actual human lives. The aim in so doing is to lay out in a more systematic way a picture of the development of faith which would attend in particular to the interaction between self-becoming and the object representation of God. This will be the project of the next three chapters.

FOOTNOTES CHAPTER FOUR

1. John MacQuarrie has argued that the proper task of a natural theology is not, as was formerly claimed, to furnish proof of the existence of God persuasive to the secular unbeliever. "Perhaps the most that natural theology would do would be to show the compatibility of the modern scientific understanding of the world with religious beliefs" (MacQuarrie, 1975, p. 138). My own argument is an effort to make a contribution within these limits.

2. On the subject of Freud's personal faith see Rieff, 1961 and Rogers, 1978.

3. This same polarity is described by David Bakan in his book, The Duality of Human Existence, in which is it described as the tension between agency and communion (Bakan, 1966).

4. Marjorie Brierly, an early British psychoanalyst, seems to have seen this when she made the interesting observation that Augustine's hunger for God may have been as much motivated by the very adequacy of his earliest experience of a beneficient reality as from any experience of deficit or loss. The passage in Augustine that Brierly had particularly in mind is from Book I of the Confessions:

> Thus for my sustenance and my delight I had woman's milk; yet it was not my mother or my nurses who stored their breasts for me, it was Yourself. . .It was by Your gift that I desired what you gave and no more, by Your gift that those who suckled me willed to give me what you had given them; for it was by the love implanted in them by you that they gave so willingly that milk which by Your gift flowed in their breasts.

Brierly wonders, "Perhaps the Saints enter the Kingdom of Heaven, after they have re-traversed the intervening developmental hells and purgatories, because they were particularly blessed in infancy" (Brierly, 1951, p. 227). This is a very different vantage on the meaning of religious yearnings than we would find in a traditional psychoanalytic model that views religion as an effort to manage a deficit in development.

5. These examples are taken from interviews and conversations with clients, colleagues and research subjects.

6. "The truth is that in the metaphysical and religious sphere, articulate reasons are cogent for us only when our inarticulate feelings of reality have already been impressed in favor of the same conclusion" (James, 1904/1958, p. 73).

7. The habit of elaborating theory closely reflecting the language of their clients is characteristic of British psychoanalytic object relations theorists (Sutherland, 1963). Because the resulting conceptual constructs exhibit more directly the actual accounts of psychic processes rendered in the analytic session, it has been suggested that psychoanalytic object relations theory represents a rapprochement between psychoanalysis and phenomenological psychology (Sugerman, 1977).

Contrasted with this enthusiasm for the descriptive power of this approach we have the contrary proposal of Schafer (1976) that what psychoanalysis badly needs is an "action language" which eliminates the mischief of reification and recognizes the status of object representations "merely as thought, ideas of information" (Schafer, 1968, p. 138). This line of reform is resisted both on the grounds that it is inadequate to the task of describing the actual clinical phenomena presented in analysis (Meissner, 1976; Grossman and Simon, 1969) and that is it based on an understanding of language function which does not comprehend the real complexity and depth of the operation of human knowing. (For this debate see Fourcher, 1977). While the jury is still out on the most radical revisions proposed by Schafer, it is not premature to accept, as I do in this book, the important corrective he offers to the more uncritical reifying tendencies in the theory. The theological wariness about the dangers of idolatry which is imported into this discussion on the boundary between theology and psychoanalysis makes us particularly alert to the problem of misplaced concreteness. To maintain a sense of the object of our inquiry as a dynamic <u>process</u> operating at multiple levels of cognition and involving an ever changing set of emotional responses seems essential if we are to avoid the error of thinking about the "image" of God as a picture that can be retouched or painted over. This excessively literal notion of the object representation of God is widely apparent in the work of psychologists/faith healers who have taken over some of these ideas through certain popular writers. (See Stapleton, 1979; Missildine, 1975.)

8. Jung's autobiographical account introduces an interesting and important problem for this research. As he tells his own story, "The Lord Jesus" was the first representation of the divine which he encountered as a very small child and to that representation became conflated his introjected father in so far as his father expressed fear of Jesuits (the name similarity is the relevant connection) and Jung's own associations to a terrible nightmare. "Lord Jesus never became quite real for me, never quite accepting, never quite lovable, for again and again I would think of his underground counterpart, a frightful revelation which had been accorded me without thinking of it" (Ibid., p. 13). Later, however, Jung's encounter with the wordsymbol "God" permits him to construct a new configuration of a divine other relatively uncontaminated by the representations which constellated around the Lord Jesus:

> While it became increasingly impossible for me to adopt a positive attitude to Lord Jesus, I remember that from the the idea of God began to interest me. I because it was a prayer without contradictions. God was not complicated by distrust. Moreover, he was not a person in a black robe, and not Lord Jesus of the pictures, draped with brightly colored clothes. . . . (Ibid., p. 27)

Jung's experience illustrates our point that one symbolization of the divine may not be available for a solution to the problem of life conservation due to its own "natural history" in the life of the individual. The material also alerts us to the fact that we must also be ready to inquire after the different manifestations of the divine Other in order to find out what happens to the God function.

CHAPTER FIVE

REVIEW AND PROSPECTIVE OF
RESEARCH METHODS ON THE IMAGING OF GOD

I.   Introduction. . . . . p. 137

II.   Freud and his Forebearers on Religion . . . . . . p. 137

III.   Post-Freudian Investigation of the Image of God   p. 140

IV.   Psychological Studies of the Image of God:
        Psychoanalytic Perspective. . . . . p. 141

V.   Psychoanalytic Object Relations Theory
        and Research on Religion. . . . . p. 144

137

CHAPTER FIVE

REVIEW AND PROSPECTIVE OF RESEARCH METHODS
ON THE IMAGINING OF GOD

I. Introduction

Before introducing the two case studies which I shall be using to illustrate an object relational interpretation of faith, it would be useful to survey some of the ways in which psychological researchers have pursued Freud's theories on religious origins. This is not intended to be a comprehensive review of the research literature. Rather it aims to present a brief overview of the approaches to the study of the imaging of God that have been influenced by psychoanalytic theory. Some understanding of the range of attempts to study this issue will help locate the clinical case study approach which I have adopted for the purpose of this project.

II. Freud and His Forebearers on Religion

The notion that human beings populate the cosmos with the productions of their own imaginations, and that this projective process is the source of religious objects, is hardly an idea original to Freud. Well before him David Hume (1711-1776) was disturbing the digestion of the religious establishment on the British Isles with his account of religious origins in a conspiracy of ignorance, anxiety and the imaginative projections of human qualities upon the unknown workings of the universe (Hume, 1956). Later Ludwig Feuerbach (1804-1872) in his monumental work The Essence of Christianity argued that religion represented the alienation of human powers and desires by their displacement onto divinity. Like Hume he called for human beings to come of age and reclaim those hopes, face those fears, and turn from being "religious and political footmen of a celestial and terrestrial monarchy and aristocracy into free, self-reliant citizens of earth" (Feuerbach, 1957, p. xi). Freud's unique contribution to this analysis of human religiousness was his location of the motivation for religious projection in the sexual and affective drama of the family romance. Freud's biographer, Ernest Jones, succinctly summarized this insight: "The religious life represents a dramatization on a cosmic plane of the emotions, fears, and longings which arose in the child's relation to his parents" (Jones, 1926, p. 195).

Summarizing Freud's understanding of religion would not be an easy task. His statements dealing with religion are characteristically unsystematic and distributed throughout his career beginning with an early essay analogizing religious ritual to the obsessive practices of the neurotic individual (1907) and continuing up to the very end of his life Jewish origins, <u>Moses and Monotheism</u> (1939). His works are also unevenly divided between some extended discussions of the phylogenetic origins of religion which encorporate questionable notions regarding the inheritance of mnemic images (1913; 1915, p. 293; 1921, p. 98; 1930; 1939) and some fewer analyses of the ontogenetic origins of religion. The latter Freud presumably based on his study of historical personages, among them Leonardo daVinci (1910), the possessed 17th. century painter Christoph Haizmann (1923), and the famous jurist Daniel Paul Schreber (1911). To a lesser extent does Freud rely on the religious material produced by his own patients, for example the case of the Wolf Man (191B). In general Freud's most eloquent and influential statements on religion are reserved for quasi-polemical writings of which <u>The Future of An Illusion</u> (1923) is probably the best known.

Despite the diversity of the material and the wide ranging character of his speculation it is less difficult to identify the ideas which Freud himself considered his most salient contributions to an understanding of religion, and the ideas which until recently have pretty much dominated psychoanalytic thinking on the subject. For Freud psychoanalysis central insight into religion is that its developmental origins are found in the vicissitudes of the oedipal complex, the young child's struggle both to maintain a relationship with and safely assert himself against the omnipotent and rivalrous father:

> Psychoanalysis has made us familiar with the intimate connection between the father-complex and belief in God; it has shown us that a person God is, psychologically, nothing other than an exalted father. . . Thus we recognize that the roots of the need for religion are in the paternal complex; the almighty and just God, and kindly Nature, appear <u>to</u> us as grand sublimations of father and mother, or rather as rivals and restorations of the young child's ideas of them (1910, p. 123).

Though the above quote mentions both father and mother in the compositions of the God image, in other places Freud seemed quite clear himself that it was the uncovering of the <u>father's</u> role in the religious process which would endure as psychoanalysis' key discovery:

> If psychoanalysis deserves any attention. . .then without prejudice to any other sources or meanings of

the concept of God, upon which psychoanalysis can shed no light - the paternal element must be the most important one (1913, p. 147).

One cannot help but be struck by the modesty with which Freud presents his central intuition in this passage and the qualifications with which he rings it. I think that it is fair to say that in later writings, and certainly in the work of subsequent psychoanalysts this reserve about the place of analytic explanation is largely missing, at least with respect to religion.

III. Post-Freudian Investigation of the Image of God

Although a number of psychoanalytic researchers expanded Freud's analysis to consider an enlarged range of religious phenomena such as Judeo-Christian dogmas and ceremonials (Reik, 1931) and the myths of saints and heros (Rank, 1914), in the main attention has stayed focused on the topic which most persistently intrigued Freud and which is also the central concern of this study - the origin and function of the personalized images of God in the human life cycle. By and large most of the studies that have been done of the God image either from an anthropological or a psychological position have been attempts to validate Freud's hypothesis concerning the intimate relationship presumed to obtain between the experience of the child with the parent and the creation and elaboration of particular images of God.

Sociological Studies of the God Image

Within the field of social anthropology, researchers have begun with Kardiner's Freudian notion of religion as a "cultural projective system" and have attempted to establish a connection between beliefs regarding supernatural beings, childbearing practices and early socialization experiences (Kardiner, 1939). Two studies utilizing representative "primitive" societies stand out as exemplary of this research strategy. Both, it should be noted, are also indebted to the field work of John Whiting and colleagues in the study of child-parent interaction in various cultural settings (Whiting and Child, 1953). Lambert, Triandis and Wolf (1959) set out to test the hypothesis that beliefs in the male volence of the supernatural world correlate positively with punitive infant and child rearing practices, while beliefs in the benevolence of the supernatural world will correlate with more nurturant practices in infant and child training. The researchers did find that societies with beliefs in aggressive deities were more likely to utilize pain and punishment in the course of normal child raising. The researchers evoked conditioning, reinforcement and conflict theory to account for their results although psychoanalytic explanations would also have been relevant.

A more ambitious study, and a more consistently psychoanalytic one, was conducted by Spiro and D'Andrade (1958). They broke down the notion of nurturance into its component parts in order to develop a description of various degrees of nurturance. In effect they come up with an inter esting operationalization of Winnicott's notion of "good-enough mothering" although his work was not explicitly cited in the study. These they attempted to correlate with a finely discriminated set of convictions about what sort of nurturance and what sort of punishment might be expected from the gods. For example, do the gods (like the mother) provide nurturance noncontingently, or must that nurturance be solicited either by the performance of certain ritual actions or by obedience to certain moral codes. The findings were suggestive in the direction of their major hypothesis, but inconclusive.

The limitations of both these studies is that they are necessarily confined to considering only "beliefs," the consensual doctrines of a culture regardfng the character of God or the divine manifestations (spirits, ancestors, etc.). What falls out of the analysis is the way in which <u>particular</u> individual's unique experience may interact with the symbolic resources of a culture in the creation of the individual's own sense of God or the transcendent. As they are, studies such as these lack a theory of human development which adequately connects the actual experience of parent-child relationship with the process of configuring a way of accounting for the findings of such studies conducted at a societal or cross-cultural level. In their favor, these studies are useful in reminding us of the social character of all believing. All belief, all religious creativity with respect to the imagings of God, takes place in a cultural context. Thus any study must remember that it is examining a "fit" between the fantasies and expectations of the individual and the collective fantasies and symbolizations of a whole society.

IV. <u>Psychological Studies of the Image of God: Psychoanalytic Perspective</u>

The bulk of research efforts from this position have been fairly narrowly aimed at an empirical investigation of Freud's claim that the image of God is an infantile residue of the child's dependence on an omnipotent father whose power is sooner or later discredited by the hard facts of life. While some of these studies are methodologically quite sophisticated, their reliance on formal psychoanalytic theory, beyond the elaboration of the initial problematic, is generally quite limited. In spite of this, the contribution of such studies has been to decisively challenge Freud's particular formulation of religious origins while supporting the projective hypothesis in its broadest form. As summarized by Beit-Hallahmi and Argyle (1975), these psychoanalytically derived empirical studies demonstrate that an exclusively oedipal explanation for the formation of the God representation is not adequate. At the same time they tend to support the notion that the individual's representations of both parents contribute to the composite image of God in Western society. [See also Godin and Hallez, 1964; Siegman, 1961; and Nelson, 1971]

Methodologically, studies seem to fall into two categories: 1) Factor analytic studies of the God-representation which analyze the responses to a question such as "What does God mean to you?" (Spilka, 1964; Gorusch, 1968; Vercruysse, 1972); and 2) Studies utilizing the Osgood Semantic Differential Test (Osgood et. al., 1957) or a variation thereof and/or Q-sort analysis (Stephenson, 1953) to study very particularly how the image of the deity relates to the image of the mother and of the father.

In this second category by far the most extensive and careful studies have been those conducted by Catholic researchers at the Lumen Vitae Center for the Psychology of Religion, Louvain, Belgium. Over the past fifteen years Professor Antoine Vergote of the Lumen Vitae and his colleagues have designed and validated a research instrument which they call the Semantic Differential Parental Scale (SDPS), originally constructed in Dutch and subsequently translated into French, Spanish, English and Italian. The SDPS has permitted a degree of cross-cultural analysis not hitherto possible. (Vergote and Tamayo, 1981)

Vergote's research differs from other empirical studies into parental/God imagery and from the approach of this project by a theoretical distinction Vergote draws between the "memory images" of parents which are the residue of intersubjective experiences of an individual's particular parents, and "symbol-figures" (Image-symbole) which describe the symbolic roles attributed to the mother and the father within the family constellation which is itself defined by a distinct cultural milieu. It is the latter which Vergote maintains contribute the essential symbolic content to the representation of God. The research design which derives from this approach pursues, as Vergote says, the "conscious" or "objective" character of

142

the God/parent representations either by asking subjects to select the qualities which fathers (mothers, God) "should have" (Vergote and Aubert, 1972) or by asking the subjects directly to describe their "symbolic parental figures". (Vergote and Tamayo, 1981)

The Lumen Vitae studies, like the social anthropological studies discussed earlier, identify a problem that is crucial to any psychological investigation of the God representation: that such an investigation necessarily straddles the realms of shared social reality and individual psychic reality, culturally shaped "nurture" and biologically determined "nature". On the one hand, our ideal-typical fathers and mothers do in large part reflect historically determined cultural conventions that govern family roles and define normative male and female family styles. Similarly, the attribution of parental qualities to the object of religious devotion is an historical-cultural phenomenon influenced by changes in political, economic and theological factors and fashions. On the other hand, it may be argued (Vergote does) that these symbolic roles within the family "field of action" serve a psychic structuring function for the developing human being which is foundational to human self-becoming and not culturally arbitrary. If this is the case, then the raw material of the religious imagination may also be said to be simply "given" in the inevitable experience of infantile dependency upon an available source of love and tenderness (Vergote's "maternal function") and in the necessity for the intervention of a relationship that sponsors separation and the entry into the wider world of social rules and responsibilities (the "paternal function"). Vergote's formulation of the way in which these two orders of experience (ie. the cultural and the biological) interact is bound to be controversial and some of that controversy will fall along ideological lines. [1] None the less the Lumen Vitae research valuably identifies the need to attend to both culture and personality. Even if, as in this study, our attention is focused upon only one of these dimensions, we must be aware of this as a problem.

The other issue which the Vergote research attempts to address by its emphasis upon "symbolic action field" and the "structuring function of the symbolic roles" is the failure of much empirical research in this area to grasp the <u>dynamic</u> character of the God representation - its place within the psychic economy of the person located in an action system of other persons. The very notion of "image" as often employed in these studies is a static one. An image is regarded as something akin to a still life portrait or a picture. Such approaches lack a theory of the imagination which recognizes that what is of real interest psychologically are the <u>affects</u>

and feelings that are given shape and direction in the ongoing process of constructing, cathecting and decathecting object representations of a reality regarded as transcendent. The Dutch psychologist of religion, Heije Faber, makes just this point in his commentary on the work of Vergote:

> In the religious field projection is not so much a matter of particular images or ideas; it is rather a question of feelings which, as the person develops in the process of his emancipation from his parents, also go through a certain development. These feelings therefore always play their part at a particular moment in the relationship to the God in whom a person "believes" in the framework of his pattern of upbringing and culture (and that means here, psychologically, the God with whom he "reckons" in his behavior); for God takes the place in a man's (sic) life which was taken by his parents before he was grown up. (Faber, 1975, p. 278)

As I have argued in the previous chapter, it is only now, with the emergence of an object relational paradigm within psychoanalysis, that the theoretical tools are available to help us conceptualize the dynamism of the God representation, to conceive within a life history the inter-relationship that obtains between an object representation (like that of God), a self-representation, and the "feelings which . .the person develops in the profess of his emancipation from his parents." [2]

V. Psychoanalytic Object Relations Theory and Research on Religion

In a review of the literature on the psychoanalytic study of religion from 1960 to 1975, William Saffady observed that research on religion guided by psychoanalytic presuppositions has, after an enthusiastic start, become largely moribund due to an unimaginative adherence to Freud's preoccupation with the oedipal origins of religion (Saffady, 1976). As observed above, efforts to validate the Freudian explanation for the origins of God imagery in the paternal complex have been unsuccessful. What is promising is the way in which theoretical developments within psychoanalysis have begun to influence the perception of religious beginnings, and in particular have brought new attention to the pre-oedipal origins of religion. As we have earlier observed, it is just this shift of attention to the significance of very early parent-child interaction for the development of psychic structure which is one of the salient features of the object relational perspective in psychoanalysis. Most of the studies which have pursued this line of inquiry have been applications of ego psychology to the study of Christian and Jewish symbols and stories. The general thrust of these studies has been to uncover the feminine or maternal aspects of the divine which are perceived to underlie both the Old Testament images of Yahweh (Rubenstein, 1963; Schlossmann, 1972; and Schoenfeld, 1962). Precedent for this line of argument is actually to be found in some of the pioneering work of early object relations theorists, prominently Ian Suttie of the Tavistock Clinic, who devoted considerable attention in his book, The Origins of Love and Hate, to an examination of the psychological determinants of matriarchal and patriarchal aspects of religion (Suttie, 1935). [3]

Studies which have taken actual clinical material and applied an object relational analysis are considerably fewer. Sandor Lorand's study of the ambivalence towards the mother which frequently underlies the psychic problems of believers entering therapy is one such study (Lorand, 1962). Other analyses of the function of religion in the psychic development of individuals have followed the pattern of using the single illustrative case study to make the writer's point (Draper, 1969; Klauber, 1974; Lubin, 1959). What has been rare to this point is the systematic application of a psychoanalytic object relations perspective to the study of individual religious development and particularly in more than just a single case study. Two exceptions to this are Philip Helfaer's study of eight male theology students published as The Psychology of Doubt (Helfaer, 1972), and Ana-Maria Rizzuto's extensive investigation of twenty patients admitted to the psychiatric unit of a private hospital which is presented in her book, The Birth of the Living God (Rizzuto, 1979).

Helfaer's research was restricted to young, male seminarians from conservative (fundamentalist) backgrounds. His research method consisted of extended interviews with his subjects and the administration of a number of projective instruments including the Rorschach and the Thematic Apperception Test (TAT). Helfaer's study, which was done under the direction of Levinson and Bellah in the Department of Social Relations at Harvard University, takes up the difficult problem of finding in the formal crises of religious doubting psychodynamic factors related to early object relations. The most original contributions of the study are its explorations of maternal identifications underlying his subjects' belief in God and their experience of vocation. The limitations of the Helfaer research are found in its very ambitiousness. Specifically, he attempts to make distinctions between liberal and conservative theological positions, relate these to

145

personality variables and then find the explanations for these positions in the psychodynamic histories of his subjects. The complexity of the task is further hampered by the lack of a consistent theoretical perspective on the role and function of object representations in the overall psychic economy of the individual.

Rizzuto's research is at once more modest and delimited in its ambition and more significant in its outcome. Her population is more heterogeneous, religiously, sexually and culturally, than Helfaer's and hence she is able to focus more narrowly and yet more incisively on the specific problem of how the object representation of God functions in the maintenence of ego integration. The result is an original contribution to psychoanalysis since, as considered in Chapter Four, her research brought her to a systematic reformulation of the theory of object representation and its relationship to processes of ego development. The methodology Rizzuto employed was to gather data on the family background, life history and religious (or areligious) convictions of her subjects from interviews, conversations with family members, and the reports of the doctors and staff of the private psychiatric facility in which the research was conducted. She also used what she called "ad hoc projective techniques" including inviting the subject to draw a picture of his or her family and of his or her God. In her book four representative cases are presented in careful detail to illustrate her theoretical formulations.

The research method which has produced the two case studies presented in the following chapter has been broadly derived from the imaginative initiatives of Helfaer and especially Rizzuto. It is also indebted to the growing research on the study of object relations by means of projective instruments, in particular the pioneering work of Alan Krohn and Martin Mayman (Mayman and Krohn, 1975). While neither of the two cases included in this book have been formally scored on scales developed by these researchers to assess various aspects of object relations, their research has influenced both the content of the interview and the interpretation of the data. Specifically included as a result of this research have been questions on early memories and dreams. An understanding of this inclusion necessitates a brief discussion of the theory behind the integration of projective test psychology and the psychoanalytic study of object relations.

The effort to tap unconscious object relations by means of projective devices can be found as early as Phillipson's work at Tavistock Clinic (Phillipson, 1955). Phillipson employed a TAT-like instrument and an interpretive schema to get at "unconscious, wished-for relationships, feared consequences, and defensive relationships." Phillipson's specific instrument seems not to have had much appeal to subsequent investigators, but the idea of discerning dimensions of an individual's object relations by means of projective devices has been increasingly fruitful. The most familiar and prominent projective device to be used. for this purpose has been the Rorschach (Ducey, 1975; Mayman, 1967, 1979; Urist, 1973). The other promising tool of inquiry, and the one most relevant for this project has been the use of the manifest content of dreams and early memories.

Perhaps because of Freud's warning that the manifest content of the dream was but the covering for what was presumed to be of greatest importance, the latent libidinal wishes, there has been a general neglect of the manifest content as evidence of psychic organization (Freud, 1900). With the maturation of ego psychology there has been increased attention on the way in which the ego is structured to handle wishes; and with the development of psychoanalytic object relations theory there has emerged a deeper understanding of what those wishes involved. The consequence for projective research has been the elaboration of scales that analyze manifest dream content. These look at the affective quality, coherence, organization, and action of the dream story for clues to the nature of the inner representational world (Brenneis, 1971; Krohn and Mayman, 1974; Langs, 1966). Early memories as reported by research subjects are dealt with the same way. On the one hand they provide an aperture through which to look to build an historical reconstruction. Lacking independent information from other sources, this may be the only way to do a case history. In the two case studies that follow I have frequently relied upon early memories in this fashion. Yet as Freud himself observed, memories as reconstructions from the vantage of the present are unreliable in the way that personal myth is always in some measure different from personal history (Freud, 1899, 1901, 1910). Even if there are actual life events that are being recalled and related with accuracy, there is a principle of selectivity going on. Some memories are being chosen and others neglected. The usefulness of early memories, therefore, is not only or even primarily as an entry to the past but as a "royal road" to the present (Langs, 1965; Mayman, 1959; Mayman and Faris, 1960; Saul et. al., 1956).

Like the manifest content of dreams, early memories may be productively, if carefully, read as expressions of the self and object representations available to the individual in time present. They are rich, as Mayman put it, in "intrusive interpersonal themes which define. . . enduring expectations of others" (Mayman, 1968, p. 304). With respect to the early memories which appear in the case material that follows, we are in what may appear to be a contradictory interpretive position. Recollections offered by the subjects of their childhood and of significant family members from childhood will be accepted as roughly descriptive of the way things were. At the same time, we shall be considering these memories not only "as autobiographical truths, but as retrospective inventions constructed by the person to conform with and confirm ingrained images of himself and others" (Mayman and Krohn, 1975, p. 160).

In the foregoing forced march through the range of research methods inspired by the psychoanalytic interpretation of religion, I am returned again and again to the clinical case study as the method which may most reward a longer visit. Other methods, with the exceptions noted, tend to isolate out a static configuration labeled the God image or God representation which is then impaled inert on a point of nosology like a lifeless butterfly. Even the projective measures discussed above have generally tended to go after the quality and character of object representation rather than chase the more elusive but livelier question, "How does it work in real life?" That is the question we have been asking from the beginning: "How does faith operate, and within its processes what is the function of the God representation?" The task of developing a systematic operationalization of object relations theory is an important one. At this state of the art, however, I think we shall find that a careful inquiry into the lives of ordinary and well functioning persons which employs a clinical discipline will yield much of interest on these issues. At the very least a clinical method will help surface the questions and insights that may later inform a research program.

FOOTNOTES CHAPTER FIVE

1. This is an important current debate that pits the Freudian left against the structuralists precisely over the issue of the possibility of the "transcendence of patriarchy," or to what extent the "maternal" and "paternal" axes are inevitable (in the sense of being biological or even ontological), or are the historical products of particular cultural processes (Vergote, 1969). See Guy B. Hammond, "Transformations of the Father Image," Soundings, 61:145-167, for an excellent summary discussion.

2.   Before discussing research applications of that paradigm, including the one that is the basis for this book, it is necessary to mention two more studies of God images which, while utilizing the statistical tools of academic psychology, nevertheless make suggestive contributions towards an understanding of the intrapsychic function of the God-representation.

Bernard Spilka and his colleagues at the University of Denver were early pioneers in a factor-analytical approach to the study of the God representation (Spilka et. al., 1964). Over the past several years they have extended their research to test theories of God image development other than those based on Freudian, Adlerian or Social Learning models. In this process they have found some evidence for a Self-Esteem theory which finds correlations between an individual's self-regard and his or her perception of God (Benson and Spilka, 1973; Spilka, Rosensohn and Tener, 1973). In a recent discussion of their work, Spilka observes: "Apparently high self-valuation is consonant with the holding images of God that are both positive, close, personal and also of a deity very much involved in human affairs" (Spilka, Addison and Rosensohn, 1975). What is significant about this research is that it has picked up an early insight of William James, namely that people not only have an image of God, but that they use their image(s) of God. Contemporary psychoanalytic investigation of the way in which internalizations can function to maintain a sense of self-worth may explain something of Spilka's findings, which themselves may serve as a convergent validation of the hypothesis that under certain conditions the internalized object representation of God has a role to play in the maintenance of a selfsystem.

The other example of academic research methods contributing to the study of an individual's unique constellation of God images is some creative work done by Bruce McKeown utilizing Q-sort techniques for the analysis of single-case studied (N=1 studies) (Bass and Brown, 1973; McKeown, 1976). While McKeown does not discuss in detail his findings in terms of theories of psychological development, he seems clearly to have demonstrated that there is a dynamic of displacement of affects and perceptions of primary objects (parents, loved ones, etc.) onto a plethora of secondary objects (God, but also Jesus in a variety of different representations).

3. Some mention must be made of a work almost unknown in this country which is perhaps the most ambitious effort to translate the work of the object relations theorists, principally Fairbairn, Guntrip and Winnicott into a usable theory of

religious development. I refer to Frank Lake's massive volume Clinical Theology: A Theological and Psychiatric Basis to Clinical Pastoral Care (London, Darton, Longman & Todd, 1966). Lake was a parasitologist who worked for years in India before returning to Britain to study psychiatry. Not surprising his book contains numerous charts on the life cycle of "interalized object relations" which resemble nothing so much as the cycles of intestinal parasites. Lake's book inaugurated in England a clinical theology movement centered in Nottingham which sponsored seminars and therapeutic groups for clergymen. Unfortunately the text, despite some very suggestive clinical insights, is woven through with Lake's own version of Christian orthodoxy which tends to be most uncritical even on its own terms. I can only speculate that this mixture of piety and psychoanalytic theory have prevented the work from surviving the trans-Atlantic passage.

CHAPTER SIX

PRESENTATION OF CASE MATERIAL

I.   Method of Collection of Data. . . . . p. 153

II. The Case of Ann B.: A Retreat to Advance

     Introduction. . . . . p. 155

     Early Childhood and Family Structure. . . . . . . p. 156

     Earliest Interaction with God . . . . p. 159

     Adolescence: The Expansion of the World
     and the Contraction of the Family . . . . p. 161

     The God Relationship in Adolescence . . . . p. 163

     College Years: Religious Moratorium and Return. . . p. 165

     Finding a Future and Beginning a Marriage. . . . . .p. 166

     The First Mission Assignment and Personal Tragedy. .p. 167

     The Middle Years and the Onset of Depression. . . . p. 169

     Return, Reconsolidation and Recovery. . . . . . . p. 173

     The Object Representation of God
     through the Depression and Beyond. . . . . .p. 175

     Towards the Future:
     Personal and Professional Horizons . . . . .p. 178

III. The Case of Stacy R; Learning to Care for the Inner Child

     Introduction. . . . . p. 182

     Early Childhood and Family Structure. . . . . . . p. 183

     Double Bind . . . . p. 185

     Handling Aloneness in Childhood . . . . p. 187

     God in Early Childhood. . . . . p. 189

     Parental Divorce and Aftermath. . . . . p. 190

151

Early Adulthood and Marriage. . . . . p. 191

Inner Work and Outer Transformations. . . . . p. 194

The Dream of the Truncated Baby. . . . . .p. 195

Towards the Future:
Personal and Professional Horizons. . . . . p. 198

CHAPTER SIX

PRESENTATION OF CASE MATERIAL

I. Method of Collection of Data

The two cases presented in this chapter were selected from among approximately twelve interviews conducted by the author as part of a larger study on the object relations of adults in later middle age (45 to 57). [1]   This much understudied group has only recently come into prominence in the emerging literature on adult life stages and the "midlife crisis" (Chew, 1977; Gould, 1978; Maas and Kuypers, 1975; Neugarten, 1968; Sheehy, 1976; Vaillant, 1977; Levinson, 1978).   Even within this generally neglected age group (from a research perspective) women of middle age have not been much considered in their later life developmental patterns (Barnett and Baruch, 1978; Bart, 1971; Fuchs, 1977; Gross, 1956; Sales et. al., 1977).   Yet what better stage in life in which to study the operation of human faith and what more appropriate segment of the adult population?

Later middle age often presents for both men and women a last critical opportunity to achieve the promises of youth or fulfill the possibilities seen in earlier life. It is also a time in life when there may be a dawning awareness of inescapable limitations and inevitable regret. Perhaps no time since adolescence is experienced as so pregnant with both possibility and danger.   In Tillich's term, it is a kairotic time in a life history by reason of the impress of what can only fairly be called religious questions and decisions: questions of ultimate meaning and value, decisions about how to live out with integrity and passion the last quarter of one's traditionally alloted "three score years and ten." For women, especially in this society, for whom the culturally assigned task of child-rearing is largely completed, the mid. to late forties can be a time of significant faith development. Crucial and still unresolved issues in the formation of the self erupt with an insistence that cannot be ignored.   The patterns of integration and equilibrium worked out earlier in life are threatened by the confluence of circumstances which hold out the possibility of a second life cycle. Negotiating these possibilities and risks means coming to terms with the resources of faith and hence with the inner representation world that has sustained one to the present moment.

For these reasons I have chosen to present for this book the life histories of two women in their mid-fifties. Their particular cases were selected for a number of factors. Both women are in the process of negotiating a significant change in life style and public role: the one entering upon religious ministry (Stacy R.) and the other completing doctoral study as a clinical psychologist (Ann B.). [Names and identifying material have been changed] They are also, by reason of their educational backgrounds and chosen fields of study, highly articulate with respect to their own interior lives, both psychological and spiritual. Finally, they are reasonably well-adjusted, competent, and emotionally balanced women. Subjects were available who could have exhibited the operation of the God representation in a more psychically fragile personality structure. It was felt important, however, to examine how faith and the relationship to the representation of God functions in individuals who , to all evidence, are successfully managing significant life transitions. As has been frequently observed in criticism of depth psychology, the study of healthy and well-functioning individuals is rare indeed, and the study of well-adapted religious individuals rarer still.

The number of apparent similarities between these two women might argue for the limited application of any conclusions that may be drawn from an analysis of these cases. I think we will see, however, that the very congruities at the surface level force us to consider the intrapsychic and developmental sources for what is more obvious about these two human beings as we listen to their life stories, and that is their completely distinct and individual ways of negotiating the issues of faith around significant life decisions.

Both subjects whose stories are presented here were given over the period of a month, three interviews of between two and three hours duration. Additionally, Stacy R. received a follow-up interview at a year's interval in order to follow the resolution of the grief work begun on the death of her mother which occurred during the first interview set. The interview format for both subjects was the same. They were asked initially to talk about what stood out in their lives - significant events, milestones, turning points, etc. From there the interviewer pursued as the topics appeared spontaneously a number of themes that had been identified in advance as being of particular significance for this research: creativity, the subject of being alone both presently and in the past, the history of the subject's relationship with her God, and her sense of the interior dialogue which accompanied her decision-making on significant issues.

The interviewer also obtained from the subjects both in the interview itself and by way of a written instrument their account of key early memories (memories involving parents, pleasant, unpleasant, fearful, shameful, etc.), and memorable or recurring dreams. The format and theoretical inspiration for these latter instruments was largely derived from the work of Mayman and Krohn. (See Mayman, 1959, 1968; Krohn and Mayman, 1974; and Mayman and Faris, 1960.) In addition to the interview material and these instruments, both subjects made available to the interviewer autobiographical studies which they had written for psychology or pastoral counseling courses in their respective institutions over the past year and a-half. The interviews closed with an imaginative exercise in which the subjects were invited to fantasize what sort of animal, historical or fictional character and object they would enjoy being. The responses to this exercise are Appendix A and B. These two case studies then are a reconstruction from the interview transcripts and supplemental written material of the psychosocial history of these two women.

II. The Case of Ann B.: A Retreat to Advance

Introduction

Ann B., age fifty-four, like an increasing number of women in her age group has late in life taken on the challenge of further education and a new career. After more than twenty years working abroad with her husband as a lay missionary of a mainline Protestant denomination, she returned to the United States seven years ago and began graduate study in counseling psychology. At the time of the interview she had begun research for her doctoral dissertation while also working several days a week to organize a pastoral counseling center involving the churches in the town where she and her husband now live.

Ann is a quiet spoken, warm woman with an unaffected and straightforward manner that at first strikes one as almost "masculine" in its firmness, although it is neither brusque nor assertive. Her self-presentation communicates an air of down-home simplicity, self-confidence and the non-nonsense practicality of someone familiar with hard labor and demanding conditions. At the same time there is nothing grim or severe in Ann's style. Even her tales of the most difficult and harrowing life experiences will be punctuated with bemused laughter directed at herself and her situation. As the interview series went on, Ann's mentioned self-confidence, though genuine, attained greater significance as it began to stand in relief against the crucial transitional event of her adult life - a severe midlife depression of several years duration, the only depressive episode in Ann's life. Although Ann has been effectively free of depressive symptoms for over four years, this experience of crisis and recovery continues to define for her the direction and focus of her work as a counselor and a researcher. Because of this the over six hours of interview time became in many respects a mutual and highly collaborative labor at understanding how the complex event of the depression caught up and carried to resolution a constellation of central life issues identifiable from early life. For both Ann and this interviewer these issues or many of them began very appropriately to gather under the rubric of faith.

Early Childhood and Family Structure

Ann was born and, until she left for college, lived all her life in a small town in a rural area of New England. She was one of two children, her only sibling being a brother born four years before Ann. Like the majority of the town, her family was Anglo-Saxon and Protestant, middle-class and solidly and respectably established in the community. Her father was a small businessman. Ann's earliest memory of her father is of a powerfully built man with his starched white business shirt rolled up at the wrists, exuding a host of comforting and familiar smells, and reading to her.

As Ann recalls her father, the defining quality of the intimacy was that it respected her separateness and need for independence. Ann writes of her early relationship to her father:

Of course I wanted to be held, but on my own terms. Dad seemed to understand this, and each night I sat on his lap while he read to me, but it was a free thing and not suffocating. My space never felt invaded as it did with my mother and with so many others. The not being suffocated and restricted was more important than the not being held.

He was a "very good father" Ann strongly asserts. Very much the center and authority of the family, he was also a man of substance in the community who would hold forth knowledgeably and forcefully on the issues of local concern: agriculture, county and state politics, and municipal government. Her father was the second oldest of six children and remained close all of his life to his father and his four brothers. Sunday dinner weekly at the home of her paternal grandparents' with a host of uncles and cousins, in attendance was Ann's regular experience of an extended family. Ann's father, in brief, seems to have been a much admired figure in her life up to the conflicts of junior high school.

Ann's mother, now eighty-four, is a much more problematic figure in her early life. Indeed, Ann's relationship to her mother continues to be an ongoing source of vexation and conflict for her because over the past year and a-half the mother has lived with Ann and her husband in their home. At the time of the interview this proximity brought Ann back into active commerce with a great many long-standing emotional issues around her relationship with her mother.

Ann's mother was described by her as a "pampered, spoiled girl with the emotional development of a five year-old." As a matter of fact, there does seem to be evidence that Ann's mother never fully separated from her own family of origin. When she married she moved in right next door to them. The possible complexity of the separation issues in the life of Ann's mother is suggested by the family history which Ann produced in the course of the interview. The mother was the second youngest of eleven children and the youngest female child. Ahead of her by two years was a boy. Following her by less than two years was another boy who, sick from birth, required constant care and died at the age of twenty. Though Ann's grandmother is described in loving terms - a strong, affectionate and universally liked woman - it is certainly conceivable that with a family that stopped just short of a dozen children, and with a youngest child in need of special attention, even this remarkable woman was spread thin in her capacity to provide maternal attention. It is probably relevant data in favor of this conclusion that at the time of Ann's mother's birth, her grandmother (i.e., Ann's great grandmother) also came to live with the family. The family story records that this woman brought additional demands and problems into the family. It must be in the light of these circumstances that we will have to read Ann's opinion that her mother had been a "pampered" child. These facts also effect how one might interpret Ann's observation that her mother had nothing unequivocally positive to say about any other human being with the single exception of her parents, whom she extravagantly praised all her life and in comparison to whom no one, not even Ann's father, ever was adequate.

When Ann tries to speak of her mother, something that does not happen spontaneously, it is with a mixture of bitterness and resignation. Her mother is described first of all as a woman who existed only in the shadow of Ann's father ("My mother thought only what my father thought"). Where father was a direct and dominant presence in Ann's early life, mother was "irrelevant to my life. . .it was difficult for her to assume authority with anyone, including me." There is a story which Ann's mother frequently told as Ann was growing up which dramatically illustrates the image which Ann had of herself and which the family in some sense reinforced - the image of the self-reliant and defiant child:

> . . .that day when you were six or seven years old
> and I went to slap you across the bottom for defying
> me, you grabbed my arm with such strength that I
> couldn't move it, and with your eyes blazing said,
> "Don't ever hit me." I knew then that you would
> never accept my authority, and you never did.

Ann's sense of being somehow older than and superior to her mother had another feature. In almost a reversal of roles, Ann felt that she has precocious responsibility for her mother. "I never felt," Ann observed, "that she could take care of me. . .I had to take responsibility for myself, but also for her." "One of us had to grow up," she remarked with an air of sad resignation, "and it was easier for me." There is little sense of inner victory in this for Ann. Referring both to her mother's capitulation before her defiance as well as her mother's communicated helplessness, Ann commented, " it gave me unprecedented power in relation to her - a constant source of anxiety for me." Elsewhere she adds with a touch of pathos and a note nearly of pleading, "It was too much power for a child."

Though the mother of Ann's representational world fails to make dependency safe, she is also little encouraging of Ann's moves towards independence and individuality. Some of the most touching and revealing descriptions of the mother-daughter interaction concern Ann's efforts to solicit a meaningful personal response from her mother. Ann describes, for example, coming home from school as a child, eager to share some event or accomplishment or to show off some newly acquired bit of knowledge. She would find her mother seated in a chair sewing or reading a women's magazine. In Ann's memorialization of these interactions, the mother would habitually dismiss Ann's requests for attention and recognition with an injunction to run along and play elsewhere. If she gave notice at all it would be with what Ann experienced as incomprehension or evident disinterest. Nothing that Ann said or did - at least as she recalls - seems to have evoked direct and unambiguous approval from her mother. Similarly, Ann claims that she cannot remember ever giving her mother anything which solicited from her an expression of gratitude or appreciation.

In spite of this consistently negative set of associations to her mother, Ann also produced evidence that she retains some positive representations of a mother capable of a greater degree of responsiveness and affection. Ann can respond, when probed, with mental representations of being held and sung to

158

by her mother when she was ill as a child. Yet even these representations are not unalloyed with negative affect. She also has images of longing to be held and sung to and yet feeling that she could not ask for that. She shares the image of herself as a little girl thinking to herself stubbornly upon the occasion of being dismissed by her mother, "Well then, I'm not getting up on your lap again ever!"

The picture which Ann paints of her mother has as a prominent feature what Ann describes as her mother's "natural timidity." Her mother was, in Ann's words, "afraid of everything. . .of the outdoors, or insects - of everything." Ann for her part is self-described as a bold and adventurous child, an early leader among the neighborhood children both male and female. One of the themes we shall be exploring in the analysis of Ann's history is this early negative identification with her mother's passivity and fearfulness. The roots of it are complex, but one element not to be ignored is Ann's perception that this aspect of her mother's character was a central element in what was wrong in her parents' marriage. Her earliest reported memory of a parental inter-action concerns her father expressing some expansive emotion, some new plan or some spontaneous happiness, and her mother making some negative comment calculated to take the edge off her father's joy. It was her father who Ann says she most strongly identified with as a child - and it was her father who she saw as trapped and hemmed in by the marriage.

Earliest Interaction with God

When invited to share her earlier association to "God," Ann went directly to what was for her the most sacred time of her childhood, the yearly celebration of Christmas. One of her earliest stated memories of any sort is of lying in her crib as a very young child on Christmas eve, looking out into the night and sensing deeply, almost intuitively, that there was "something loose out there that was a tremendous security. . .it was more than Santa Claus." Ever after Christmas involved for Ann some period of time when she would be alone and could get in touch with that special sense of benign mystery. God, she says, was largely a protective presence in those earliest years. Hence, when she was tormented by nightmares and apprehensive about thunderstorms, particularly because of the stories her older brother would tell her about the origins of thunder and lightning, she would nevertheless get up in the middle of the night and go to the window to watch the storm. Though the spectacle was awesome and frightening, yet somewhere was a very deep and secure feeling that that Presence was out there in control - "the One who came on Christmas, that was aware of what you did all year 'round, that loved little children and that represented the baby and the whole thing nice and secure."

As Ann documents her own religious development, she connects this sense of the security that enables fearlessness specifically with her father as opposed to her mother:

> My memory at age five was that my father did not invade my space, but allowed me to come to him in my own way and on my own terms. My mother seemed a suffocating presence, weak and leaning; whereas my father's presence was freeing at this stage. <u>God's presence took on this characteristic, and was a great source of strength and security</u> - dependable, loving and accessible. I never doubted He would be there when I needed Him. Like my father. On my terms. (emphasis added)

In the train of her associations to the questions about God, Ann spontaneously introduced the theme of aloneness. From her earliest recollections she says she always cherished time to be by herself in the course of the day. Bedtime in particular she claims was welcomed because it was the avenue of entry into a private fantasy world. Her nightly ritual began at the bathroom mirror, acting out a role or character part, and continued into going to bed where she would play along the particular fantasy until she fell asleep. One of the oft-told pieces of family lore concerning Ann describes her practice as a child of only two and a-half of leaving her grandparents' home during the evening and going next door to her own home, climbing the stairs, and putting herself to bed by herself.

When Ann first shared this story it was in illustration of the point that she "really liked being alone" from very early in life. As the interview progressed, Ann's relationship to this story began to display the more ambivalent dimension of her early capacity to be alone. On the one hand the story reflects her identification with the strength and self-confidence of her father and says something important about her internalizations supportive of a creative sense of secure presence. On the other hand it may also represent her defenses against her mother's failures in nurturance - ("Well then, I'm not getting up on your lap again ever!") - as well as her negative identification with her mother's "natural timidity." The problem is that having become part of her public persona and her own self-representation, it had become a trap. It was a posture from which she could not retreat without a loss of self-esteem.

"Fearless," they would say. Later when I began to have I couldn't tell anyone, because I couldn't bear to be thought a coward.

The leading edge of Ann's faith development might be read as the slow development of the capacity to acknowledge dependency and admit an image of herself as a person who can be both strong and needy, fearless and fearful. The emergent object representation would be one that would begin to fill somethin of the longing which she acknowledges "is still and probably always will be there; to be held by a mother who will not push me to the ground with her leaning."

Throughout Ann's life, not only in her dealings with God but in her relationship to individuals and organizations of all kinds, there is to be found the motif of this struggle to be separate and independent and yet not abandoned or unheld. Ann speaks of it as the issue of control and explains how one early sense of God as the Being in control of life gave her a feeling of freedom to explore and to expand. In a representative childhood story she describes going cross-country skiing and of being outdoors at dusk touched with "such a sense in space of that Being in charge and in control." She adds to this the thought that "perhaps the reason that from the earliest I've never felt or allowed another person to control me and yet felt under control was that I had this tremendous sense that God was in control - and everything around me convinced me of that."

Ann's private religious life in early childhood appears to have been fairly rich and developed, but she was influenced in important ways by formal instruction as well. She went regularly and loyally to the local Protestant church to which her parents belonged. Her father carried on periodic disputes with the pastor and from time to time would stay home in protest, but her mother sang in the choir and was a faithful attender. Though later in junior high school Ann would experience strong disillusionment with the character of her parent's faith, she appears to have retained through most of her youth an independent attachment to the Church.

Adolescence: The Expansion of the World and the Contraction of the Family

The issues that sound across Ann's account of her adolescence are variations upon a central theme: her struggle to deal with the disillusionment and the coercion of limits and controls. There were two situations in which she had to fight for herself (and literally for her "self"). The first was in her family where she discovered the limits of their understanding and tolerance of persons different from themselves and their consequent attempt to restrict Ann's freedom of association. The second was in school where she ran headlong into society's limited vision of the possibilities for women and the set of controls it attempted to exert on the behavior of females.

Ann's community was hardly pluralistic. In the whole New England town of her birth there was, by her reckoning, only two Jewish families and one Black family - all of whom were regarded from a condescending distance. The only sizable minority by New England standards where the Roman Catholics. Until junior high school, however, Ann never came in contact with this group because her town did have a parochial school to which most Catholic parents sent their children. In the one local junior high school parochial students integrated with public school students for the first time. Here Ann had her first real experience of religious and ethnic diversity. The occasion also unfortunately brought with it the disillusioning discovery of her parents' racial and religious prejudices. When, as a freshman in high school, she began dating a Roman Catholic boy, she suddenly found herself in conflict with her father's prejudices against Catholics. She recalls angry exchanges and dinnertime arguments]n which she would leave the table in tears and anger. If, as Erikson proposes, adolescence is typically a time when he developing person looks for a confirmation of values worthy of loyalty and ideals worthy of trust, the realization of a serious discrepancy between the espoused values of the family and their actual judgments would understandably precipitate a crisis of faith (Erikson, 1964). For Ann this conflict had implications wider than just the issue of religious prejudice:

> It was as though the whole area of trust was gone. . . that those people who taught me that all were created equal suddenly were saying they're not all equal. The ideals that had seemed important for them and were important for me were qualified. I began to wonder what else was qualified.

In other areas as well Ann was beginning to run up against the limitations of her father's capacity to understand and respond to her ideals, affective commitments and emerging intellectual interests. Heretofore he had been the one parent who could be counted on to give her questions a respectful hearing and to be responsive to her logic. Now when the questions deviated from regional politics or farming he would find ways of ignoring or avoiding them altogether. Up to now persuading her father was a matter of finding the right argument and the proper logic. In high school, however, Ann for the first time was treading issues that her father could not deal with intellectually or emotionally, and the trusted method of father-daughter negotiation not only failed but became a positive source of conflict.

In school Ann rudely encountered another set of limitations and attempted controls. Also for the first time in her experience she began to receive the clear message that to be a female was "just not a good thing." Specifically in her words, "it was to be forced into channels and behaviors that were not what I wanted for myself." It was, in a word, to be "restricted." In her rebellion against the apparent constriction of life choices, a crucial turning point for Ann was her felt alliance at age twelve with an unmarried female teacher who became an important role model. Significantly, when in the course of the interview Ann was asked to cite crucial life milestones, it was the friendship with this teacher that she immediately cited as the decisive event in her life. Of this influential association Ann recalls:

> She helped me to integrate what it meant to be a girl and a woman and to like that idea, and still feel that I had choices to make with respect to my life so that I wasn't totally demolished when I learned at age twelve that you were supposed to be a young lady - not a tom boy or as active as a boy - that what it meant was a restriction. . .She taught me that as a woman you could have choices and responsibilities even though you didn't win popularity contests.

The pattern of going beyond the immediate family to look for sponsorship and support in her moves towards autonomy was a common one in Ann's early life. Even before meeting the remarkable female teacher mentioned above, Ann had drawn inspiration and encouragement from her relationship to her two grandmothers and several maternal aunts who were well educated and professionally competent women- Now in high school it was not only her mother that she wrote off as an emotional and intellectual resource, but her father as well. There was a sense of sharing so little with her parents that she could say that effectively "they were in my life but not of my life."

There was one other significant ally in this struggle over independence of thought and action which Ann specifically cites and we shall give special attention to that relationship. The ally was God.

The God Relationship in Adolescence

Throughout high school Ann continued to be very active in her local church. That involvement now was quite independent of her parents' interests in the church, and indeed she confesses a strong sense at this time that both of them somehow seemed to miss the point of it all. Her mother she recalls as being mainly concerned with church going as a social occasion, an opportunity to acquire and exchange local gossip. Her father would periodically drop out of regular attendance over some disagreement with the preaching or politics of the current minister. In any case, Ann recalls recognizing at this point that whoever God was for her parents, He seemed to be different for her - or at least she hoped so.

In her own felt relationship with God in adolescence the emphasis she says shifts to a more abstract relation associated in some way with her expanding experience of new persons, ideas and cultural possibilities. "I was most aware of God," Ann remembers, "in music, poetry and feelings towards friends - particularly friends." The important continuity with the earlier representation of God, and the one that seems directly relevant to her deepening disappointment with her parents, is the sense of God as the ultimate controller. It was this awareness, to the extent that she could be aware of it and trust it, that enabled Ann as she put it "to bear my imperfect parents." The dynamic appears to be that cited earlier. Where God is finally in control the attempted controls by inadequate or inept human persons is relativized and rendered tolerable if not powerless.

I have said of this representation of God as benign controller, "to the extent that she could trust it," because as Ann spoke of her interactions with God in the adolescent years it appears that two or more competing, even conflicting representations of God may have been operative at this time. This confirming and supportive sense of God appears to have coexisted with another representation of God who was the target for the disappointment Ann was feeling towards her parents in general and her father in particular.

God came in for His share of my disillusionment too. . .God loved all people, then He loved all people. Even so, this increasing awareness of the fallibility of the adult world around me and the rapid pace at which they were changing, put me in a great state of tension with God. His image changed from one who respected my autonomy to one who knew everything and had the power to punish, not just for now, but for all the transgressions of way back.

Poised on the verge of her adulthood and first decisive physical separation from her family, Ann's barely conscious questions of faith are eloquently asked in the terms of her

164

competing representations of God. Is God/Reality/Life such as finally to support me and sustain me in the passage to autonomous selfhood that I have undertaken, or will I pay the price in guilt for this self assertion and for all the other efforts at independence going "way back" - some of which caused pain and loss for those adults I also loved? If we speculate that the rememberances Ann shares also participate in the structure of the inner representational world in time present, then we may also see the same questions being asked afresh today. Indeed Ann's present situation at the time of the interview parallels no earlier time in her life so much as this time between adolescence and adulthood. Once again she is on the brink of claiming a new kind of life for herself and once again the developmental spiral passes over the issues of separation and individuation.

When we consider the tension that Ann is in with her God representation as she leaves high school, it is perhaps not surprising that in the next stage of her life she will take leave for a while of all conscious interaction with the representations of God until one emerges what can claim univocal loyalty.

College Years: Religious Moratorium and Return

Ann graduated from her local high school at the height of the Depression. Her father tried to make it clear to her that as he saw it college would be an impossibility and she would, like her brother, have to go to work to support herself. For Ann, however, there was never any question that she was going on to college. The most important woman in her family had been an unmarried maternal aunt who had been college educated and whose extensive personal library had been an important source of intellectual stimulation for Ann. There was also the example of the much admired female school teacher. No, Ann was going to college and that was all there was to it. With a conviction that defied logic Ann plunged into scholarship applications and soon won a substantial scholarship to a good school in a major metropolitan area. This pattern of an overwhelming internal conviction that almost denies circumstances but is validated in results is one that Ann finds elsewhere in her life. Indeed it might well describe her present successful doctoral work at age fifty-four. She says of this, "This is something I've experienced all my life. . .When a decision is right for me it would happen, it would just unfold."

In college Ann majored in education and became enthusiastically involved in the multiplicity of activities that were available to her in her first encounter with a major urban area. The one activity she deliberately avoided, however, for the whole of her four years of college work was the church. Where in high school she had been actively involved in church work, now while away at school she did not attend services, take courses in religion or associate with actively religious students. It was for her a kind of drying out period in which her active involvement with her God was not so much denied or repressed as it was simply ignored and set aside for a while. At least with respect to her religion this is a period that has all the characteristics of what Erikson describes as a psychological moratorium (Erikson, 1968, p. 156).

The end of college brought with it an experience that occasioned the end of the religious moratorium as well. Ann was invited to attend a summer program for graduating students by the Danforth Foundation. While on the program she and the other students were given a brief test designed to measure their knowledge in matters religious. When Ann sat down to discuss the results of the test with a counselor she was shaken by the information that, at least in the area of religious knowledge, she had not developed much beyond her secondary school training. Given her studious avoidance of religion courses in college this should hardly have been surprising; still the effect of hearing it was disturbing to her. At one level she was simply abashed to learn that there was an area of her life hitherto of some importance that was "unstructured and untutored." At another level, more subtle and more significant, the experience re-evoked some of the older and more personal yearnings. "It woke me to the fact," she put it, "that I missed God." Summarizing the import of this summer experience she concluded, "It reopened and reconnected me with so much of what was important to me."

Finding a Future and Beginning a Marriage

If Ann reconnected with her God upon leaving college it could not have happened at a more crucial time. Just as in adolescence God appears to have been evoked and experienced as an ally in her maintenance of a sense of connection and personal value over against her "imperfect parents," so at this stage God was again pressed to the service of helping Ann stand firm against a considerable set of social expectations. Specifically, Ann encountered the uniform expectation that she would return to her hometown and settle down into the career and the social style of a small town school teacner. While Ann loved the teaching process itself, she disliked intensely the conditions under which teachers worked. "Teaching required you to be a restricted person without choices and without control over one's own life" she felt, and restriction was the last

166

thing she wanted for her life. College opened up horizons that had to be investigated. In her words, "I just wanted to get out there and touch the world. I didn't want to know two years or five years from now what I would be doing." Ann's criterion for post college employment was simple enough: "That it seem important to me, that it involve working with people, and that it give me the maximum number of choices." God at this time represented to Ann a claim that contravened the opposing tide of family and professional opinion. His sensed claim was not well articulated but it had to do with realizing inner potentials which Ann felt were gifts of God to be unwrapped and used.

The job that Ann took out of college was as an agent for the Department of Agriculture. In this capacity she traveled widely in New England advising families and communities on educational and social problems. There were several important relationships during the two years of this job, three of which resulted in engagements. As Ann explained it, at this time and in this social setting there was just no way of getting to know what you wanted to know about a prospective partner or to discuss serious plans unless you were engaged. In each case Ann broke off the engagement at the point she determined that her fiance's image of her role in the marriage was at variance with her own. When she did finally marry two years out of college it was to a young man who shared her desire for a marriage that combined the raising of a family with the maintenance of two separate or joint careers. Ann's new husband, Ted, happened to share with her from the beginning of the marriage a sense that what he would like to do is work as a lay missionary for the church in some Third World country. The marriage that took place began then with an horizon of travel and adventure and a promise of some very wide-ranging sorts of opportunities. That promise was not disappointed.

After the marriage Ted went into engineering school and Ann worked to support the family which soon included a baby girl, the first of the four children which Ann and Ted had decided would be their goal. A year's post-graduate internship in engineering was followed by seminary, in the last year of which Ann and Ted had their second child, a girl. The trip to their first assignment abroad was in fact delayed several months because of the policy that children be at least three months old in order to travel.

The First Mission Assignment and Personal Tragedy

Between their first and second children, Ann suffered three miscarriages. One consequence was that having children became, in her terms, "almost an obsession." She and her

167

husband were delighted, therefore, when during their first year at their first mission station they found that Ann was again pregnant. Less happily the conditions under which they were living at that first assignment were strenuous beyond their expectations. As it turned out they were being sent in as troubleshooters to rescue a failing mission in the back country of an impoverished Third World nation. They arrived at their station to discover that it was in financial chaos, that the other Western couple at the station were emotionally unstable and inept, and that the native community was largely apathetic and unmotivated. A series of harrowing accidents and illnesses began to plague them. Ted and their first child, then five years of age, became ill with mushroom poisoning. Then their youngest baby went into convulsions from a malarial fever and for a while appeared in danger of dying. For Ann the worst horror, however, was the feeling that she and her husband were trapped in that situation, and trapped in part by reason of the incompetence and irresponsibility of the church leadership that had assigned them there. As a newly employed missionary couple without money of their own Ted and Ann literally had no way of leaving the mission station until Ann's pregnancy finally required them to be brought back to a larger town in which there was a hospital.

At the hospital Ann delivered her third child. Three weeks later the child died suddenly of malarial fever. It was only then that Ted and Ann learned that it was common lore among both missionaries and indigenous peoples that no child born to missionary couples at that particular mission station ever survived the first year. They had not been told.

The total experience was a crisis for the young couple at several levels. Compounding the trauma of their loss was the bitter sense of disillusionment in the hierarchy and administration of the church that they felt had set them up and then failed to provide for them. For Ann it was an experience that recapitulated her earlier crises of faith when she ran up against the experienced inadequacy of her parents and their capacity to put her into the position of feeling trapped. Here as earlier the sense of a God who was somehow beyond the limitations of finite persons and greater than, certainly other than, the church itself was a crucial factor in enabling Ann to deal with the crisis.

At the completion of their tour Ann and Ted returned to the United States on furlough and debated the decision whether or not to continue with mission work. Laboring with strong ambivalences they finally sat down and made a list of reasons for and against returning to the continent they had just left. When the list was complete they found they had to add one last item to the pro side which "once we threw it in made the whole exercise obsolete." This item, as Ann talks about it, was "our faith in Jesus Christ and what God wants us to do." When asked at the time of the interview to discuss what this meant to her at the time, Ann resisted the more personalist language that would render this phrase as something like "the Lord calling you." Instead she now says:

> I have a difficult time with the notion of any personified being calling me to do anything. But there was a clear sense that we had a purpose for going that was above and beyond anything that either of us could understand or articulate. . .So that not to go was in a real sense not to be faithful.

Reflecting back now on the decision to return to the mission after this experience of deep personal loss, Ann still speaks with an almost steely firmness of her conviction that in returning she had to be clear that she was not going to re-entrust herself to the fallible hands of fellow humans.

> The only anger I was conscious of was whether I was entrusting myself to, putting myself under the control of persons or whether I was in God's framework. It made a difference for me who was calling the shots. No way was I going to let that happen again. . .that I would feel trapped and have no choices. What I saw was the possibility that I could be placed by some person in the position of being faithless in my relationship with God.

It was thus only in so far as Ann was able to feel that a return to the missions was a decision made somehow in partnership with God that she could tolerate an imperfect church even as earlier she had to be able to tolerate imperfect parents.

The Middle Years and the Onset of Depression

Ann, Ted and their two children returned to the foreign missions and were reassigned to work in a different country from the one to which they had been originally sent. In sharp contrast to their earlier assignment, this second term was "a tremendously rich and joyful experience." For the next twelve years the life of Ann and her family was a rhythm of work abroad punctuated with furloughs of several months back in the States during which Ann usually picked up several graduate courses in her field. Though she did not speak extensively on these years in the interview it appears that they were indeed full and satisfying ones. A third child, a boy, was born during their time abroad. One catches the sense in the interview of Ann in these years as a competent and energetic wife, mother and missionary. As a wife she played the role of encourager, visionary, and spokesperson for the shared religious vision. As mother she seems to have been very available to her growing children who relied upon her not so much to do things for them as to be one who could be counted upon to do things with them. Finally as a missionary she worked primarily with the emerging educated leadership of the nation to develop schools in the areas of their assignment. The family flourished. Ann and Ted developed a reputation in the church as a solid and reliable team who could indeed be counted on as troubleshooters competent to take on difficult situations.

Seven years prior to the date of the interview Ann and Ted were once again returning from a Stateside furlough and preparing to reenter the field, this time in a very different cultural setting from any place they had hitherto worked. Ann was forty-seven. According to plans she and her husband were to be sent to a predominately Muslim region in a desert area to attempt to reorganize and reenergize a struggling school, church and hospital run by a conservative branch of their denomination. The other aspect of their assignment which would make it significantly different from earlier placements was that for the first time they would not be accompanied by their children. All three children having reached secondary school age or college, they would have to remain behind in the States or in schools in the capital city of the country to which they were being assigned.

In preparation for this assignment the entire family was sent to Paris where Ann and Ted took a crash course in Muslim culture while waiting for the approval of their visas. Since their wait was to be of indeterminate length, they were housed during their stay in a venerable old boarding house in an historic section of Paris. From the moment Ann entered the old house she felt strangely and deeply affected by the setting. As she describes it the experience had almost an uncanny quality to it, although it was by no means unpleasant for her. "It felt," she explained, "as though I were returning to a place I had lived in before and loved." Returning to the security and comfort of this lovely old home at the end of a day of sightseeing or classes felt to Ann "like getting into a warm bath and unwinding." Even now as she describes her several weeks in this home Ann's voice takes on a warmth and vibrancy.

One morning during the stay in Paris Ann awoke and found that she was, in her words, "immobilized." "I didn't have an ounce of energy or motivation," she recalls. "I just wanted to

170

sit in front of the fire with the BBC on the radio. . .I didn't want to talk to anyone. . .I didn't want to meet anyone's expectations." As the days of waiting wore on Ann's sense of inertia and desire to withdraw increased to the point that it required extraordinary effort to mobilize herself to do the various errands and tasks in preparation for departure. While her family regarded her uncharacteristic listlessness as something unusual, it appears that no one in the family, including Ann herself, was as yet alarmed or overly concerned.

When the time came to actually leave France for their mission assignment Ann rallied and felt sufficiently energized again to handle the complexities of once more setting up a new household, this time in the middle of a desert area. Once settled in, surrounded by the awesome, uninterrupted expanses of land and the ancient unchanging ways of an Islamic society, Ann felt herself slipping back into that sense of timelessness and motionlessness that had absorbed her in France. She got up in the morning and discharged her responsibilities at the mission school, but without enthusiasm or great interest. Her interaction with the other faculty and staff of the mission she kept to a bare minimum and she found that even talking with her husband was burdensome and draining. Mostly she just wanted to be left alone with her thoughts. She would sit for hours on the porch of the mission cottage and gaze off into the desert and write. She wrote extensively; indeed she says of this time that she has seldom felt as creative or energized for writing.

There was little in the mission itself to encourage Ann. Once again she and her husband had arrived to find that they were expected to be the saviours of an impossible situation. The mission team that met them was composed of Christians much more conservative theologically and socially than Ann and Ted. In a cultural milieu highly resistant to traditional Christian evangelization these other missionaries were attempting to carry on just that sort of project, while those activities that might have been of more direct service to the people, the educational and medical functions, were about to be taken over by the government. Compounding the problem was the personal instability of the other Western couple assigned with Ann and Ted. Remarkably duplicating the circumstances of the very first assignment, the other woman on the mission team was in the midst of a serious nervous breakdown.

A natural break in the mission tour occurred several months into the assignment when Ann and Ted returned to the States for the marriage of their oldest daughter. By now Ann's mental state had become alarming to her. The sense of retreat she experienced in France had felt like a return to a time earlier in her own life, but in the desert her sensation was of being drawn back to some primordial age. Ann's description of this feeling is eloquent:

> There was a tremendous overwhelming sense of encapsulation . . .It was a moving back into a space that was timeless, that had no restrictions, no mental or emotional restrictions. When people came I gave them short shrift. At first it was good, I couldn't get enough of it. . .of this being in myself, into this aura.

> It was as if in Paris I was moving back in time, but it was a time not too far back, a time that was within my own life time of experience. But in the desert I went further back. At first it was good, but then it got scary, because I found it increasingly difficult to come back. It was getting to the point that I couldn't will myself back to the present though I wanted to and needed to.

Though her husband had also become aware by this time that something was seriously wrong, even he refused to believe Ann when she insisted that she could not return to the overseas assignment. "There was this myth," she observed, "that somehow or other I could surmount anything." The myth that traps Ann now as an adult is the old story of the fearless little girl who never needed anyone else's help. The important difference is that at this point Ann can no longer believe this of herself even though it continues to govern the perceptions of her family and friends.

Against her better judgment Ann agreed to return to a different mission station, but only for four months. The new assignment proved to be located in a remote area even more desolate and isolated than the previous one, inaccessible by any means except airlift for six months out of the year. Ann served her four months there and at the end of the time, true to her statement, she returned to the United States. Up to the very day before she left there were still friends at the mission station who were saying things like, "You're not really going to go through with this, are you? You're not really going to leave your husband here?" For Ann there was now no choice. It seemed to her that her very sanity was at stake. "All I could think of," she remembers, "was to get myself back to some place where I could be responsible for myself. . .have some sense of motivating power, some sense of future."

Return, Reconsolidation and Recovery

The very act of boarding the plane back home brought an immense sense of freedom and relief to Ann. "It was," she says in a revealing analogy, "like sitting in front of that fire in France." When the light touched down in the United States she found waiting for her at the airport her in-laws with some sad and unexpected news. The day prior to her arrival her father had died suddenly at his retirement home in Arizona. The last conversation she had with him on the occasion of her last visit to the States had been a bitter argument in which her father had harped on a familiar theme for him - his resentment of Ann's missionary career for having robbed him of the experience of seeing his grandchildren grow up. Now he was dead. Ann pulled herself together quickly and reassumed the role of leader, comforter, and manager in the family. She handled the details of the burial, settled the estate and saw that her mother, who stayed in Arizona, was taken care of. Ann says of the death of her father that it was likely not until much later when she began her own therapy that she began to genuinely grieve her father. For the moment the loss was but one more in a complex of losses to be dealt with.

After a few weeks Ann returned to her home state and took a small apartment by herself not far from the state university. For the next several months she lived by herself, entered therapy, began attending classes at the university in counseling psychology, and in general took up the slow process of rebuilding her life. When Ann talks about the six month period in which she lived alone prior to the return of her husband, it is with a very evident sense of awe and appreciation. It was a time of significant insights and personal breakthroughs. There emerges in her telling of her story a dual aspect to the healing character of this time. The first factor that she underscores is that it was a time of self-chosen solitude. The second is that this aloneness was lived in the ambiance of an old and familiar environment; the area of New England in which she had been raised and on which she had determinedly turned her back nearly twenty years before.

The theme of self-chosen aloneness as a requirement for psychic recovery is prominent in the interview with Ann. She had made the decision to leave the mission field over the protests of her colleagues and with the trusting approval but likely only the slenderest comprehension of her husband. It was motivated by the deeply felt sense that she needed to go somewhere where she could be alone in a way more creative than the withdrawal which she was enacting while surrounded by the demands of family and associates. She says of this sense of an inner work to be done:

> I had to have the distance. There was no way I could stay in the presence of my husband and children and their expectations of me. Nothing had changed in my feelings towards them. I've been rich in my husband's devotion to me, my children, my family. . but I had to be alone in order to do what I had to do.

Once settled into her small apartment, Ann enjoyed for the first time since her marriage the freedom from being accountable to the expectations of any other person. She learned to relish the liberty to set meal times and rest times for herself. Once returned to the States and after her father's funeral, her mood took on the character of an agitated depression (her designation). She felt considerable energy and was able to function successfully enough in the courses she was taking that no one who did not know her immediate past history gave her any indication that they were aware of her problem. The worse moments of Ann's day, if they occurred at all, came at dusk when she would be seized with a strong desire simply to run. It was a sense of anxiety near to panic that made her feel like jumping in her car and going off in any direction. Her way of dealing with these feelings was simply to take a sleeping pill and go to bed. Invariably, she said, she would wake up in the morning feeling refreshed and unanxious. Ann took no other medications during this time, and at no time did she identify herself as suicidal. [2]

The other aspect of this six month period which was highly significant for Ann was that it was, at many different levels, homecoming. The town she chose to live in was proximate to the small town in which she had grown up. As she settled into her life alone Ann discovered that she was alert and aware as she had never been before to the impact of her surroundings. She describes for example the fresh delight she found in the most ordinary rituals of life and the most mundane occasions. Making her own breakfast, eating a sandwich at lunch gazing out at the trees on campus. . . "everything became ritual and I felt fed and refreshed in a way that was more than food.' The changes of season, the vegetation and foliage of New England, all took on a meaning or were disclosed as having a beauty that she had hitherto not appreciated. Sometimes the wonder of it all was an almost palpable sensation: "My fingertips tingling at the sight of the familiar grass and trees. . .it as like a whole new sense of my surroundings as part of the world and God's gift to me."

For Ann this sense of returning to see the old things of home in a dramatically new way was captured in a line by T.S. Eliot which she frequently carried with her during this time and which she took to be a symbolic statement of the process she was undergoing:

> We shall not cease from exploration,
> And the end of all our exploring
> Will be to arrive where we started
> And know the place for the first time.

The Object Representation of God through the Depression and Beyond

Not surprisingly, Ann's relationship with her God was a prominent factor in her traversing of this major life crisis, even as God had been there in all other earlier critical periods. The changes which that representation itself underwent in the process, however, have only become apparent retrospectively.

In the midst of the depression Ann found herself unable to pray in conventional ways. She never felt entirely bereft of an underlying sense of God, a sense which she says has never deserted her. Yet at the same time she felt deeply alienated and put off by formal worship. One striking example of this incapacity was that for a period of time while abroad she was quite literally unable to pronounce the words "Our Father" that begin the Lord's Prayer. She had no idea at the time why she was so blocked. It was only after she returned to the United States by herself that she began to feel with a special intensity that the whole experience of the depression was in some way intimately related to her relationship with God. Significantly the way she has come to understand this connects her relationship with God to the whole dynamic of her negotiation of closeness and distance.

As Ann regards her own development from the vantage of the interview, she feels that the major transitions in her life have been defined by shifts in significant interpersonal relationships - the loyalties and commitments they have evoked, the sense of personal worth and value which was derived from those relationships. Her discussion of this process seems, at first, fairly abstract. It is run through the categories of Niebuhr, Kierkegaard and others who have been companions to her thinking. Yet between the lines one can discern the anguish that is being described:

> There is the need I have for people who give me a
> sense of being valued and there is a point that it is

175

no longer enough. The transition. . .they were no longer the object now, they are the sign post - pointing towards another person. Relationships became more complex, involved, demanded more from me. . .Every time you move out of a relationship with a significant person. . .(pause). . . there is in that a convenantal relationship demanding faithfulness, and the moment that changes and you invest in another. . .like the movement from parents to friends, to husband, to children. . .there is someone who has to receive primary love and faithfulness. It isn't that you lose them from your life but the priority changes. Yet because of the nature of faith there must be an experience of guilt because there is a violation of faithfulness, particularly when the other person is not in the same place.

The above discussion is not easy to follow. It is disjointed and moreover cast in a theological language. Nevertheless as the interview progressed, it became clearer what sorts of changes Ann is trying to describe. Ann already discussed the realignment of loyalty from her parents to her teachers and friends that occurred in high school. She then described how, when she got married, she had to work through the shift of loyalty and attention from a close girlfriend to her husband. Later there were her children to incorporate whose needs adjusted the primary relationship she had with her husband. Later still she says she shifted emphasis back to her husband as her children became mature and demanded less of her. Through all this, up to the period of the depression, her relationship with her God was experienced as complementary and not competitive with these other significant object relationships. As Ann expresses it, "For a long time it was not a question of who's first; rather God operated in terms of enabling you to value these other relationships." The relationship with God was a point of continuity that paralleled these other relationships and emerged in greater relief only during those periods of relational transition during which Ann reoriented herself in terms of defining relationships.

With the onset of the depression, but most clearly during the six month period of self-selected solitude back in the United States, Ann became aware that for the first time she was experiencing her relationship with God as relativizing all other relationships including her relationship to her husband and family. This sense followed in the train of a growing awareness that she had reached a point where what she wanted for herself in life could not be satisfied by investing herself wholly in any other single relationship as she had attempted to do throughout her life. In describing this feeling Ann compares herself with other women her age who have undergone similar depressive episodes:

> What it was was the awareness that God was essential, that no human being could satisfy me now, could meet my needs, could be enough. This is the common element I am finding with other women I know who have gone through a midlife depression as their only depressive episode. They arrive at a point or are coming to the point of being aware that no other person is really enough for them, can be for them what they want. . .They are essentially separate - it is contact with that vital reality that you are indeed separate. And the struggle is to get the distance you need to move into the religious, the spiritual, the God relationship.

Read in the light of the above statement Ann's turn away from family relationships and demands to be by herself must also be seen as a turn towards towards the intensification of her relationship with God and the claiming of a wider set of responsibilities. Ann asserts that in the years between the resolution of the depression and the time of the interview her relationship with God has become a more comprehensive reality in her life. Prayer, which was once a specialized activity requiring a particular setting is now, she says with a broad smile, "more like breathing." At the same time she says that the sense of a competition between her relationship with God and her other relationships has mitigated. Whether this is true or not, it is evident as we shall see below that the whole process of the depression and the recovery has brought about a renegotiation of the structures of dependence within Ann's family so that she does not have the exact same impingement of demands as she experienced before.

The other two lasting consequences from this period of her life are a change in the position of Jesus within the economy of the spiritual life and a further shift in her perceptions of the church. Since both of these are emblematic of shifts in Ann's inner representational world they deserve more attention.

Throughout Ann's seminary experience she found herself both immensely attracted by and alienated from the simple direct faith in the person of Jesus Christ which characterized the piety of many of her colleagues. On the one hand the idea of a relationship with a personal savior had a definite appeal. On the other hand Ann was painfully aware that such a piety just did not seem to work for her. God was real to her to be sure; but Jesus - or at least the Jesus related to by others - seemed remote and unavailable. On her final mission

177

assignment, surrounded by evangelical Christians with just such a personalist piety centered in the emotional relationship to Jesus, Ann found herself back in the quandary she had left unresolved years before. When Ann started back to graduate school as the depression was beginning to lift she recognized that Jesus had become a positive block to her in her experiencing of God. "He gets in the way," she observed. "I feel more at home and in tune with Job, (Viktor) Frankel, and Buber than I do with the New Testament, with the possible exception of the Gospel of John."

The other development visible to Ann is a change in her attitude towards the church. As Ann now views it, much of her life has been a series of approaches and withdrawals from the structures of the Christian church.

> Being a person you need other people and want them there. The church was a way of being in relation to other people. I didn't need the church to be in relation to God, but the church helped me bring the three together. . .but I had to go through. . .sort of like that image of spiraling. . .At one point when the church or people seemed inadequate. . . then you have to get a sense of yourself alone in relation to God without either one of them. . .then you can move back into relation with the church and with other people, but its always on a different level and in a different way.

While Ann has continued to attend church in her town, her general relationship to it remains problematic. As she looks ahead to possible professional connections with the church she finds that its organizational aspects have less and less meaning and that getting distance seems important.

Towards the Future: Personal and Professional Horizons

Six months after Ann returned by herself from abroad her husband completed his tour and himself came stateside, rejoining Ann. Because Ann had already made it clear that she would not do another overseas tour, Ted retired from mission work and took his first secular professional position since college. Ann and Ted then negotiated together the decision that she would go on and do doctoral work in counseling psychology.

The first year back together in the United States with one child for a while still at home was a series of difficult adjustment for the entire family. Though Ann did not say so directly in the interview, the impression she communicated was that Ted's return was greeted with definitely mixed emotions. Ann had begun to enjoy the experience of solitary independence and likely resented its loss. Hence she was determined that life together with her family would not be business as usual. For one thing she quickly found that the jobs she used to enjoy as part of her servant/leader role in the family were no longer satisfying but burdensome. Because of this, she reports, "One of the tasks I consciously took on for myself was of making my family more independent of me." The stresses of that first year revealed that this was an easier task to declare than to accomplish. Her children had developed an expectation that their mother would be a party to their major and minor life decisions. Now she made it clear that she would no longer be unconditionally available for consultations. Her husband's adjustment was perhaps the most difficult of all.

Ted and Ann had developed a highly successful and adaptive system for managing their life together. Ted was the sixth of eight children born to traditional Eastern European immigrants and the only child in the family to have completed college. At the time Ann met him he was basically a quiet, competent, socially inexperienced young man who nevertheless had a spirit of adventure waiting to be ignited. Ann was then and continued to be the spark in Ted's life that kept it interesting and motivated. She was, he used to say, his sun. He relied upon Ann to supply the starting energy, vision, and theology for their work together. As the more aggressive and socially adept partner, Ann also had sole responsibility for creating and maintaining their shared social life and friendship circles. Ted made no friends independent of those Ann introduced him to. By contrast, if Ann was Ted's source of both head and light, he was, in her words, her "rock." His down-to-earth practicality, delight in ordinary things, and humble sense of shared humanity keeps her, she feels, rooted and anchored in everyday life. With Ann's beginning doctoral study the couple for the first time in their married life are moving in radically different circles. "It was not easy to tell Ted that I'm not going to be responsible for your enthusiasm and happiness. . .I can't carry your emotional well-being by myself. You (family members) are going to have to start helping one another."

At first Ted was hurt by Ann's readjustment of the unspoken rules of the marriage, and she for her part had to wrestle with her guilt over no longer being the supplier of energy and motive. Over the several years of the doctoral program they appear to have come to an arrangement that provides, at least by Ann's account, a satisfying and viable common life. Ted has taken a professional position which moves him in different company, but he shares vicariously in the excitement of Ann's work by long and regular periods of conversation. They also structure into their lives times of mutual recreation and play. Ann for her part has taken on the challenges of graduate school with evident delight and success. This requires of her a good deal of commuting and several nights a week away from home; but at the time of the interview she was within sight of the last stretch of the program.

As Ann looks ahead to her own future she identifies two key issues with which she shall have to deal. The first is a personal issue that concerns her responsibility for her failing mother. The second involves her private and yet not illegitimate fears that despite her energy and competence she is entering a field in which her age and late arrival will limit her opportunities.

One of the unexpected events of the last year prior to the interview was the rapid incapacitation of Ann's mother following an accident which the elderly woman had in her retirement home in Florida. Seeing that her mother was no longer able to care for herself, Ann and Ted made the decision to invite her to live with them. They built a home for themselves that included a separate wing for the mother. Ann gave up the summer she had set aside to prepare for her general examinations and used it instead to move her mother north. The arrangement has not been a happy one on either side. The mother for her part complains about being left alone because of the professional responsibilities of Ted and Ann. Ann on the other hand feels the serious and growing impingement on her own capacity to move professionally. She protests, "I came to school to give myself more choices and degrees of freedom, and what her presence does it to take it away."

Ahead of Ann is the difficult decision of what to do when her mother becomes so incapacitated that she will require constant care. No relative in either Ted's or Ann's family ever finished his or her life in a nursing home, and both feel the burden and expectation of that tradition. At the same time it also seems to Ann as she assesses her own psychic resources and the nature of the interaction between herself and her mother that the decision to keep her mother at home might end up making both of them bitter and miserable. It is not simply a rationalization when Ann observed that given her mother's current protested discontent it is not clear that she would be more unhappy in a good care facility.

Psychically, the conflict between having to be responsible for her mother and trying to be responsible for herself has resurrected in Ann the ghosts of much older conflicts with this parent. Here once more is the mother, this time legitimately, as the helpless child. The threatened outcome, as Ann

180

experiences it on the _Anlage_ of her earlier object relations, is once again to thwart her moves towards competence and autonomy. To Ann's credit she is able to identify many of the strands of this conflict and the major dynamics of her vexed relationship with her mother now entering its last chapter, or at least its last chapter in the living interaction of the two.

The other issue which this conflict with the mother raises relates to Ann's launching at fifty-four of her own professional career as a psychologist. Like any man or woman entering at late midlife what is, effectively, a second professional life cycle, Ann has moments when she must confront her fear that somehow she has missed an opportunity and that in spite of her strenuous efforts she has arrived at this time of life "too late." Practically speaking there are a whole host of very real problems which she knows she will have to face and which she has in fact already begun to encounter. How will the professional establishment regard her, a newcomer to the discipline at an unconventional age? How will she handle the misunderstanding and resistance that meets any woman who deviates from expected roles? Will there be a place for her in the profession and will she be free to pursue her own interests in her own way? Finally, does she have whatever it takes to complete the last and most demanding stage of the graduate work she has thus far managed so successfully?

There is a dream which in various forms Ann has had repeatedly in the course of her graduate studies. It is a dramatic statement of the unconscious fears that attend the momentous and difficult business of choosing a second life. In the dream Ann sees herself arriving at the door of a classroom for a class which she thought would be at a certain hour and for which she had expected to arrive on time. Looking into the classroom she finds to her horror that the class is already in session and that only her seat is vacant. On entering the classroom her classmates ask her where she's been and inform her that she has arrived too late. Going to her place she finds it covered with unfamiliar mathematics problems and in a moment of panic she wonders whether she can possibly catch up. In some versions of the dream she sets to work, in others she despairs of ever being able to manage. On two occasions when Ann had this dream, the next day she re-enacted the very scenario by arriving an hour late for classes which she had consciously thought she would be on time for.

Ann's dream could well represent the feelings and fears of a great many persons her age who late in life have taken the risk of embarking on a new and difficult way of life, one that requires significant adjustments in established relationships and carries them into areas of new mastery. In this life

181

passage as in others that have come before, I will suggest that it is Ann's faith that will be a crucial personal factor in the successful traversal of these dangerous opportunities and opportune dangers in the direction of a fuller, richer life. While much was still at risk in Ann's life at the time of the research interview and the developmental outcome is not settled, still the signs are there of a gathering new strength and self-assurance that will take on the many difficult tasks ahead. The dream of "too late" has become less frequent and in fact has been absent for over the last two years.

III. The Case of Stacy R: Learning to Care for the Inner
      Child

Introduction

      Stacy R. is a fifty seven year-old woman whose present life situation bears certain evident similarities to that of Ann B. Like Ann, Stacy is married and has raised to maturity three children. Also like Ann, Stacy has made the decision late in life to undertake a radical shift in career. Before that Stacy had been a homemaker, increasingly active as a layperson in the local and eventually the national affairs of the mainline Protestant denomination of which she is a member. About three years prior to the time of the interview, however, she began the process of seminary education in preparation for possible ordination to the ministry. Stacy's denomination, like many in the Christian communion, is one in which it is still unusual to find a woman serving as an ordained minister. Hence her decision was in context an unusual one and even a courageous one, made as it was without the uniform support and encouragement of her community. The interviews upon which this case study is based were conducted over a period of twelve months between the fall of Stacy's second year of seminary and the second semester of her third year.

      Both Ann and Stacy are, in their own ways, accomplished and competent individuals who appear to command the respect of their professional colleagues. In personal style, however, the women are quite a bit different. As contrasted with Ann's relatively more reserved New England demeanor, Stacy appears outgoing and on occasion even outspoken. Her manner carries that paradoxical touch of the flamboyant and dramatic coexisting with a deep sense of social propriety and formality that is so typically Southern. Nevertheless, under these two varied self-presentations Stacy and Ann share a deeper commonality. For both women their present self-assurance and centeredness is the hardwon outcome of a complex, ongoing faith journey in which they have had to struggle to become whole and integral selves. Despite their diverse cultural and religious backgrounds (New England pietism and Southern fundamentalism), both women received rather similar messages while growing up regarding what was proper and improper for a woman to do and to become - messages which emphatically did not include the sort of leadership roles which they are now assuming. At a deeper level of analysis still, we find that the richness and distinctiveness of these two lives, confronted with comparable sociological realities as women of the same generation, is defined by the unique relational experiences of each woman which generated different inner representational worlds. Thus the dynamic issues which faith has to address in both women's lives are quite distinct. For Ann the dynamic conflict that plays as a recurrent theme through her life story might be set as a question: "Can I be a self if I admit, alongside of my protested sense of autonomy, an awareness of my dependence and neediness?" For Stacy the problem for faith is also one of maintaining fundamental self-esteem and relatedness, but it is accented differently. Stacy's unspoken question would appear to be something like, "Can I be a self if I claim my competence, distinctiveness and goodness?" Cast in terms of the interplay of self and object representations the life issue for both women might be said to reduce to the heart's common query: Who or What is there that will allow me to be as I am?

In the faith activity of both Ann and Stacy the object representation of God has had from the very beginning a prominent role to play. As one reads these cases, however, it should begin to be clear that each has come to have her own very personal, multifaceted and evolving God representation. In Chapter Four we discussed the constructive character of the imaging of God. With Stacy as with Ann we begin to catch some idea of the diversity of the psychic "raw material" which has gone into this construction: the objects and part-objects internalized from early experience; the symbols and stories available in the formative, religious environment, the familial presentations of God. In the story of Stacy, more clearly perhaps than with Ann, we will encounter evidence of yet another source for the permutations of the God representation and, simultaneously, the self representation. In Stacy's history we find a number of distinctive religious experiences. These are experiences to which Stacy herself does not attach preeminent significance, but which make the point that an individual's interaction with their God can have about it all the potential for surprise and new learning that is the distinguishing character of any living relationship.

Early Childhood and Family Structure

We observed that Ann's early life and family history was characterized by all the stability and sense of historical continuity that landed New Englanders accept as the unquestioned heritage of a long rootedness in a single piece of geography and an enduring social structure. In contrast, Stacy, the only child of parents who divorced when she was thirteen years of age, suffered an instability and uncertainty that was a function both of her parents' special circumstances and a wider historical phenomenon. Stacy's first years witnessed the dislocation experienced by a class of white Southerners dispossessed from the land by economic conditions and longing for the permanence and propriety of an earlier age. The mobility and sheer unpredictability of Stacy's first thirteen years of life has its particular antecedents in the family background of both parents.

Stacy's father was the oldest of four children and the only son born to a struggling Southern farm family. His father (Stacy's paternal grandfather) was a "disappearer" - a man who would reappear to father a child and then take off for anywhere from a few months to several years. The family was held together by Stacy's paternal grandmother, a small, wiry, strong-willed woman of deep religious faith. Life was difficult. The family lived hand to mouth, picking cotton and scratching out a slim living from an unwilling soil. Stacy recalls the wistful yearning as well as the hatred - with which her father would describe his own father who he barely knew and who Stacy knew not at all.

Stacy's father became a rural school teacher and at twenty-five married Stacy's mother whom he met at a local church social. In his own life he, too, became a wanderer and eventually a "disappearer" like his father. During Stacy's first thirteen years her father moved the family repeatedly as he pursued political positions in the state. He eventually obtained a law degree from an ivy league law school and then tried unsuccessfully to establish a practice during the depression years. During the latter half of her parents' marriage, Stacy's father would also take off for periods of time to pursue affairs with other women. Eventually when Stacy was thirteen he abandoned the family in a new town to which he had moved them, and filed for divorce.

Stacy's mother was also the youngest of thirteen children born into a family characterized by its own form of instability. Stacy's maternal grandmother was the third wife of a farmer who Stacy describes as having "worn out three wives

184

having thirteen children." Stacy's maternal grandmother died in childbirth when Stacy's mother was two years of age, leaving her to be raised by the older sisters in the family. Stacy's summary description of her mother's life was that she was "brought up by older sisters, spoiled early, but then abandoned." Actually Stacy's mother appears to have been repeatedly abandoned since the pattern of her upbringing was to be mothered by the eldest daughter until that daughter married and left home, turning the parenting over to the next oldest female child. Through all this Stacy's mother was expected to play the role of adored china doll. The older children doted on her appearance and made much of her being "beautiful." Eventually when she was thirteen her father forced her to leave school and look after his needs, all the other sisters having been married. When Stacy's mother recalled this event later in life she expressed resentment towards being taken out of school, but would also counter this with stories of how her father always made certain that she "looked nice."

The Double Bind

The invitation to supply an earliest memory of father elicited from Stacy the observation that most early images of her father she knows to be reconstructions from later life. She then added the comment that from thirteen on she had only her mother's stories about her father as a contact with him. What she does produce is this story:

> The earliest one I am sure is a memory is my father bringing our dog into the kitchen to warm up. He had been out hunting on a cold rainy day and the dog was wet and cold. Mother didn't want the dog living in the house so Bess had her own house outside. Daddy sat by the stove rubbing and drying Bess and I enjoyed the treat - having my friend in the house. I remember her nails clicking on the linoleum. The sound made me laugh.

Other associations to her father suggest that in Stacy's experience his solicitude towards the family dog did not always extend to her. It was not that either of her parents were physically abusive or neglectful. The trauma which Stacy experienced at the hands of her parents was of a more subtle psychological sort. In his dealings with Stacy, the father was on the one hand severe and exacting in terms of the standards of performance which he expected of her, and on the other hand he took it upon himself to ensure that Stacy did not become "conceited" by ever taking pride or feeling satisfaction in her performance.

My father had extremely high expectations, and I
never measured up to these expectations. I was
supposed to be the prettiest, and the most talented
at everything. And because he also had this thing
about pushing me forward "My little girl can recite a
poem or make a speech" or whatever. And then. .
.well as I think about it now, he would always bask
in what people would say about me. But then it was
like he would get worried that I would get too puffed
up or whatever. So that when we got home, he would
start out, "Well, that was nice dear, but. . . ."
Then I would hear about every mistake that I made, or
that I didn't look right - I could have stood better,
or my hair wasn't right that day.

Many years later, as a middle-aged woman at the time of
the interview, Stacy is able to see how she had internalized
the attitude of her father and mother and turned it against
herself.

It was that when I was little it was so painful to
have my father poke at me that I would always try
either to do that to myself first, thinking that it
wouldn't hurt so much when he does it if I already
know that I wasn't as intelligent or this or that or
whatever. In other words, to do that number on
myself first and that way it wouldn't hurt as much
when he did it.

The internalization of the parental attitudes made it
impossible for Stacy as a growing child, and indeed long into
adulthood, to feel unequivocally positive about herself or
anything she did.

So every time I thought that I had done something
well it would just last for a second, and then guilt;
"I shouldn't be thinking this because it isn't true.
. .I'm just puffing myself up." . . .That's just the
eleventh commandment in the South, or maybe it's the
first: "Thou shalt not think well of thyself." That
was the worst thing you could say about someone -
she's really stuck on herself, or, she thinks she's
really something, or, she's conceited.

Eventually Stacy's defense against these feelings of guilt
took the form of denial, avoiding entirely compliments or
positive attributions which might provoke this reaction of
self-diminishment.

You wouldn't believe it, but up until a few years ago
I could not really hear a compliment, could not hear
if anyone said anything really nice about me.
Because if I heard that it meant that I would have to
deal with that and put myself down. If I didn't hear
it then I wouldn't have to go through that process.

Stacy's memories of her mother, like those of her father,
are also stamped by ambivalence. That the relationship with the
mother had over time laid down some measure of positive
presence in Stacy's representational world is perhaps evidenced
by the earliest memory she offers of her mother:

I am being toilet trained. It is winter and the
potty rim is cold (no indoor plumbing). I'm
squatting, so I don't have to sit on the cold potty.
Mother is holding the potty, tilting it so I can
squat, not sit. She is patient. I think it takes a
little while for me to get started. I feel like it
is morning, but the day is cloudy and the kitchen is
dark. The stove is nice and hot. I feel comfortable.

Coexistent with the representations of the patient mother
in the warm, winter kitchen are other more negatively affective
internalizations. Stacy's mother apparently shared her
husband's concern to communicate the message: "Do well and
excel, but at all costs never become 'puffed up' or think well
of yourself." There was an added contradiction in the mother's
advocating of this position that caused Stacy pain she is only
now dealing with. While her mother taught Stacy to dismiss all
compliments, Stacy asserts that she recalls her mother taking
great pride in comments her hairdresser would make praising her
mother's beautiful hair. Stacy says she had to listen to an
ongoing litany of those compliments while being herself
effectively forbidden to mention or acknowledge any such
comments as might come her way.

Handling Aloneness in Childhood

Because of her father's job hunting during the time her
parents were together, the family moved around a great deal and
Stacy frequently had that most dreaded of all childhood
experiences, being the "new kid." This combined with a certain
precocity that put her in school considerably ahead of her age
group made her through much of her life a double outsider: a
stranger to the community and a stranger among her classmates.
The latter sense she observed has become a permanent feature of
her own self-representation.

The fact that I've moved around a lot is significant
in my development. My childhood was not really happy
in a lot of ways. I grew up more introspective than
many people. I was younger than many people. I was
younger than everyone, an old child.

I started kindergarten at three and first grade at
four - so I was always younger. The teachers at this
special school thought that I was ready. Like W.H.
Auden who once remarked that at sixty he always felt
like the youngest person in the room, I still
sometimes feel that way. I know I am older than that
(but) I generally didn't have the feeling that I'm
here and I know something. Part of moving a lot was
I was always beginning again.

The picture which Stacy paints of her childhood is of a
very lonely child who worked overtime applying her imagination
and not inconsiderable creativity to the project of trying to
feel alive and in some connection with an affirming world.
This is not to read as sheerly defensive expressions of the
aggressive curiosity and creativity of a talented child. It
is, however, to observe that often in Stacy's accounts of these
acti vities there is an element of driveness which suggests
they were in some measure overdetermined.

I can't remember being bored as a child. I loved to
read and read from a very early age. . . .As a child
I painted and made ink blots, or I would be out in
the yard just reflecting, looking at things. I had a
pretty good time in my head. I used to play
dress-up. I would put on whole plays in which I was
every character.

Stacy's inventiveness as a child seems proportionate to the
degree to which she felt herself deprived of the unequivocal
approval of her immediate family. One of the few places where,
in Stacy's memory, such approval was available was with her
paternal grandmother. She invented a game which enabled her to
recreate a sense of her grandmother's loving presence when she
needed it:

I had the most marvelous way of giving myself strokes
that I couldn't get first-hand. I read that
television had been invented, so I fantasized that
there was a television that you could turn on and be
watching other people. I fantasized that my
grandmother and my aunts could watch me, and they
would say, "Doesn't she look pretty," and "Doesn't
she look sweet." Then I thought there is a way they

188

could tune into my thoughts and I could send them
messages. I'd tell them things I'd been doing or
thinking. I'd tell them about the good times I had
with them.

Stacy then added to these reminiscences a poignant afterthought
which summarizes what emerges as a recurrent theme in her
struggle with self-becoming:

We moved so much that the one place that was stable
was my father's mother's house. My grandmother
thought that I was great. I felt that she really
loved me, thought that what I did was great, and I
got so little at home. I was so good and yet I
thought I was so bad. I've tried to get back
recently and love myself.

God in Early Childhood

There is discernible in Stacy's presentation of her
earlier representations of God at least two discrete sets of
representations. The earliest are of a companionable God whose
all-seeing is a comfort and a security and whose care is
freeing rather than confining. This representation appears to
be linked to two parental memories. The one is of her mother's
bedtime ritual which went: "I see the moon, the moon sees me,
God sees the moon and God sees me." God here is a face as
benevolent and as available as the face of the man in the moon.
The second memory concerns her father tending a baby bird with
a broken wing. After a time, when the bird was well, he
explained to Stacy that the way God intended things was that
the bird had to be free to grow up and be itself. Stacy
associates this scene with a very early sense of God as
benevolent and compassionate.

To these parental representations we might reasonably add
the representations of the paternal grandmother whose approving
presence can be summoned in the television game. Additionally,
Stacy's grandmother is explicitly identified in her memory with
religious faith for she was a woman of firm and simple beliefs
who early impressed Stacy with a sense of a provident God.

Overlaying these earlier object representations of God,
and until adulthood the more dominating sense of God, was one
allied to a very different set of memorialized parental
interactions. Her first set of associations are to her mother:

If mother didn't like anyone she'd say, "They're just
trying to show off." I was particularly
self-conscious, trying always to examine my motives,

189

feelings and behavior - feeling under the microscope. God wanted me to do that, it seemed, and that was how I would be able to create myself into a beautiful person. And yet a lot of this simple compassion from childhood was still there. I recall entering into puberty and thinking that God the Father had to stay out of the bathroom

On another occasion in the interview process Stacy links her childhood perceptions of God to the interaction with her father discussed above, where God not only carries the demands for perfection but also enforces the need to be self-denigrating.

For me mixed up with God is the judgmental factor. I was praised a Southern Baptist. Probably mixed up with perceptions of my father. I felt he loved me, but laid great demands upon me. . .I was supposed to be the prettiest, the best, but in the Southern culture you're never supposed to think you're those things. He pushed me to excel, but then would tell me everything I had done wrong. I was never able to feel I did anything well. . .I would critique myself, I would look for imperfections. That continued as a habit.

I got the picture of God, still striving for perfection in God's eyes. The major difference was God was fairer. There were times when my father would say I was lying, and I knew that God would know better.

I was not supposed to think well of myself or God would zap me. . .Suppose you did allow yourself a good feeling, when it got burst I'd think I was getting too puffed up. I'd think that God sent that person to me. I have vestiges of that attitude, the old behavior. Under pressure I regress. But now I can say, "Hey, God, see how I'm behaving."

In examining Stacy's later life we will be concerned to understand the sort of interpsychic developments which now allow Stacy a measure of perspective on her earlier object relationship to God and which have mitigated that relationship in the direction of a less persecuting, more affirmative one.

Parental Divorce and Aftermath

Stacy's parents' relationship appears to have begun to deteriorate fairly early on. From about age six her parents slept in separate rooms and Stacy shared her mother's bed. This appears to have continued up through the time of her parents' separation. Among the traumatic memories that Stacy carries of her parents' relationship are those associated with her mother's frequent threats to commit suicide. On at least one occasion Stacy recalls having to go with her father to bring back her mother after she had threatened to throw herself in the river. Stacy felt both terribly responsible, as though there were something which she had to do to save the marriage, and yet at the same time utterly inadequate and helpless. Both parents made her their unwilling and overwhelmed confidante. At one point her father charged that her mother was not a virgin when they married. Her mother, for her part, told Stacy many stories of her father's misadventures.

At thirteen Stacy's parents finally divorced. Stacy's mother never remarried. Her father moved on to a new town, returning to visit three or four times a year. Eventually he remarried, in fact several times, and became progressively more distant. For years, however, Stacy felt she had to maintain the public fiction that her parents were not in fact divorced or separated. At that time and in the social situation in which Stacy was raised, divorce was still quite uncommon and to be identified as a product of a "broken home" carried a certain stigma. Perhaps another child might have handled it differently, but with Stacy's already fragile self-esteem she felt the admission of her parents' divorce would have been the last blow. Consequently for several years she developed an elaborate myth about how her father's position required him to travel constantly. As one might imagine, this strategy for surviving psychically on one front had a huge price in terms of Stacy's guilt and distress over her own duplicity. As we shall see, one of the breakthroughs in her later life will be to accept and understand the pressures that brought her to this pass as a child.

Early Adulthood and Marriage

The divorce was hard on Stacy's mother. She felt cheated and remonstrated bitterly against life and the treatment she had received from her husband. She was forced to go to work for the first time to support herself and Stacy. Stacy graduated from high school again at a precocious fifteen. From there she went on to junior college for two years, worked as a movie cashier, and assisted a speech teacher in running a creative drama group for children. Except for the period of junior college, Stacy continued to live with her mother. Marriage at age twenty to Mike was a life landmark for Stacy, significantly the one she cites immediately after mentioning her parents' divorce. She acknowledges that much of her passionate investment in her own marriage relates to the desire to undo something of the trauma of her parents' failed marriage. She says of this:

> I'm one of those children of divorce who decides "I'm going to stay married." If I had married someone who didn't give me room I'd have knuckled down. If I had tried to live that life I'd be a mess. I'm willing to endure an awful lot for a commitment.

Within the first year of their marriage Stacy became pregnant, and when their first child was a month old Mike was sent overseas for the duration of the war. Stacy stayed with her in-laws whom she accepted as the intact family she had long wished for. At the same time she was scared, missed Mike desperately and went into a prolonged depression. This was the only period in Stacy's life when she felt the need to seek professional help.

When Mike returned from the war Stacy supported him through college. For a period of time she became involved in theatre and recalls that Mike was jealous of this activity, resenting the way in which this took her away from the house. The conflict disappeared with the advent of another child, and Stacy devoted herself full time to the raising and educating of her three three children.

Stacy's children were the primary focus of her creative energy for a number of years. However, an incident when she was thirty-five and the children were all in school pointed out to her an unmet and ascendent need to find a locus of creativity independent of her children. She was washing dishes at the sink when she suddenly began to cry. The question formed in her mind, "What am I for me?" As she reflects on this experience in the present she interprets this question in these forms:

> I was giving all these parts of myself to others, but it seems important that I give something for me. What could I be doing that would be a part of what I would become?

One of the more practical consequences of this self-revelation was that Stacy began to become more active in voluntary associations and projects. Among the volunteer activities that began to engage her energy and interest was the work of the church. This reinvolvement with the church was, in retrospect, a fateful decision, but by no means an accidental one. As we have seen, Stacy had from fairly early on a vigorous if vexed relationship to her God. At seventeen she made the independent decision to change denominations and join a more liturgical, more formal Protestant church, one in which she felt "more at home." She says of her first encounter with this alternative Christian tradition:

> Almost as I entered the door, I knew this was home for me. The decency and order, the quietness and beauty - this was what my soul needed. To have prayers in a book, the same prayers which came out of reflection as well as conviction, instead of Baptist deacons explaining what was wrong and telling God how he should fix it.

For a short year, between nineteen and twenty, she effectively ran the mission church of the denomination in the small Southern town in which she lived. The church could not afford to hire a full time minister and so Stacy was the combination lay leader, organist, sexton and secretary. It was her first major experience of adult responsibility and she loved it. For a while she seriously considered going into the area of religious education - the only church work open to women in those days. With marriage and family those dreams faded and during most of the years her children were at home Stacy and her husband were both inactive in the church.

In some measure the withdrawal from an active engagement with formal religious life was, for Stacy, a consequence of the experienced dichotomy between her childhood religious views and the operation of her critical intellect. In an autobiographical essay she writes of this time:

> My fundamentalist, literalist background got me into trouble later. In my twenties, I began to question a lot of things I was saying or proclaiming during the service. I was not certain what some of them meant, so how could I stand up and say, "I believe. . ."? I also didn't see what was going on in the church as having much relationship to the teaching of the Gospel. I knew I wasn't acting that out very well in my own life; just going to church every Sunday and being very busy didn't seem to be the answer. I began to feel hypocritical and that I didn't belong. My husband had his own reasons for dissatisfaction and we just stopped going. We sent our children to Church School and drank coffee and read the New York Times.

> I did not stop believing in God, but was less and less sure what that meant. There was still a sense of Someone, but it was mostly on the feeling level.

193

A combination of circumstances and redecisions - the kitchen sink experience, the discovery of a parish with an excellent pastor, the realization that the message to their children was "religion is only for children" - all came together to re-engage Stacy with formal religious observance and with her God. The Church and its mission became increasingly "a part of what (she) would become." Here I want to re emphasize that in our examination of this life, the becoming we are most interested in is not Stacy's becoming an ordained minister or even an active church person, but her becoming a self.

Inner Work and Outer Transformations

At the time the interview picks up Stacy's life, she is engaged in an endeavor of some real risk and challenge. She has gone from being a polite, hard-working and deferential church matron to being a leader in the church, an official lay delegate to three national conventions of the denomination. Now she is embarked upon the step of becoming a candidate for the ordained ministry. In attempting to reconstruct from the interview material the process that built to this change, it soon becomes apparent that the external transformations in style and status parallel a sequence of interpsychic developments related to shifts in Stacy's object representations of God and their attendent self-representations.

Although this has been a gradual process, and one which Stacy herself would have to acknowledge is far from complete, it has been punctuated by a series of religious experiences. In presenting these experiences it is important to observe that it is not clear to Stacy how these experiences relate to psychological developments involving her relationship to other people, organizations and circumstances in her life. In some cases the experiences appear to initiate a process of self-acceptance and integration that carries on beyond theeventitself. In other cases they are signs of a psychic and spiritual movement already underway but brought to particular consciousness.

One of the earliest of these adult experiences which suggests the direction Stacy was to travel occurred ten years prior to the interview during what she describes as "one of those dry periods." Feeling like she needed a quiet place to pray she had gotten in her car and driven to the church:

Not that I thought God was any more there than elsewhere, but I needed the quiet. I was reading Psalm 119 and came to the words, "take the rebuke

that I am afraid of." I was praying those words, and
I cried and cried. This God who loves me; what am I
afraid of? I had a picture of God looking at all of
us fig trees and He could see that these leaves were
made of plastic, He could see it. . .I was afraid
that God would see that I wasn't worthy. . .a
relieved kind of crying thank God that I don't have
to carry around this burden. I started then and it
has been slow working out. That was sort of the
beginning.

The fig tree reference in the above quotation in context
seems to refer to the famous (or infamous) fig tree in the
gospels which was cursed by Jesus for its failure to bear fruit
(Matthew 21:1B-22). The comment by Stacy appears to express
her fear of being "found out" as phony or "plastic" by an
all-seeing God, even as her high school years were lived under
the torturous fear that her fabricated family story would be
exposed. The hope half-guessed, the gift half-understood is
that she might be acceptable as she is. The relief she sensed
in this experience comes from an anticipated release from the
impossible expectation that "I was going to take all this pile
of shit and get it in order. . .then, on the Day of Judgment, I
was going to present myself all fixed up."

The process of this sort of psychic transformation was a
slow one, but there were in the intervening years moments when
she would unexpectedly break through to the feeling she
describes as "not having to be one's own creator." One such
moment she recounts as taking place while seated in a
restaurant after a session with her spiritual director (a
woman), eating a favorite meal. Suddenly she heard a voice or
somehow sensed the communication, "I love you." It was not an
auditory hallucination, more rather a very powerful sense of a
communication as clear as if spoken. The words were
scriptural. "You are the apple of my eye." Stacy had a deep
and contented sense of being loved of God that did not just end
with her. As she left the restaurant she recalls looking
around her at all the other people on the streets and thinking
with tender affection, "All you other apples too. . .and I hope
you know it!"

The Dream of the Truncated Baby

The process of moving from the tyranny of the question,
"What kind of person can I be that this person will like me?"
or "How can I be acceptable in this person's eyes" to a freeing
sense of some order of acceptance and adequacy was one that was
protracted over the last ten years of Stacy's life. There has
been a curious sort of psychic litmus which has recorded the

work and the changes taking place. The symbol for Stacy of the gradual psychic transformation which has occurred over the years is the development in a singular, recurring dream which Stacy refers to as "The Dream of the Truncated Child":

I don't know for how many years I had been having a dream that I called the dream of the truncated child, because it was about a female child of about three or four years of age but squished into baby size, so that it was sort of peculiar looking. I had been having that dream for several years and in whatever the other circumstances of the dream, I was always neglecting that child. In my dream I might be thinking, "Here it is almost lunch time and I haven't fed the baby yet." Or "I haven't give the baby a bath in a week, or fed it or changed its diapers since yesterday." So in the dream this baby is usually undernourished, sitting in a pile of shit, being neglected. Yet the baby is never protesting. I can remember thinking in the dream, "If that baby would only cry, then I would have paid attention to it." In the dream when I would come to it to tend it, it would just smile, and know you in this kind of feeble state. So I was trying to figure out what that was about.

The dream remained a mystery to Stacy although its appearance always brought with it some degree of anxiety. Then, about two and a-half years prior to the research interview Stacy had an unusual experience while on retreat that triggered the release of a flood of affect and insight.

I was on a weekend, silent retreat. And I had gone out for a walk one afternoon. In trying to figure out how to deal with my mind in the silence I had decided just to pay attention to everything and write about it in my journal. So I was just walking around, felt a bit funny stopping to pay attention to a leaf or a tree. And I was thinking of all these things that I was paying attention to, but that meant all these things that I was not paying attention to, and it still felt artificial.

But then something happened. A leaf fell off a tree and just landed on me [gestures to her breast], and it was like, "Oh, that's my leaf." You know, it had sought me out in a way. But it was like I did not have to choose which leaf to pay attention to, the leaf had chosen me. And somehow in that, that sense of consciousness of self was lost, and I was able to walk around and look at everything and feel free and spontaneous. There was a cedar tree growing there, and it had peeling bark. I just took off a piece and began nibbling at it. And that took me back to the time when I was a little girl and we had a cedar tree in the backyard and I used to like to nibble on it.

All of a sudden it was just like I was a little girl again. And I walked along. . .you know, I was looking at everything in this sort of careless way, and I was stopping here and there and really doing something with somethings, just very spontaneous and free. I felt like a little girl. I came to a place where there was a barricade on the trail set up to keep people from going further on a certain path. And I remember running across this barrier, and I looked at it and thought [whispers] "Should I go across that or should I turn around?" I turned around, and as I turned around I became an adult again. The child. . .would have gone over. But even as an adult again that sort of noticing and freedom stayed with me. And I was having a great time discovering all sorts of things.

When Stacy returned to her room at the retreat center she began writing about this experience in her journal. She wrote, "It was fun getting in touch with my little girl self again. . .I liked that." Suddenly, as she was writing, she began to cry. What she realized is that at another level she did not like being in touch with her little girl self, because she did not like the little girl she had been, or had to be in order to survive. Stacy's crying, prolonged for several days, was a mourning of sorts for the little girl she had been forced to become. In the sequence of the interview itself it was precisely as she shared her feelings about the little girl she was that she discussed the double messages of both her parents as well as the fictions about her absent father which she was forced to construct in high school.

In the course of retreat Stacy allowed herself to look at the negative feelings she had about herself and her childhood. In the train of this reflection came a fantasy which stands out for Stacy:

On that retreat I had this little fantasy. . .
experiencing myself in the birth canal, and it was
God's birth canal. A good feeling. I was feeling
good. Just went on walking as though a burden had
been lifted. It was kind of a new birth.

197

In the months subsequent to the retreat experience Stacy began to have a series of dreams that replaced the old dream of the truncated baby. In each of these dreams she had a baby, but was able to take care of it adequately and in fact felt abundantly providing. In one of these dream sequences she was at the annual general meeting of her denomination and discovered that the baby was with her. Much to her surprise she found in the dream that she was able to nurse and look after the baby even while being fully involved in the work of the general conference.

Towards the Future: Personal and Professional Horizons

Stacy, at the commencement of the interview process, like Ann B. faced two immediate difficulties. The first was familial and, again like Ann, involved her mother. The second was professional and concerned the uncertainty that attends a late life career change. Stacy's mother had lived with her and her husband for nearly ten years. During that time she had become progressively more enfeebled physically and mentally. Stacy shared with Ann the emotionally torturous question about whether or not to commit her mother to a nursing home. Shortly after the first major set of interviews, Stacy's mother took ill, failed rapidly, and died. Stacy called the interviewer after this happended and there was an extended conversation that dealt with her feelings around the sudden loss of her mother. There was then one more follow-up interview a little over a year after the death to see how the grieving had been resolved. The following observations are made from notes made on those two occasions.

Several comments Stacy made at the time of her mother's death suggested how her sense of God was enabling her to to manage the grief work involved in mourning this very ambivalent mother-daughter relationship. Stacy was able to say that she felt that on balance she had done well for her mother in her declining years. She had enabled her to avoid the "final indignity" of a nursing home. Still Stacy was left with her share of "If only I had's" - regrets which she acknowledges, if only intellectually, may be reflections of her perfectionism. In the midst of this what gives her comfort is the line from the funeral liturgy, "Thou art doing better things for them than we could do." The thought came to her: "I did my best, but didn't always succeed in making her happy - now God is doing better things for her." Accompanying this thought was an image which she found appearing in her imaginative prayer in the days immediately following her mother's burial. It was the image of Jesus holding her mother to his breast where she, like a baby, smiles at him in delight. [3] There was, it would appear, an object representation of God available to Stacy to help ease the burden of reparation by taking up the caring task and doing it more adequately. The image of the maternal Jesus offers the hope that the resolution of Stacy's grieving might be laying aside the responsibility for her mother's well-being which she, rather like Ann, was precociously given.

The year that followed Stacy's mother's death was full of difficult anniversaries and periods during which Stacy felt considerable psychic stress of an indeterminant nature. Two months before the actual anniversary death date, for example, Stacy had a brief attack of dizziness and irregular heart beat while traveling to the seminary - serious enough that she ended up in the emergency room of the hospital. No physical causes of the attack could be determined. She subsequently began cutting back on extensive church and school commitments and eating regularly and more carefully and exercising, treating herself to small periods of rest and relaxation. The other thing that she has begun to do for herself is to buy, from the money left her in her mother's estate, a good, professional wardrobe. Perhaps more than any other single action, this outfitting of herself in attractive clothes appears to represent an enlarging capacity to use the "good" inheritance from her mother for mature self-enhancement.

The other life issue which faces Stacy concerns her potential future as an ordained minister. The path to the acceptance of a sense of calling has not been an easy one for Stacy. Interiorly she has had to wrestle with that chronic sense of inadequacy which tells her, "God couldn't call someone like me; He would call someone more religious and better." These intrapsychic conflicts have their analogue in her apprehension that her gifts and contributions will not be recognized or affirmed by the Church. Practically speaking it is a legitimate concern at a time in the history of a denomination that has many times more ministers than it can employ. Yet at the same time this uncertainty about her future taps into a very old and painful memory which, one suspects, stands for a whole series of experiences of not being taken with real seriousness by parents unhappily preoccupied with securing their own fragile self-esteem. Stacy's account of this memory merits retelling as an example of the vividness and emotional immediacy with which representations of supposed past events survive in the representational world.

I am four. I'm in the first grade, so I can read and write and add. I have been bugging my family (according to the way they told it) to let me go out and get a job. (My feeling now is that I had heard a lot of talk about being poor, but I get a trace of feeling that "I'm ready to do something"). When my father asks what kind of job I want, I say "I want to help the minister at the church." (I think this dialogue has gone on for a while.)

One day my father says, "All right," and has my mother pack a little lunch for me in a brown paper bag (little). He puts me in our Model T and drives me to the church, lets me out, says goodby and drives away. I go up the walk to the BIG front doors, knock for a while, then kick and bang the doors. Nobody comes. I am crying a little, but persist. After a bit, I know that if there is anyone in there they can't hear me. I feel very alone - on my own. They can't hear me, my daddy has left - all there is is me and my lunch bag. I sit on the steps and cry. I feel totally alone - is there anyone, anywhere fore me? What will happen to me?

In the midst of crying, even though I want to just cry and cry forever, I'm thinking: there are other doors to the church - if I walk around the building and bang on doors, maybe someone will hear - and want me - I still want a job. Or - can I remember my way home, when I've always gone in the car before?

My big cry has diminished as I weigh my alternatives. Just then, my father drives up - relief - but he is talking about it as though it's funny; it doesn't feel funny to me. I thought I had been abandoned, bereft - there's something I don't understand. I am home - I will not eat that lunch in the brown bag, even though I know food is precious. No, No. Daddy and Mother laugh - for several weeks (months?-years?) the story is told to friends and relatives.

No one ever asks about my feelings - it's a cute story. I'm ashamed - I'm different. Everyone else thinks it's funny there must be something wrong with me±. I am not supposed to act up," I am supposed to enjoy the story with everyone else. I'm ashamed - I shouldn't be feeling the way I do when the story is told. I'm ashamed - I pretend that I think it's funny too - I'm acting a part, I'm lying. I'm guilty of something - but what? What's the matter with me?

Now that I'm hoping for ordination, I wonder sometimes if my end is in my beginning - will I knock and kick and not be heard? Will I sit on the step, holding my little gifts? Now, I prefer the steps to the Model T.

This story recapitulates many of the salient themes in Stacy's development: the longing to be recognized and the sense of not being allowed to make a contribution, the precocious sense of responsibility for the well-being of her family, the experienced demand to conform herself to the expectations of her family and community with the painful sense that she is guilty of a double failure. At one level she wonders what is wrong with her that she is both the butt of everyone's humor and yet can't see the joke. More deeply she knows her gifts are not to be despised and in pretending to laugh along with the others at herself she experiences a betrayal of self.

There are, however, two distinct ways in which Stacy believes herself to have developed with respect to the identity and self-esteem issues that ride upon her professional future. One is that if she fails to see her hopes for ministry realized she is determined not to interpret that as a joke upon her for not knowing her value or her place. In the imagery of her tale, she has come to "prefer the steps to the Model T." The other change, which may in fact help support her sense of the integrity of her own calling, is that she does see that her reception or nonreception by the institutional church will not reflect her value and worth in the eyes of God. As she expressed it in the interview, now if she is turned down and left outside the doors she is secure in the knowledge that it is a human institution that has locked her out and that she has, for her part, been faithful to God. To translate this into the language of emotional life, her sense of self and inner conviction about her own goodness does not reside in an ultimate way on the judgments of others.

FOOTNOTES CHAPTER SIX

1. This study was supervised and conducted by Dr. Lee Helena Perry, Program in Counseling and Consulting Psychology, Harvard University Graduate School of Education. The interviews for these two cases were conducted between October 1979 and February 1980.

2. According to Ann one of the first things she did for herself upon returning to the States was to have a complete medical examination in order to determine whether the depression was menopausal or had some other physical source. The determination was apparently negative on all counts.

3. The image which Stacy spontaneously describes bears remarkable resemblance to an iconographic convention frequently found in late medieval paintings of the death of the Virgin or of a saint. These portray Jesus in heaven cradling in his arms a small child, representing the soul of the person whose dead body, surrounded by mourning disciples, is painted in the lower portion of the painting. For example, see Fra Angelico, "Death and Dormition of the Blessed Virgin Mary," (15th century), Gardner Museum.

CHAPTER SEVEN

AN OBJECT RELATIONS ANALYSIS OF FAITH DEVELOPMENT

I. The Emergence of a Psychoanalytic
   Theory of Object Relations

   Two Stories of Failure and a Revolution in Theory. p. 204

   Fairbairn and Winnicott:
   Internalization for Defense vs. Primal Creativity. p. 209

II. Case Analysis: Infancy and Early Childhood

   Prelude to the Drama: Setting the Stage . . . . . p. 214

   Birth and the Origins of Basic Trust. . . . . . . p. 217

   The Separation Individuation Process. . . . . . . p. 221

   Traditional Object Phenomena, Play and God. . . . p. 225

III. Play Age Through Adolescence

   Stacy: God and the Judgmental Factor. . . . . . . p. 230

   Ann: God the Controller. . . . . p. 234

IV. The Crises of Adult Life

   Ann and the Long Way Home. . . . . p. 237

   Stacy and the Child of the Dream. . . . . p. 241

V. Concluding Reflections. . . . . p. 245

CHAPTER SEVEN

AN OBJECT RELATIONS ANALYSIS OF FAITH DEVELOPMENT

I. The Emergence of a Psychoanalytic Theory of Object Relations Two Stories of Failure and a Revolution in Theory

Even a summary history of the progressive development of the object relational perspective within psychoanalysis is beyond the scope of this book. [1] However, a flavor for the revision that object relations theory represents over classical psychoanalysis might be obtained by looking at two brief vignettes. They are not the sort of stories that therapists or spiritual directors like to tell on themselves. These are accounts of failure, the failure of an individual to be therapeutically or salvifically present to another human being. Like other stories of failure (and one recalls here Freud's famous case of Dora), these incidents raise critical questions regarding the theory that informs practice.

The first story is taken from an autobiographical sketch by the Jewish philosopher Martin Buber who describes an incident which he locates at the emotional well spring of his career as a philosopher of dialogue:

> . . .after a morning of "religious" enthusiasm, I had
> a visit from an unknown young man, without being
> there in spirit. I certainly did not fail to let the
> meeting be friendly, I did not treat him any more
> remissly than all his contemporaries who were in the
> habit of seeking me out about this time of day as an
> oracle that is ready to listen to reason. I
> conversed attentively and openly with him only I
> omitted to guess the questions which he did not put.
> Later, not long after, I learned from one of his
> friends - he himself was no longer alive - the
> essential content of these questions; I learned that
> he had come to me not casually, but borne by destiny,
> not for a chat, but for a decision. He had come to
> me, he had come in this hour. What do we expect when
> we are in despair and yet go to a man? Surely a
> presence by means of which we are told that
> nevertheless there is meaning.
>
> Since then I have given up the "religious" which is
> nothing but the exception, extraction [Heraustritt]
> exaltation, ecstacy; or it has given me up. I
> possess nothing but the everyday out of which I am
> never taken. . . [Buber, 1976, pp. 3-4]

The second story of failure is the case study which stands at the head of the published theoretical papers of the Scottish psychoanalyst, W.R.D. Fairbairn (1889-1964). The case, "Notes on the Religious Phantasies of a Female Patient," dates to 1927 when Fairbairn was just beginning his practice as a young psychiatrist (Fairbairn, 1952a, pp.183-196). The unmarried woman in the case was thirty-one at the time she came to see Fairbairn for analysis. She was the youngest child in a family in which the father was an alcoholic who had disappeared at the time of her birth. Her mother died when the patient was nineteen. She suffered from age twenty one from severe hysterical symptoms that were periodically disabling. She also had developed an intense and compulsive habit of masturbation. The "religious phantasies" which alternately terrified and consoled her were largely woven around sexual themes. In these visions and dreams she was often either directly identified with Christ as the favorite child of the Father, or felt she was to be the Mother of Christ by an act of miraculous impregnation by the Father, or felt chosen to be the bride of Christ. Fairbairn, it appears, attempted to interpret the material his patient presented according to classical analytic doctrine, as the expression of sexual and aggressive drives seeking discharge.

Somewhat later than this particular case another patient protested Fairbairn's orthodoxy with the words, "You're always talking about my wanting this or that desire satisfied; but what I really want is a father" (Ibid., p. 137). The women in the 1927 case similarly expressed, but in a more tragic and decisive way the failure of Fairbairn's therapeutic interventions to touch the heart of her real need. She discontinued analysis and fell into a state of neurasthenic decline. When Fairbairn was called to her home to see her it was to her deathbed. He records:

> When I went to the house, I found her in the state of extreme weakness which I have already described; and, although neither her own doctor nor a consultant physician who had examined her could find any evidence of organic disease, it was obvious that she had not long to live. During the next few days I visited her regularly; and my last visit was on the day before she finally faded away and died. . . .I was not able to learn a great deal about the experiences through which she was passing. I remember, however, that she was perfectly rational and perfectly oriented in time and space. I can also remember that she was experiencing no ecstatic or horrific visions; but, unless my memory deceives me, she was definitely entertaining sexual phantasies.

Be that as it may, it is quite certain that she was
in a state of extreme sexual desire; and, when I left
her moribund on the occasion of my final visit,
almost her last words were, "I want a man."
(Ibid., pp. 195-196)

Both Buber's and Fairbairn's experiences of failure are
convergent upon a common insight, the irreducible centrality of
the human for relationship. Human beings can die,
psychologically if not physically, for want of confirming,
self-validating relations with other persons. Buber went on
from this experience to spend a lifetime studying the
phenomenon of human meeting and dialogue. Fairbairn made
reflection upon the implications of such phenomena the real
starting point for a systematic revision of Freudian theory in
the direction of "the emancipation of the core of psychodynamic
thinking" - the primary object relations for the psychic
development of the human person (Guntrip, 1971, p. 33).
Fairbairn captured this insight in his epigramatic assertion,
"Libido is essentially object seeking" (Fairbain, 19522, p.
162). By that I take him to mean that the primary energy
interest in living is directed from the beginning towards
seeking mutuality with other human beings and is only
exclusively sexual or aggressive in the presences of
frustration of that primal goal. In other words, "A preoccupation with establishing and maintaining object relations
is the human motive sine qua non" (Goethals, 1973, p. 92). [2]

Interestingly, where Buber's discovery of the primacy of
the personal meant a turning away from the religious (or at
least the piety of his earlier formation), for Fairbairn the
comparable discovery represented something of a return.
Fairbairn's recovery of the object relational core of
psychoanalysis represents a reappropriation of theological
influences that antedated his medical training. Fairbairn had
graduated from Edinburgh University in Philosophy in 1911 and
spent three years after that studying divinity and classics
both in Edinburgh and on the continent before the First World
War permanently interrupted his philosophical and theological
education. One of the key influences on Fairbairn in Edinburgh
was the theologian John MacMurray, whose Gifford Lectures, The
Form of the Personal, were a major effort to introduce the
relational paradigm into fundamental theology (MacMurray,
1957). It was MacMurray who wrote:

That capacity for communion, that capacity for
entering into free and equal personal relations is
the thing that makes us human. . . the personal life
demands a relationship with one another in which we

can be our whole selves and have complete freedom to
express everything that makes us what we are.
(MacMurray, 1935, pp. 63, 97)

Fairbairn sees that modern psychoanalytic theory in
significant ways adopts MacMurray's theological agenda by
attempting to concretely understand the developmental blocks to
our capacity for communion. Religion intuited first that what
is saving in human life is the power of relationship and
psychoanalysis follows by rendering that insight in scientific
form and embodying it in a system of therapy that emphasizes
the effective presence of the therapist. Fairbairn therefore
allows what Freud would never have considered, that understood
rightly religion and psychoanalysis aim for the same results,
and under some circumstances religion may be the more effective
of the two.

It is the verdict of history, and particularly of
religious history, that effective psychotherapy can
take place in the absence of all scientific
knowledge. . .I consider further that what is sought
by the patient who enlists psychotherapeutic aid, is
not so much health as salvation from his past, from
bondage to his (internal) bad objects, from the
burden of guilt and from spiritual death.
(Fairbairn, 1955, pp. 155-156)

Religion has always stood for the saving power of the
good object relationship. Religion is distinguished
from science as the historical form under which the
therapeutic factor for personality ills has been
recognized and cultivated.
(Guntrip, 1953, p. 116)

The revision of Freud's instinct theory is only one side
of Fairbairn's object relational perspective. The other aspect
is the insistence that the relationships which influence and
define us are not simply the ones conducted with discrete
others in time present, but those we carry on unconsciously
with all whom we have ever loved and left. This attention to
the enduring relationships carried on with past significant
others recasts the problem of the unconscious as the problem of
inner and outer reality. Fairbairn says of this, commenting on
the work of Melanie Klein:

On the basis of the resulting concept of internal
objects there has been developed the concept of a
world of inner reality involving situations and
relationships in which the ego participates together

207

with its internal objects. These situations and relationships are comparable with those in which the personality as a whole participates in a world of outer reality, but the form which they assume remains that confered upon them by the child's experience of situations and relationships in the earliest years of life. . . .The fact is that, once the conception of inner reality has been accepted, every individual must be regarded as living in two worlds at the same time - the world of outer reality and the world of inner reality; and whilst life in outer reality is characteristically conscious, and life in inner reality is characteristically unconscious, it will be realized that Freud's original distinction between the conscious and the unconscious now becomes less important than the distinction between the two worlds of outer reality and inner reality. (Fairbairn, 1952b, p. 124)

The idea that psychic life is patterned on our actual experience with parents and other significant persons in early life is not original to Fairbairn. It is precisely his claim that Freud produced this insight although his bondage to drive theory prevented him from fully appreciating the significance of his discovery. Specifically, Fairbairn and other object relations theorists point back to Freud's postulation of the superego as his recognition that psychic structure is formed by the process of internalization. [3]

A portion of the external world has, at least partially, A portion of the external world has, at least partially, been abandoned as an object and has instead by identification, been taken into the ego and thus become an integral part of the internal world. This new psychical agency continues to carry on the functions which have hitherto been performed by people in the external world.
(Freud, 1933/1965, p. 205)

Ironically, if Fairbairn had taken a clue from the content of his first published case study and gone directly to Freud's papers on religion, he would have found there the essential components for a theory of object representation and internalization (Rizzuto, 1976). As it was he built his own theoretical revisions upon the pioneering work of Melanie Klein, whose explorations into the fantasy life of children uncovered the dramatic reality of the pre-oedipal internal world (Klein, 1948). While Fairbairn's debt to Klein is considerable his disagreements are substantial. It is in part 4because of Fairbairn's need to do battle with Klein's notion of internalization as an innate process that his theory of object relations has some major limitations. The problem with Fairbairn's work which is most relevant for this project concerns his postulation of the motives for internalization, why the child creates an inner world in the first place. We shall briefly consider Fairbairn's ideas as a bridge to introduce D.W. Winnicott, the object relations theorist whose work will be the principal "tool to think with" in our analysis of the two case studies.

Fairbairn and Winnicott: Internalization for Defense vs. Primary Creativity

For many object relations theorists it is the highly imaginative but controversial work of British child analyst Melanie Klein that marks the great divide in the development of psychoanalysis, "the decisive contribution which marks the transition from classical to present-day psychodynamic research" (Guntrip, 1969, p. 409). Klein began, like Fairbairn, from an orthodox Freudian position. Also like Fairbairn, however, she was forced to develop psychoanalytic theory in new directions in order to make sense of her experience with her patients. In the case of Klein this experience chiefly involved her extensive analysis of the rich fantasy lives of very young children and her discovery that children from early in life live within both an outer world of relations and a secret inner world organized around the twin fantasies of good or protective and bad or persecutory objects. She speculated that these objects were "internalized" as a way of dealing with the experience of relationships in the real world which were alarmingly ambivalent, i.e., that were both frustrating/terrifying and satisfying/exciting. Strictly speaking, the emphasis on Kleinian psychology is not upon the actual quality of the parent-child interaction so much as on the child's _experience_ of that relationship, which is colored by the child's projection of his primary aggressive instincts upon the maternal environment.

Fairbairn was decisively influenced by Klein's work on internal and external object relationships and their interplay in fantasy. Where he parted company with Klein was over the motivation for the internalization process. For Fairbairn the Kleinian notion of the projection of innate aggressive instincts, Klein's adoption of Freud's highly speculative idea of a death instinct, in effect made the child's real experience with actual human objects irrelevant. All the weight came down upon "nature" and none upon "nurture." As Harry Guntrip, Fairbairn's protege and principal interpreter put it, Klein had developed a theory of "ego development by hereditary predestination," as opposed to a theory of "ego development by

209

environmental object-relations" (Guntrip, 1969, pp. 411-412). Fairbairn's effort to redress this imbalance was to re-emphasize the formative experience of the child's actual involvement with the parenting others.

The issue then becomes what sorts of experiences initiate the process of internalization. Here Fairbairn shows himself to be closer to the spirit of Klein's work than he is generally willing to acknowledge. For Fairbairn, as for Klein, internalization is a psychological dynamic employed in the interests of defending the self against intolerable anxiety. The crucial factor for Fairbairn is the degree to which the child was able to experience himself as dependably loved for his own sake. Parents could fail to provide this experience in one of several ways. They could be genuinely neglecting of the child or unresponsive to the child's need to be recognized as a separate self; or they could be so oversolicitous and possessive that they rob the child of the integrity of his or her own experience.

If for whatever combination of circumstances the parent is not there for the child as a reliable and satisfying object during the first stage of life, then to that degree the child experiences him or her and the world at large as frustrating and "bad." Fairbairn theorized that the way the child dealt with the experience of intolerable frustration and anxiety was to split the image of the parent into a good ("idealized") and a bad ("exciting and frustrating") object. The latter was internalized in order that it might be more safely controlled. This process of internalization is accompanied by an attendent process of ego splitting (Fairbairn, 1952, pp. 94-102). Although there is a real question whether the idea of "ego splitting" can be made metapsychologically coherent (see Pruyser, 1975), the phenomenon Fairbairn is pointing to is clinically evocative. He is describing persons for whom part of the capacity to love and to be in relationship is withdrawn from active engagement with other persons in the world and instead is attached to objects in fantasy. This defensive preoccupation with inner reality is the central feature of what Fairbairn termed the "schizoid" characteristics of personality.

Fairbairn's idea that internalization is a defensive measure adopted in response to an unsatisfying environment has implications for his vision of human health, his theory of therapy, and ultimately for his understanding of the meaning and ends of religion. The problem with the schizoid defense, as Fairbairn sees it, is that the individual is constantly "finding" his good and bad internalized objects in the external world, in other words distorting reality to meet the requirements of the defensive structure. "The sub-ego structure. . .coerces these people into the role of the inner object. . .such objects are not permitted to have any real independence or individuality; they have to fit the inner image" (Sutherland, 1964, p. 117). The achievement of psychic integration or wholeness would mean in some sense an "emptying" of the contents of the inner representational world so that one is whole-heartedly in relationship to the total, undistorted reality of the individuals one actually encounters. The influence of both MacMurray and Buber is particularly evident here. The never completely-achieved psychological ideal for Fairbairn would presumably be a person free of repressed bad objects and hence capable of an outgoing, spontaneous interaction with others perceived in their own wholeness and actuality. Therapy, then, is frequently described by Fairbairn with the metaphor of exorcism. "It becomes evident," he writes, "that the psychotherapist is the true successor to the exorcist, and that he is concerned not only with the 'forgiveness of sins,' but also with 'the casting out of the devils'" (Fairbairn, 1952, p. 70). The "devils" in this metaphor are those aspects of an object relation which had to be repressed as bad, i.e., threatening to the integrity of the self.

Fairbairn's theological training and positive perspective on the function of religion have already been commented upon. The significance of his work for an interpretation of religion was made explicit in the commentaries on psychoanalytic object relations theory written by Fairbairn's protege, Harry Guntrip. Before entering upon the study and practice of psychoanalysis, Guntrip was a Non-Conforming minister in England who had become dissatisfied with the resources for effective pastoral counseling available to him in a purely ecclesiastical context. Like Fairbairn, Guntrip was also very much influenced by J.C. Fugel, John MacMurray and Martin Buber. A Melanchthon to Fairbairn's Luther, Guntrip wrote as an interpreter, extender, apologist and popularizer of Fairbairn's psychoanalytic manifesto. One of his aims was expressly to develop the idea that Fairbairn only suggested, i.e., that religion and psychology have achieved closure in the insights of psychoanalytic object relations theory (Guntrip, 1949; 1956).

Guntrip begins his analysis of religion with the central insight of psychoanalytic object relations theory, that "human beings have an absolute need for a personal environment that values us as persons, if we are to be able to become and survive as persons" (Guntrip, 1969, p. 328). This assertion repeats the position of our work with respect to faith, that the first question of faith is not "what is there?" but rather "who is there for me?" Religion then is on a continuum with the experience of the benevolent interpersonal universe of infancy. It is, in Guntrip's words, an experience of personal relationship, which extends the 'personal' interpretation of experience to the nth degree, to embrace both man and his universe in one meaningful whole" (Ibid., p. 325). Human religiousness is therefore "a way of experiencing the universe that does not condemn us all to meaningless schizoid isolation, but relates us to a personal heart of reality, that we refer to by the indefinable term 'God,' experienced, but not explained, the 'ultimate indefinable mystery'" (Ibid., p. 331, emphasis author's).

There is certainly much to be endorsed in Guntrip's interpretation of what the essence of religion is about. The burden of my argument to this point has been to make a very similar claim - that the character of human faith is decisively marked by the nature of the human person as object seeking and of personality development as a process of object relating. As one reads Guntrip's accounts of what qualifies as religion, however, one senses a kind of religious positivism of a curiously ingenuous sort. Religion, like mature interpersonal relationships, is about the full experiencing of all that is really there in the "external world." It is exactly modeled on the paradigm of a mature object relationship. In fact it is held out to be "the one full answer to alienation. . .the basic religious experience of the universe as not alien to our nature as 'persons,' a sense of oneness with ultimate reality akin to the experience of human love" (Ibid., p. 332). Although Guntrip has asserted that religion differs "in range" but not "in type" from human personal relations experience, he is in fact unable to give an account of how in the process of ordinary religious development we might arrive at this basic experience of "oneness with ultimate reality." Not surprisingly the only religious exemplars he can point to are the mystics, persons who presumably have very concrete experiences of an encounter with the divine other.

The problem can be traced back to Fairbairn's proposal that the formation of an inner world is a defensive process which hence must be "undone" or at least significantly modified in order to permit mature interpersonal relationships to occur. When one builds a theory of religion upon this structure one ends up with Guntrip's positivist notion in which one somehow "finds" God or the universe rather than simultaneously "creating" and "encountering" the reality of the divine in a more complex process of introjection and projection. The important theoretical corrective was applied by D.W. Winnicott (1896-1971). Winnicott, an eminent pediatrician and analyst and a contemporary of Fairbairn's, criticized Fairbairn for his emphasis upon internalization as a psychic process which only occurs in reaction to a frustrating interpersonal environment.

"It is difficult to see," Winnicott observed, "how the human being could build up inner sources of strength, or the basic stuff of the inner world that is personal, and indeed the self, simply on the taking in of 'bad objects' through the operation of a defense mechanism" (Winnicott & Khan, 1953). What Winnicott proposed, and developed as a concept in a lifetime of creative analytical writing, was a process of "primary psychic creativity" whereby the child creates the maternal object in the case where a satisfying or "good enough" mother provides a secure basis for the child's primary activity of psychic construction.

In the analysis of the two cases which follows I shall rely heavily upon the work of Winnicott and in particular upon two of his original formulations, the idea of "transitional object phenomena" and "True Self/False Self formation." I want to point out at the beginning, however, that this further development in psychoanalytic object relations theory beyond Fairbairn, [i.e., the recognition of the primary, integrative dimension of internalization] has a broader significance than even that suggested by the work of Winnicott. This is the recognition I have earlier referred to that the inner representational world functions constructively as a kind of map or model, which enables us to identify not only danger but safety, not only enemies but also potential friends and lovers. Hence the psychoanalytic dictum that "object finding is object refinding" (Goethals, 1973) no longer needs to be seen simply as a commentary on distorting projective mechanisms or the human proclivity to recreate earlier relational patterns. The inevitability if not the essentiality of projective mechanisms as a way of finding a path through a world of unlikeness must have profound consequences for the study of religion which heretofore has dismissed God as "merely" a matter of projection. [4]

Let us now turn to an examination of the data of the two cases presented as Chapter Six. By considering them together in a longitudinal fashion we aim at a better understanding of how the dimensions of faith explored in Chapter Three develop and unfold in the course of a human life, and in particular how these relate to the creation, elaboration and reconstruction of the object representation(s) of God.

II. Case Analysis: Infancy and Early Childhood
Prelude to the Drama: Setting the Stage

It is commonplace to regard the action of an individual life as beginning with the event of birth. In a formal sense this is true, but it is misleading. Perhaps a more adequate understanding of human development would follow from taking seriously the clue Shakespeare offers in his metaphor of the world as a stage. Let us for a moment entertain the idea that a human birth is something like the entrance of a new character onto the stage. The drama is one that began well before his or her arrival and which will continue indefinitely after the character utters his or her last lines and departs the stage forever. The setting, the props, the other characters and the suggested scripts by no means strictly determine the plot of the play (which is, within limits, largely improvised). They do, however, account for much that will shape and influence the course of the life story.

How is the stage set? Some new human actors make their entrance on a set constructed of tin roofs and mud floors, others in the antiseptic brightness of a hospital labor room. There is a college fund waiting for some, and a welfare check for others. Who is on stage to welcome the new member of the cast; or is she welcomed at all? Is this the first-born, long-awaited and urgently desired, whose entrance on stage is greeted with an expectant hush? Or does the infant player arrive to find himself one of a score of supporting actors, his entry barely noticed amid the clamor and chaos of action happening elsewhere on stage? Worse still, perhaps the child arrives to find her appearance an unpleasant surprise, a disappointment, a burden.

The matter of expectations awaiting the new infant is a complex matter. On the one hand there are each parent's conscious and unconscious fantasies of who the child is and will become. The child may be regarded as the possibility for the parent to vicariously live out his or her own wishes and desires ("My son/daughter is going to have all the chances I never had"). [5] The parent may also hold the unconscious fantasy that parenting the new infant will be providing the nurturance he or she longed for in their own infancy and childhood. That longing psychically survives in the inner representation of a self that as a needy child lives on in the timelessness of the unconscious (Benedek, 1959). It is this representation projected onto the newborn child which makes the child for a time a narcissistic extension of the self. There are also shared parental expectations which the child all unknowingly runs into. This may be the child whose birth is

214

expected to cement a failing marriage or infuse meaning and stability into a faltering relationship.

We might image these cumulative expectations as the script which the baby is handed upon entering life. Some children, mercifully, are handed a script with few if any instructions. "Just be yourself and we will be there for you" the instructions read. Then the child begins his drama of development in a state of omnipotent improvisation, supported by a responsive and resourceful cast of adults. Only gradually does he have to recognize that there are other actors and other life scripts to which he must adjust. Other babies are handed, by contrast, rather detailed scripts that elaborately define how the child must be to merit the love and acceptance of the parent. "You shall be the perfect, pliant, adoring and adorable baby," one script might read, "whose first role is to respond to all my ministrations so as to confirm me in my ideal identity as the all-competent mother or father." The waiting script may go on for many acts and many years. In the case of Ann, for example, she discovered that it included a whole set of expectations regarding female life role, religious and political beliefs and social style. How is it that life scripts are in fact communicated to the child has been the special object of study of the object relations theorists. As we shall briefly discuss, it is a complicated business that begins early and subtly, well before the advent of language. It is no exaggeration to say that from the very onset of life the emergent human being is being catechized into a cosmology - a sense of the way the universe runs and his or her place in the scheme of things. "Is it the case," we ask ourselves, "that I am a special and unique human being, destined to play a meaningful part somewhere in the drama?" Or is it our sense, as I've heard a man remark with resignation of himself, that "my assigned role appears always to be the third spear carrier, second row back, right behind the elephants in the chorus from Aida?" [6]

Pressed to a deeper level of analysis, the matter of scripts and expectations may be seen to be a function of a more primary variable the competency of certain key members of the cast to play the role of primary caretaker. The role is demanding, difficult and unrelenting, yet no special training or prior experience is necessarily needed to play the part. It is not even clear that one sex has any a priori advantage over another (Chodorow, 1978). What the parenting part does require is that the involved parties have adequately enough mastered their own developmental issues, and be sufficiently supported by a network of social meanings and structures (including economic) to be optimally available through the period of the child's extended dependence. This means, as we shall shortly

215

discuss, that the parent must be able to adjust his or her affective availability to the child according to the child's own developing needs and capacities. At first this availability, like the infant's dependency, is absolute. Later the adult must be able to gradually modulate that availability in order to permit the child to securely separate and claim his or her own selfhood.

In the terms we have been employing in this work, what is being proposed is that <u>the faith of the child has its foundation and origins in the faith of the parenting other.</u> The parents' sense of availability for loving self-donation and their capacity to tolerate ambivalence are absolutely crucial factors in sponsoring into being the child's nascent self. Optimally, the parent must be able to give recognition and attention to the child from a position of strength and a sense of fullness, not from a posture that unconsciously fears the child's needs will deplete the parents' resources. Behind this must be a more fundamental sense that the parent and the child exist in a universe where they are not in competition for a limited supply of the good things in life. Additionally, the caretaking adults must first be able to accept in themselves as they have had to accept in their own parents - the fact that human beings are capable of both love and hate, even towards the child of their own flesh. The parent must then be able to absorb without anxiety the anger and rage which the child will express towards them from time to time in the course of growing up.

Our evidence for the level of faith development and self-integration of the parents of both our subjects is circumstantial and must be inferred from a careful reading of the admittedly one-sided accounts of their daughters. Nevertheless a picture does begin to emerge of the psychological strengths and liabilities which these adults brought to their role as parents. Ann's mother it appears entered upon marriage having only incompletely and ambivalently separated from her own parents. She was by turns doted upon, dominated and deprived by three very powerful older sisters and a competent but overstrained mother whose primary caretaking responsibilities had to be directed towards a sickly youngest sibling, born two years after Ann's mother. The much protested devotion and uncritical praise which Ann's mother seems to have directed towards her parents, coexisting with a general mood of disappointment and resentment towards other persons, is suggestive of a defensive splitting of object representations for the purpose of containing her own deeper frustrations and yearnings. [7]

Given this history, it should not be surprising that when Ann's mother herself has children, and especially a daughter, this female child would be unconsciously regarded as another competitive sibling, another claimant for a limited fund of love and approval, and hence a potential target for projected anger? Ann's father presents a more subtle and less clearly disturbed clinical portrait. He, too, has built a life security within the orbit of an extended family dominated by his parents and, after Ann's eighth year, by his mother alone. Outside the home he has become a biggish personality in the smallish world of rural New England. Within the home he was, by Ann's account, "entrapped" and undermined by the passive aggressive attacks of his wife. We would not be surprised to find (as was in fact the case) that he is more readily sponsoring of Ann's autonomy and separation from the mother. What will happen, however, when Ann's trajectory of development threatens to move outside of his locus of control and authority? How will either one of them handle that challenge to the psychic security of their respective universes?

Stacy's mother, like Ann's, knew the seduction and the defeat of being the youngest of a large family where her role was to be doll-like, pretty, and submissive. Additionally she experienced not only the radical abandonment of her mother, who died in childbirth when Stacy's mother was two, but the successive abandonments of a series of older sisters who would pick up the role of mother and then "pass along" the child whenever the oldest sister would leave home to be married. When she has a child of her own will the family territory be big enough for two needy children? Stacy's father presents the complex and tragic picture of a young man whose only model of fatherhood was an inconstant and depriving father who trapped the family in poverty. Stacy's father refuses to accept "his place" at the bottom of society and struggles his way through local politics, state politics and finally an ivy league law degree - only to be defeated by the onset of the Depression. In the midst of his own difficult attempt to climb out of a hateful past, will he be able to regard with empathy and understanding a child climbing out of her own weakness and dependence?

The stage is set. The cast is in place. The new actress wonders and wanders upon the boards, blinking and wailing and acting rather astonished to find herself alive after the rude passage from her dark comfort in the wings of the womb.

Birth and the Origins of Basic Trust

As we discussed in the third chapter, the research into early child development of Margaret Mahler and others has made us aware that the human person enroute to becoming a self has to negotiate two birth passages. The first is the actual event of parturition without which the child lacks life in its literal biological sense. The second passage is what Mahler has termed the "hatching" process, or the psychological birth. On the successful negotiation of this passage, which commences at about the second month and continues through the first three years of life, depends the human being's sense of "aliveness" or, as I have called it in Chapter Three, the "sense of being real." This sense of feeling alive is a developmental accomplishment of the parent-infant interaction. Though its foundation is laid in the events of the first few years of life, indeed the first few months, it is an aspect of self-becoming that is renewed and reworked at successive life stages.

The child even after birth remains psychically fused with the mother or whoever is the primary caretaking person. [8] Although it is impossible to know for certain what the child's inner experience of these first few months of life is like, it is hypothesized that it is something like what Michael Balint called the "harmonious interpenetrating mix-up" (Balint, 1968). The child is not aware of distinctions between himself and the parenting other, where his boundaries end and the mother's begins. The human infant begins life then in a state of undifferentiated physical/psychic awareness. The infant's universe, as Winnicott suggestively observed, is not mother and baby, but only mother-baby.

The nature of the baby's undisputed attachment to his mothering object has been a matter of some debate among analysts (Ainsworth, 1969). Following Freud's discussion of primary narcissism, some theorists have held that the infant is at first wholly self-absorbed but gradually comes to recognize the caretaking parents as those whose ministrations are reductive of the tensions due to hunger, wetness, physical irritations, etc. The attachment of the child to the parent is regarded therefore as "anaclitic" or "leaning upon" the satisfaction of more primary drives. My own view follows more closely that of John Bowlby and Alice and Michael Balint who hold that there is a primary and fundamental sociality in the infant that cannot be reduced to another more basic need (Bowlby, 1969; Balint, M., 1965). It is not that the infant has already identified the parent as the object of this primary love. Rather, there is posited a general libidinal cathexis of the interpersonal environment out of which the infant progressively identifies the unique configuration of the parenting others.

In the beginning of life then the child is in a relationship of absolute dependence, "a state at which the infant exists only because of the maternal care together with which it forms a unit" (Winnicott, 1965, p. 42). Mahler describes the first two to three weeks of extrauterine life as the stage of normal infantile autism, the period when the neonate is shielded from excessive stimulation by a total absorption in maintaining homeostasis. From about the second month on into the sixth month the child is in what Mahler termed the "symbiotic phase," Spitz referred to as the period of "unified situational experience" (Spitz, 1965), and Winnicott called simply, "the holding environment" (Winnicott, 1960). It is during this time that the ministrations of the primary caretaker "made uniquely responsive by reason of love" (Winnicott), function as a kind of auxiliary ego for the infant. The solicitude of the parent anticipates the child's needs with an adequacy that continues the child's sense of still being somehow at one with a benevolent and provident reality.

As Winnicott saw it, the human sense of "continuity of being" or what Federn called "ego feeling " (ich-gefuhl) got its essential start in the child's safe anchorage within the maternal matrix (Federn, 1952). "Good-enough" mothering was simply care which protected the child from having to make premature or precocious adjustments to environmental and interpersonal impingements. The origins of the "True Self sense", the capacity for feeling real, creative and spontaneous, are to be found in the careful modulation of the process by which the child is brought to realize the existence of an external world. By contrast, the False Self configuration is characterized an inner sense of unreality or futility which derives from the infant having to make a premature adjustment to the schedules, wishes and whims of the caretaker (Winnicott, 1952, pp. 140-152). In its most severe form the False-Self sense is a central characteristic of the borderline personality or what Fairbairn called the schizoid personality (Chessick, 1974; Searles, 1960). It is a haunting sense of not being alive inside, a lack of a sense of being, of entity, of being in doubt not about who I am, but more fundamentally that I am (Mahler, Pine & Bergman, 1975).

The symbiotic phase of development is the stage of life which Erikson has identified as foundational for the establishment of a sense of "basic trust" (Erikson, 1963). It is in this basic trust that Erikson locates the origins of the virtue of hope: "the enduring belief in the attainability of fervent wishes, in spite of the dark urges and rages which mark the beginning of existence" (Erikson, 1964, p. 118). It is also the stage in which the psychic raw material for the later

219

creation of a representation of God is made available by the adequacy of the holding environment. Erikson paid particular attention to this process of the proto-representation of the divine. He found its paradigm in the ritual of greeting between parent and child. Erikson writes of this:

> I would suggest, therefore, that this first and dimmest affirmation, this sense of a hallowed presence, contributes to man's ritual making a pervasive element which we will call the "Numinous." This designation betrays my intention to follow the earliest into the last: and, indeed, we vaguely recognize the numinous as an indispensible aspect of periodical religious observances, where the believer, by appropriate gestures, confesses his dependence and his childlike faith and seeks, by appropriate offerings, to secure a sense of being lifted up to the very bosom of the supernatural which in the visible form of an image may graciously respond with the faint smile of an inclined face. The result is a sense of separateness transcended, and yet also of distinctiveness confirmed. (Erikson, 1968, pp. 714-715)

By the time this mutuality of recognition has begun to occur between primary parent and child, anywhere from the fifth to the tenth week of life, it is a sign that a specific bond has been formed and that optimal symbiosis has set the stage for a sense of "confident expectation" (Benedek, 1938). The basis for that sense of expectation is the total sense of well being which is reinforced and ritualized in the special greeting of parent and child. It is this sense of basic trust, with whatever admixture of mistrust may accompany it, which is the core of faith development.

Evidence from both case studies suggests that Ann and Stacy were fortunate in receiving from their mothers during this symbiotic phase the care adequate to lay down a foundation of basic trust. In part this is a deduction made from the absence of serious pathology of the sort that would presumably be evident if the subjects had suffered serious trauma during this crucial developmental period. The positive evidence is found in the subjects' accounts of their representations of God. As one listens to the interviews one catches the glimpse of what might be called a "pre-ambivalent representation of God," aspects of God that evoke for the subject that primal sense of secure unity, oneness, "separateness transcended" and "distinctiveness confirmed." [9] In Stacy this appears in her associations to the poem from early childhood, "I see the moon, the moon sees me, God sees the moon and God sees me." The theme of "being seen" and its negative variation, "being found out," are central developmental motifs in Stacy's life. Their prevalence testifies both to some foundational experience of being seen/being held (in the child's experience the two are functionally equivalent) that was "good-enough" to be a longed-for restitution, but vexed enough later to be the cause of ongoing conflict. The religious experience in the restaurant in which Stacy imagines a voice assuring her that she is the "apple of God's eye" is one other instance where the idea of being seen and being loved evokes resonances of the security of the symbiotic period. In Ann's case I would point to more subtle comments of a more recent period in which she testifies to a sense of God as surrounding her, of being everywhere, and of uplifting or sustaining her. This feeling appears to be another face of that inchoate impression she locates as an earliest memory that there is "something loose out there that was a tremendous security."

The Separation-Individuation Process

One day something is different. Sometime around the fourth or fifth month, the infant begins to exhibit a new look of alertness, a new kind of persistence and a new air of goal directedness. The child has begun his or her first steps towards unmooring from the symbiotic anchorage, hopefully with the capacity "to use the mother as a beacon of orientation in the world of reality" (Mahler, 1968, p. 7). The separation-individuation phase, according to Mahler, lasts from about five months to around thirty to thirty-six months. Actually, Mahler prefers to consider separation-individuation as a process that is open-ended at the older end. She maintains this not only because the developmental schedules of human infants are highly variable but because in an important sense the consolidation of individuality and the achievement of ego integration is a life-long process. "As is the case with any intrapsychic process, this one reverberates throughout the life cycle. It is never finished; it can always become reactivated; new phases of the life cycle witness new derivatives of the earliest processes still at work" (Mahler, 1972, p. 333). In the terms of this book, the problem of separation-individuation has been further identified with the life issue of becoming a self which we have defined as the central matter of human faith. Hence what we are examining in these dramatic first three years of life is how the terms of an individual's faith struggle are laid in interpersonal experience, though the outcome is in nowise determined.

Once the infant begins the process of the differentiation of self from the external world, he or she rapidly begins to move out into that world, touch it, taste it and finally traverse it on uncertain legs. The responsibility of the primary caretakers at this point must be modified accordingly. Optimally they will continue to provide the quality of attention and secure regard which allows the child to slowly become disillusioned of his or her infantile omnipotence, which is to say on a schedule that the developing cognitive and psychic apparatus can handle without excessive anxiety. The potential for False-Self development is present here as in earlier life. The matter is whether the parents will allow the child to explore and appropriate the world on his own terms and in his own time, or whether they force the child to be compliant with their interpretations not only of external reality but more crucially of the child herself. The role of the parents in this stage has been described as a mirroring function (Kohut, 1971). The child looks at them to learn about her own competence and capacities and her own inherent goodness or badness. In them she sees reflected the character of the world with which she has to deal, its fearfulness or its fascination. As we discussed earlier, the capacity of the parent to adequately mirror the child depends on the extent to which they have successfully negotiated their own developmental issues. Having provided a more or less secure holding environment, will they now be able to permit the child to move away - and return - in that dynamic of retreat and advance which is the child's strategy for taking on the world of unlikeness?

The failure of parents to allow their children to differentiate can take a number of different forms. One sort is the parent who will attach or "appersonate" to the child (Spelling, 1944). The child remains bound to the mother (or father) who for their own purposes cannot permit the child to have a separate existence. The classical example of the mother or father who, when the child falls, cries as though she or he were themselves injured illustrates a dynamic which effectively robs the child of the reality of his own experience, even of his own bodily experience. The other problems with differentiation are related to parents who provided satisfactory symbiotic stages but who when the child began to make movements towards separation push them prematurely towards separation and a precocious but tenuous "autonomy." From the evidence of the research interviews I would suggest that both Ann and Stacy fall into this second category, although in different ways.

Ann shared with the interviewer the observation she had once made that her mother was excellent with very small infants but "terrible" with toddlers. Whenever they got old enough to walk away, she commented, her mother would feel hurt and angry. This observation may very well be an aperture into the situation of Ann and her mother when Ann herself began the process of separation. We have already sketched a clinical picture of Ann's mother that would make inconsistent mothering a plausible if not predictable outcome. The "adored" but emotionally neglected youngest daughter of a large family, Ann's mother appears never to have completely managed the process of her own separation-individuation. Object relation theory's rendering of Freud's idea of repetition compulsion is that we return again and again to unsatisfying relationships, either in face or in fantasy, until we "get it right," i.e., until we obtain the love and recognition we longed for and did not receive (Fairbairn, 1952, p. 166). Ann's mother may well represent that hope, lived out in her life-long attachment to her own family of origin and unwillingness to admit that anyone else in her life could be as satisfying as her idealized parents. When a daughter is introduced into the picture we appear to have the reactivation of the fantasy that somehow in mothering the infant she will herself be remothered. The fantasy is bound to fail once the child becomes old enough to make the first halting steps towards a life of her own while yet needing her mother to manage the world.

Ann describes her mother as "a suffocating presence, weak and leaning," and acknowledges her own deep yearning "to be held by a mother who will not push me to the ground with her leaning." The words suggest that from fairly early on in the process of achieving separation Ann was forced to feel precocious responsibility for her mother's emotional needs. "One of us had to grow up," Ann ruefully observed, "and it was easier for me." With the life of the self at stake Ann had no choice. The alternative to growing up prematurely would be to be engulfed by the presence of a mother who likely made two conflicting demands. On the one hand she wanted her daughter to stay little and fearful like herself and to that end she mediated a world full of unknown terrors and dangers. On the other hand by communicating her own fearfulness to the child she was saying in effect, "take care of me." Fortunately for Ann the emotional availability of her father permitted a set of positive identifications that allowed her an escape from the symbiotic suffocation represented by her mother. [10]

There was a price to Ann's escape, however. The price was the construction of a modality of False Self. The denied aspects of her True Self were those which were impossible to experience and express in her early relationship with her mother. Principally Ann had to bury (or project) aspects of her self-representation that involved feeling dependent, fearful, weak or "leaning." The dynamic is eloquently expressed in what seems to me to be a very significant screen memory: Ann's recalling of times when her mother would hold and rock her and other times when her mother would fail to do so and Ann's defiant inner protest would be "See if I get up on your lap again ever!" Such defiance has its intrapsychic forms and they are preverbal. They would be the child's repressed identification with the weak but urgently desired mother. What would remain in consciousness and in the public persona would be a protested independence and autonomy. The faith necessary to tolerate dependency is severely undermined then by this configuration of self and object representations originating in the separation-individuation phase of development.

In our earlier discussion of Stacy's parents we considered a number of different factors which could make it difficult for them to sponsor Stacy's moves towards autonomy. In order to appreciate how this might have taken place it is necessary to examine more closely how the parent-child interaction involves a mutual activation and a reciprocal response.

The mirroring process by which the child comes to know herself as good in the reflected appraisal of the parent ("I am loved = I am lovable") works both ways. The child's intuitive, imitative capacities will naively but often quite accurately reflect back to the parent both desirable and undesirable aspects of the self. Where these aspects are acceptable to the parent there is a reinforcement of what Benedek referred to as "the positive arc of emotional symbiosis" (Benedek, 1959). "That's my boy/girl," the parent says proudly, feeling a deep sense of confirmation about himself as well as his progeny. However, when the child's playful imitation exposes aspects of the parent's self that have been denied, then the character of the parent's response is directly related to the parent's capacity to integrate those split-off self and object representations, the "ambivalent core of the personality." [11]

> It can also happen that the parent is shocked by the child's imitative behavior when the child reenacts representations of negative experiences, sometimes with threatening hostility. Imitation of the parent by the child then stimulates, and by repetition may reinforce the negative arc of the emotional symbiosis. It depends upon the maturity of the parent and the genuineness of his love for the child whether such a warning is heeded or whether it leads to rejection of the unloved self/unloved child. (Ibid.)

Benedek's discussion of emotional symbiosis seems particularly useful in further understanding the nature of the interaction between Stacy and her parents. Both Stacy's parents, we have observed, were deprived as children of recognition as selves loved in their own right: Stacy's mother by the event of her mother's death that relegated her to the role of family pet, Stacy's father by the uncertainty of his father's presence and the financial exigencies that early defined his significance in terms of being simply another hand for the harvest. While both parents appeared to have pushed Stacy onto the stage and precociously into the classroom, it may well have been that her talent for acting mimicked only too well their own anxious striving for recognition and applause. Thus while the mother would report in delighted detail the compliments her hairdresser paid to her, she would be ruthlessly vigilant to see that any compliments on her appearance that Stacy brought home were undone by the stern injunctions about humility. Her mother's (and her father's) inability to come to terms with their own False-Self configurations set Stacy up for a comparable problem. How will she be able to accept in herself those needs, fears and yearnings which her parents could not themselves tolerate? The issue, in the terms of our analysis, involves one dimension of faith - the achievement of the capacity to tolerate ambivalence.

For Stacy this issue is represented by the image of the truncated child in a recurring dream. Not surprisingly, this dream first appeared while her daughter was in adolescence and going through turmoil both at home and in school. It would be reasonable to speculate that this conflict in her daughter's ' life put Stacy in touch with the unresolved issues around the "little girl self" she had to be to survive and yet could not abide. When we examine at greater length the processes that point to the resolution of this developmental conflict we shall find that they involve the modifications of self and object representations in the presence of an object (i.e., God) who permits a space of play in which the True Self can finally emerge.

Transitional Object Phenomena, Play and God

The problem of self becoming may be seen as the problem of how to simultaneously "hold on" and "let go," how to experience oneself as separate and independent while maintaining the sense of inner sustainment and connectedness which assures one of meaning and enduring place. After years of closely observing the interaction of normal, healthy mothers and children, D.W. Winnicott proposed that optimally this passage to selfhood was a matter of the internalization of good parental objects. This process structured the inner representational world in such a way as to permit the human child to carry with him the assurance of well-being which was reflected in early life by the actual presence of the parents. This particular idea Winnicott shares commonly with Balint, Bowlby, Kernberg and other psychoanalytic theorists. Winnicott's own most original contribution was his imaginative interpretation of the actual process by which the child manages this business of separation. In particular Winnicott paid attention to the nearly universal phenomenon of early childhood in which the young child will invest a teddy bear, blanket corner or special ritual with an unusual private significance. The sensitive parent generally allows this to take place and leaves the child's relationship with this chosen article undisturbed. The parent observes that the teddy bear, or doll, or piece of fabric, which sometimes may be given a special name by the child, has a remarkable capacity to sooth and comfort the child in moments of anxiety and at bedtime. After a period of time the hallowed article, now worn, frayed and tattered, is gradually used less and less and finally one day left behind, neither rejected nor destroyed. It was Winnicott's unusual clinical perspicacity that saw in this ordinary rite of childhood a crucial developmental event. He called this transitional object phenomena. It is the key to understanding the developmental origins of the object representation of God.

The transitional object may be an actual "thing" discovered in the environment like a teddy bear or it may be a particular practice, like sucking one's thumb in a special way while stroking one's nose. Whatever it is, it owes its developmental significance to the power it has to evoke for the child the sense of the security associated with the ministrations of the "good-enough" parent. It is the prototype for symbolic activity. The object is transitional in two senses: first it is transitional in so far as it appears between the child's experience of himself in undifferentiated merger with his interpersonal world and the later experience of the parents as separate and distinct from himself. But transitional object phenomena is "transitional" in a second sense which does not limit its relevance to the first few years of life. It represents the transitting from involvement with purely inner reality to engagement with strictly external or shared reality. Transitional phenomena represents "an intermediate area of experiencing, to which inner reality and external reality both contribute. It is an area that is not challenged, because no claim is made on its behalf except that it shall exist as a resting-place for the individual engaged in the perpetual human task of keeping inner and outer reality separate yet interrelated" (Winnicott, 1971, p. 2).

The very condition for satisfying transitional object phenomena is the secure presence of the parent who provides an arena of safety, a space within which the child can genuinely play. Play for Winnicott, as it was for Erikson, is the serious work of childhood. It involves trying on roles and identities, experimenting with a range of possible emotions, manipulating the external world for the satisfaction of an inner vision. More generally it means relaxing one's need to respond and react and instead acting out of a spontaneous, creative core of self. Clearly the capacity for play is compromised to the degree that one's experience with the parenting adults was such as to require the defense creation of a False-Self position as a way of maintaining the fragile integrity of the self.

Winnicott held that one does not outgrow the need for the space of transitional phenomena, the play space. Rather, while particular transitional objects serve their purpose and are left behind, the capacity to use transitional phenomena enlarges into the ability to creatively use culture and religion.

> . . .in health the transitional object does not "go inside" nor does the feeling about it necessarily undergo repression. It is not forgotten and it is not mourned. It loses meaning, and this is because the transitional phenomena have become diffused, have become spread out over the whole intermediate territory between "inner psychic reality" and "the external world as perceived by two persons in common," that is to say, over the whole cultural field. (Ibid., p. 5)

> This intermediate area of experience, unchallenged in respect of its belonging to inner or external (Shared) reality, constitutes the greater part of the infant's experience, and throughout life is retained in the intense experiencing that belongs to the arts and to religion and to imaginative living and to creative scientific work. (Ibid., p. 14)

Prominent in the cultural field and potentially available for the integrative work of a transitional object is "God." As discussed in Chapter Four, God arrives in the train of a whole troop of fantasy characters (Bettelheim, 1976), imaginary companions (Nagera, 1969), and images from popular culture which begin to populate the child's world from the time of the achievement of symbolic function (Piaget, 1951) through to latency. Unlike these other figures, the reality of the character of God is testified to by a whole social environment, even one that takes God relatively unseriously.

Winnicott himself was given a striking insight into the possible significance of God as a transitional object in a remarkable conversation with one of his clients. The session was reported by Winnicott in some detail. It is one such moment that Winnicott may have been thinking of when he dedicated Playing and Reality "to my patients who have paid to teach me" (Winnicott, 1971).

The patient in this session is a young woman whose presenting complaint is that she feels empty, unmet and somehow not alive. It is "as though there isn't really a ME" she laments early into the long (three hour) session. Later the following exchange takes place (Ibid., p. 62):

> She said, "It was in my mind: 'Don't make me wish to BE!' That's a line of a poem by Gerard Manly Hopkins."

> We now talked about poetry, how she makes a great deal of use of poetry that she knows by heart, and how she had lived from poem to poem (like cigarette to cigarette in chain smoking), but without the poem's meaning being understood or felt as she now understands and feels this poem. . .I referred her to God as I AM, a useful concept when the individual cannot bear to BE.

> She said: "People use God like an analyst - someone to be there while you're playing."

> I said: "For whom you matter." and she said, "I couldn't say that because I couldn't be sure.

> I said: "Did it spoil things when I said this?" (I feared I had mucked up a very good session.)

> But she said: "No! It's different if you say it, because if I matter to you. . .I want to do thing to please you. . . you see this is the hell of having had a religious upbringing. Blast the good girls!"

> As a self-observation she said :"That implies I have a wish not to get well."

Winnicott is dealing with a person whose dominant psychic configuration is the schizoid position, the False Self in its most severe form. He is in a difficult position as a therapist. He must in effect recreate a holding environment which will allow his patient the security to re-experience her own repressed and denied True Self. To do that he must take care not to make interpretations which are intrusive and rob the patient of her own creativity and spontaneity. In brief he must not appear to exact the premature compliance that the patient's parents did at the vulnerable period in her development. This is the concern behind Winnicott's comment, "I feared I had mucked up a very good session." His acceptance of her as she is must be so unconditional that she does not even have to fear that getting better might be done simply to please him. If that happens then ironically a protest of health on the part of the repressed True Self would be to remain ill. That is the significance of her own last self-observation.

The amazing and highly relevant insight on the part of the patient is that for some persons God functions as that all accepting Other who, like the analyst and the good-enough mother, is the guarantor and preserver of that background of safety which makes possible play. In Winnicott's terms, that God serves as that transitional object which allows the person to experience and express the True Self. This woman is aware of this fact in the painful absence of such a God. At the same time she has some understanding of the God that must be absent for her to live, even in the painful and unsatisfying state that she is in. The clue is in her remark about "the hell of having had a religious upbringing." In the history of this woman the self and object representation of God quite evidently gathered on the side of all those internalized others which enforce the compliance of the False Self. God is for her a greater and perhaps more insidious representation of mother, father or early religious authority figures which are aligned against the True Self.

Whether or not the child is able to use an object representation of God to protect play, i.e., for the faith that supports self-becoming, will depend on multiple factors. Most primary is that there be that foundational sense of trust which can be a referent for the representation of God. Winnicott spoke of this when he observed that there was no possibility for "belief in God" where there was no "belief in," no sense of there being a fundamental reliability in life (Winnicott, 1965, p. 94). The second condition is that the child's introduction to God must respect his own primary religious creativity. God cannot be given to the child let alone forced upon him. God is discovered/created by the child in the transitional space. Winnicott's few published thoughts on the subject of religious education are an eloquent plea for parents and religious educators to respect the integrity and the timing of an individual's private creation of a God that preserves a sense of inner goodness.

> Religions have made much of original sin, but have
> not all come round to the idea of original goodness,
> that which by being gathered together in the idea of

God is at the same time separate off from the individuals who collectively create and recreate this God concept. The saying that man made God in his own image is usually treated as an amusing example of the perverse, but the truth in this saying could be made more evident by a restatement, such as: man continues to create and recreate God as a place to put what is good in himself, and which he might spoil if he kept it in himself along with all the hate and destructiveness which is also to be found there.

Religion (or is it theology?) has stolen the good from the developing individual child, and has then set up an artificial scheme for injecting this that has been stolen back into the child, and has called it moral education. (Ibid.)

With the help of Winnicott we are now in a position to see how the constellation of object representations of God unique to Ann and to Stacy are intimately implicated in the various dimensions of faith as self-becoming. Some aspects of their respective God representations are, like the good analyst, someone to be there while they play. Such representations support the emergence of the True Self and mediate the faith that makes it possible to tolerate dependence, accept ambivalence, embrace aloneness and love unreservedly. Other aspects of the God representation we will see allied to the False Self organization. The history of each woman's faith development might be summarized as the progressive victory of the God who permits play a victory not finally secure or completed, but clearly underway.

III. Play Age Through Adolescence
    Stacy: God and the Judgmental Factor

The need of every emerging human self is to be seen and valued as one is. God, presented in Western religious culture as the omnipresent and omniscient Being, is the obvious candidate to serve that function at the point where the child comes to recognize that the parents who he had looked towards for unconditional approval are fallible and limited. Yet as we look at the childhood of Stacy given in her own self-report we see the coexistence of a least two representations of God. One countermands the severe judgments of her family. The other elevates the moral scrutiny enforced by her parents to a cosmic level. Both demand to be understood.

The first representation of God we have already connected to a positive, pre-oedipal inheritance of self and object representations in which Stacy feels unequivocally loved. These appear to be represented in two linked memories. The one is of an injured bird who her father heals and allows to fly free (explaining that God wants it that way). [12]   The other is captured in the ritual bedtime poem, "I see the moon, the moon sees me; God sees the moon and God sees me."   The poem is a perfect evocation of the ideal mirroring function of the parent and by extension of God.   This mirroring Stacy imaginatively works into the television game which she invents as a way of being seen and complimented by her adored grandmother whose love and whose homestead were among the few constants in Stacy's frequently disrupted early life.   The television game appears to be the lineal ancestor of a Catholic devotional text which Stacy discovered and employed for a period of time as an adult, Brother Lawrence's Practice of the Presence of God.   In this meditative practice the individual is enjoined to call to mind multiple times during the course of the day, "God is watching me; I am in the presence of God; God is here."

The powerful and persistent emphasis upon being seen by a benevolent other has a quality of pathos when read against the two other currents in Stacy's early experience.   The first I surmise to be a fear of abandonment by one or both parents. Hence the need to assure herself of being seen by God, whether graciously or in judgment, may be the surface expression of a need to be assured that her parents are not out of her sight. Stacy grew up with her father's stories of being abandoned by his father and was fairly early made the confidante of the information that her mother had not been a virgin at marriage (and hence might be deserving of desertion?).   Her mother was a woman who threatened suicide and who came to the family with her own stories of being left by the death of her mother.   The second factor which gives particular poignancy to Stacy's hope for the benevolent all-seeing God is that it stands over against another more prominent representation of God, one whose omniscience comes as a demand and not a relief.

This second representation of God appears to be more oedipal in its features.   It seems to have consolidated in the period when the child begins the final internalization of the rules and mores of the parents in order to become self-regulatory, that is, the resolution of the oedipal phase. The particular rules which Stacy felt enjoined upon her were inherently self-contradictory.   On the one hand she was expected to strive for perfection in all areas and expected to provide her parents' pleasure and pride by drawing the approval of others.   On the other hand she was led to understand that feeling pride in any accomplishments or becoming "stuck on

231

yourself" was the worst of all sins. Both parents reinforced this by frequent critical remarks designed to make her feel humble. We have examined earlier possible reasons for this attitude on the part of the parents. The effect on Stacy was to provide her with the developmental material for a relentlessly critical God, a God who wanted her to "strive for perfection," examine her motives "under a microscope," and who would "zap" her if she permitted herself to feel good about herself.

Stacy's description of the process by which she came to accept and adopt her father's standards of judgment for herself is revealing:

It was that when I was little, it was so painful to have my father poke at me, I would always try either to do that to myself first, thinking that it wouldn't hurt so much when he does it if I already know that I wasn't as intelligent, or as this or as whatever. In other words to do that number on myself first and that way it wouldn't hurt as much when he did it.

That was very painful. Then too the thing that went along with it was. . .you wouldn't believe it but up until a few years ago I could not really hear a compliment, could not hear if anyone said anything really nice about me. Sometimes it happened literally that I couldn't hear. Because if I heard that meant I would have to deal with that and put myself down.

The account follows the form of a classical psychoanalytic description of the internalization of taboos against forbidden sexual and aggressive impulses. The developing child "identifies with the aggressor" (Anna Freud, 1966) and finds it safer to punish himself before he is found out by the omnipotent parent. Finally the problematic impulse itself is repressed entirely and the need for overt punishment is avoided, at least as long as the repression barrier holds. There are two limitations to this account as a full explanation for the dynamics of internalization in this case. The first is that what is being denied to awareness here is not a sexual or aggressive desires but an element of the child's self-esteem, the refusal of which results in a diminishment of the child's positive self-representation. The second problem is that this account does not help us understand why God must be evoked as the omniscient judge and father surrogate.

A more adequate explanation for the origin of Stacy's negative representation of God is found in Fairbairn's discussion of the "defense of guilt" (Fairbairn, 1952). The beginning premise is that the one intolerable admission for a child is that his or her parents are bad or inadequate. When the parents have literally constituted the known world for the child from birth, to acknowledge their deficiency would be tantamount to despairing of goodness in existence. Fairbairn evokes an explicitly religious metaphor to explain this process but in our analysis the metaphor becomes an exact description:

> It is better to be a sinner in a world ruled by God than to live in a world ruled by the Devil. A sinner in a world ruled by God may be bad; but there is always a certain sense of security to be derived from the fact that the world around is good. (Ibid., pp. 66-67)

Stacy's concern is how to maintain some hope that she might eventually be found pleasing to the father (and the mother) whom she must see as perfect. The existence of a representation of God who is "just like father, only fairer" holds that hope intact. Witness the number of times Stacy refers to the fantasy of presenting herself on the Last Day made over new and finally acceptable ("I was going to take all this pile of shit and get it in order. . .then, on the Day of Judgment, I was going to present myself all fixed up"). The problem of course is that if this object representation of God keeps alive the hope of ultimate acceptance it also maintains in place the introjections which form the False Self structure. The only way through this dilemma would be a reworking of the representational world in a way which would uncover those aspects of God which are accepting of Stacy's True Self, that is, a self capable of unapologetic creativity and some degree of healthy narcissism.

It is important here to emphasize that the False Self organization of personality as described by Winnicott is placed on a continuum of psychic organization. At one end the False Self is set up as real and the individual is aware only of a nagging and debilitating sense of personal unreality, a sense of the betrayal of an inner truth or failure to realize a potentiality for living. In relative health, however, the False Self is built upon identifications which enable the individual to maintain a restrained, disciplined and effective social self even while aware, sometimes painfully, of the discrepancy between this public self and the secret self. The capacity to endure this dichotomy when it cannot be avoided requires a sense beyond words that somehow the secret self is known and held. [13] At least until developments in their adult years, both Ann and Stacy maintained aspects of a False Self organization somewhere between the more pathological denial of the True Self and the capacity to recognize those aspects of the False Self which are a cultural or situational adaptation. With both women the mitigation of the False Self is a matter of faith, the growth of an inner assurance that they can live out of their True Selves and not risk being undone.

As we follow Stacy through the oedipal dilemma and latency and on into adolescence, there are indications of some of the multiple roles which her God representation is called upon to play. One ongoing developmental issue for Stacy is the achievement of what Erikson refers to as "ego actuality," the individual's involvement in "the world of participation, shared with other participants with a minimum of defensive maneuvering and a maximum of mutual activation" (Erikson, 1964, p. 165). It is this progressive achievement which was discussed as "the sense of being in relationship to a real and meaningful world" (Chapter Three). Central to ego actuality is the trust that somewhere someone will be there to receive the gift we have to offer. Stacy's story of her effort to work for the church at age three can be read as a statement about her hope, both in early life but in present time as well, that she will be respected as having a contribution to make. The church, and by extension God, is the place Stacy turns to in an early effort to locate her place and identify her offering in the social world. As a teenager the church, the house of God, becomes for Stacy the first arena in which she trusts herself to make an adult decision and assume adult responsibilities. Her independent decision for "conversion" is an assertion of her adolescent right to "sustain loyalties freely pledged" (Ibid., p. 125). Her particular choice of a "prayerbook church" may be a way of affirming that representation of God that is "fairer" than father, i.e., more objective, less vulnerable to the whims of arbitrary human beings. The church was also the first place where as a teenager she held a position of responsibility. When we pick up the story of Stacy again in adulthood we will find the church once more serving as that locus of a self's struggle for recognition and acceptance.

Ann: God the Controller

The dynamic configuration of Ann's family, as we have observed, was defined by a mother who was by turns clinging and dismissive and a father who was emotionally available but also in some sense trapped by the passive manipulations of his wife. In this situation an internal representation of God emerges that has two functions to serve. On the one hand God was the sponsor of autonomy. Like Ann's father and, we presume, like Ann's grandmothers and distinguished aunts, God was for Ann "dependable, loving and accessible. . .on my terms." The qualifying phrase is crucial. God must help satisfy a deep need for a consistent, available, loving object and at the same time must help defend her against the intrusive efforts at control exercised by her mother. God must be a presence, but not too present. On the other hand, God as a transitional object representation must help defend Ann against the opposite threat to the integrity of the self - the terror of too much freedom and not enough limitation. Ann, we recall, added to her description of her mother's lack of authority over her the pensive reflection that this power was "a constant source of anxiety for me. . .it was too much power for a child.

Young children, as Melanie Klein has particularly observed, carry unconscious fantasies of the extreme destructiveness of their own rages (Klein, 1957). The parents in general, and the mother in particular, must give evidence by the constancy and stability of their presence to the child that they are not destroyed or injured by the child's powerful emotions and aggressive energies. The child is actually comforted by recognizing that in at least one area he is powerless. He is powerless to destroy with either his love or his hate. Ann's mother, by what we presume was her emotional withdrawal at the age when Ann was beginning to assert her willfulness (Freud's anal-sadistic phase), was not able to give Ann this full assurance. God then is evoked as an inner warrant that Ann will be able both to make her own way and yet not get "out of control," i.e., hurt loved others.

> . . .perhaps the reason that from the earliest I've never felt or allowed another person to control me and yet felt under control was that I had this tremendous sense that God was in control."

God's being "in charge" allows Ann to express choice without evoking the fear that her choices will finally cut her off from the possibility of closeness with her parenting others. At the same time the need to have God "in control" represents an adaptation to a certain developmental failure, the lack of a mother strong and resourceful enough to permit a secure identification.

The God who accompanies Ann into the turmoil of adolescence has made a pact with her. God will endorse her choices and empower her to face danger and the unknown (as she did when, as a small child, she would force herself to look upon thunderstorms). Ann for her part will not admit to herself let alone to others that she could ever be needy or scared or vulnerable. The self-representation linked to the object representation of God the controller is Ann the fearless and the independent.

In adolescence Ann faces the challenge of a "second individuation process" (Blos, 1967). She must disembed herself from the conventions of her family and establish an identity that does not conform to the standard expectations of what young women will and (especially) will not do. We have observed how her identifications with a number of strong and self-reliant women at this time in her life gave her the assurance to manage this transition. The other inner resource, however, appears to have been her representation of God. God the ultimate controller enables her to "bear (her) imperfect parents," perhaps by defining an arena of authority more inclusive than that of the parents' and thereby radically relativizing their claims. The ideological perspective of adolescence which demands that the world conform to fairly definite standards of right and wrong cannot accept the moral inconsistencies of the parental authorities and particularly, in Ann's case, her father whom she had hitherto depended on for understanding and example. This last disillusionment with finite authority might very well complete the task of religious creativity begun with the first dawning awareness of the limitations and finitude of the parental objects. In point of fact, however, we observe that Ann's representation of God is not entirely unequivocal. Coexistent with the God who appears to sponsor and even inspire autonomy is a shadow representation of a God who "knew everything and had the power to punish, not just for now, but for all the transgressions of way back." Who is this God and what does he represent? That is the most subtle and yet most central question which can be asked of Ann's faith development. It is the question which will be the focus of our analysis of the critical event of Ann's adult life, her experience of depression and recovery.

IV. The Crises of Adult Life
     Ann and the Long Way Home

The key to understanding Ann's faith journey in adulthood appears to lie in two strikingly insightful and eloquent passages from autobiographical reflections which she made available to this researcher. In the first selection she refers to her life as:

> ". . .the history of the dissolution of a deep, hard
> core of anger; the history of an obstinate,
> persistent determination to be that which I felt an
> inner compulsion to be; the record of the necessity
> to defend and protect the integrity of that being all
> the way; the history of the intense need and
> agonizing search for a model, a heroine, an ego ideal
> consistent with my certainty of what a "real" woman
> must be, and <u>the need for a God, whose presence I</u>
> <u>could allow to pervade my space and to whose</u>
> <u>authority I could entrust all that I am.</u>"
> (emphasis added)

In the second passage, written about three years prior to the research interview, she observes:

> I have lived all my life on probation, never quite
> willing to accept any authority but my own, barely
> avoiding some awesome punishment, yet rarely feeling
> guilty (is this arrogance?) - but feeling as though
> something had been withheld from me. Will I never
> stop seeking that which I do not have?

If one were to have observed Ann in her early middle years, one would have seen scant evidence of a woman who feels she is living "on probation. . .barely avoiding some awesome punishment." Ann led the sort of adventurous and mobile life that other men and women look upon with a measure of awe and envy. As the mother of three children, lay missionary and wife, most of her adult life was spent entering and leaving difficult assignments in a cultural environment that could not be more different from the rural New England of her youth. The feeling she testifies to would not have been visible in behavior. It is a sense that Ann herself was likely not fully aware of until the sudden onset of depression at the age of forty-seven forced it to her attention. What Ann describes as a gnawing sense of something "withheld" is the sensation of inner fragility and impairment that is the nucleus of False Self organization. What has been withheld is the inner sustainment provided by parenting which would permit Ann to own a legitimate dependency. Instead Ann was forced to live with two public and private deceptions. The first, as we have observed, is the persona of the all-competent and fearless woman who can pull up stakes and move courageously into new and demanding situations. The secret is Ann's denied True Self. The second secret is that God the Controller is not really in control, or better, that God's control is distrusted.

One possible option for the God representation when implicated in problematic parenting is that the child becomes herself identified with God, becomes her own God or at least shares both God's power and God's immense responsibility (Rizzuto, 1979). This appears to be one aspect of Ann's earlier God representation. Her relationship with this God was a partnership, one that rarely allowed her to completely relax and rely. The sense of "some awesome punishment just barely avoided" maybe the eruption of the dread that accompanies the awareness that one is involved in a kind of psychic charade, a living beyond one's limits, a usurpation of the role of God. The experience of Ann's midlife depression was a crisis of faith precisely because it made her aware of this dread. It precipitated a sequence of psychic reintegration that has meant the progressive dismantling of the False Self organization of the psyche. A central dimension of that process has been the recovery or re-creation of a God "to whose authority [Ann] could entrust all that [she is]."

Let us quickly review the circumstances of Ann's depression. She and her husband were enroute to another Third World assignment where they would again be trouble-shooters in an outlying mission post. Three things made this mission different from previous positions. First it came on the heels of a full year assignment in the States during which time Ann did a major project designing and teaching a sex education curriculum for a public school. It was a demanding, creative and yet rewarding task from which Ann reluctantly withdrew to return to the missions. Second, this assignment was to be to a predominantly Muslim region and hence Ann and Ted had to take an intensive course in Islamic culture in Paris prior to going abroad. Third, this would be the first time that their children would not be able to accompany them. It was in Paris during an indefinite wait for the clearance of their visas that Ann experienced the precipitous onset of her depression. The immediate circumstance, as Ann recounts the episode, was their lodging in a venerable and cozy boarding house which Ann felt strangely she had lived in before.

Even Ann cannot say for certain what complex of preconscious associations were evoked by her experience of the old home. Whatever they were, it seems reasonable to theorize that Ann unexpectedly got in touch with some very early yearnings for security and comfort. The house in effect recreated a "holding environment" in which Ann allowed herself to relax and feel a measure of protection and rest. In this situation it is likely that a number of unconscious affects and identifications were mobilized and defended against by depression. One was possibly Ann's negative identification with her own passive and dependent mother, the entrapping presence Ann had vowed she would never resemble. Hence Ann cannot admit to herself that she is tired and in need of a respite from a life of constant beginnings and endings. The other affect that is perilously close to consciousness is her own anger: her anger at having to leave one more project in which she had been deeply invested, her anger at her mother for failing to provide her adequate resources to manage mature dependence, and her anger at her father/husband/church for the contradictions in which she has been complicit. Most basically Ann's depression may be read as a statement of protest from her own unconscious to an overextension of psychic resources. The False Self system is strained to breaking. The lethargy and inertia of the depression are in effect a psychic sit-down strike, a signal that the effort to play the super-wife, mother and missionary can no longer be funded.

The repressed anger against the constellation of father/husband male church becomes clearer when Ann actually goes to the mission field. It is symptomatically symbolized in her inability to say the words, "Our Father." What is happening is that from both the male dominated Muslim culture, as well as from her evangelical Christian colleagues in the mission, Ann is receiving a double message. On the one hand she is being told in a variety of different ways that as a woman she is dependent upon and subservient to the male, on the other hand she is also faced with the expectation that she will perform miracles to save the failing mission. The messages too closely resemble the contradictory self and object representations which form her own inner world. There she is both identified with God as partner in omnipotence and negatively identified with the self that longs to be able to lean upon the greater strength of an other. The God she cannot bring herself to pray to is the God who enforced this False Self structure. We can now see that one significant element in that God representation is the representation of her father who affirmed her in her independence but not in her resemblance to her mother, and who finally withdrew from her in adolescence when she introduced emotional issues he was not equipped to handle.

At first the withdrawal which accompanies the depression is experienced as a great relief and a welcomed friend. The terror of it enters in when Ann feels that she could, if she permitted herself, regress to the point of the dissolution of ego boundaries and the absorption of the self. I read this as the fear in fantasy of merger with the longed for mother and a one-way retreat from the relational world. Ann's way of dealing with this seems intuitively correct. She recognizes that she must put herself in a situation in which she can, without guilt, set aside aspects of the False Self structure. This means principally fleeing from the obligations of family and friends. As she observed, this was no easy proposition. Her family and associates could not readily accept that she might be for once on the needing side of a relationship. Her return to the United States and six month sojourn alone in the area near her birthplace is a homecoming at many levels. Most primally it is what the literature of the desert fathers referred to as <u>redire ad cor</u>, to return to the place of the heart, the core or center of the self (Squire, 1973, pp. 159-171) In her period of solitude Ann in effect begins the process of renegotiating the faith that undergirds both the capacity to be alone and her sense of being real. It is an effort at recovery of the True Self.

The liberation of the True Self, I have argued, requires a presence in the inner representational world that permits play. For Ann this presence is what she calls God. We must ask at this point how best to understand the process of the reworking of this representation which is initiated by Ann's depression. At one level it is both plausible and appropriate to interpret the therapeutic process which Ann undergoes as a regression to the resources of basic trust which, as Erikson put it, "in retracing firmly established pathways returns to the present amplified and clarified" (Erikson, 1958, p. 255). More specifically, Ann's need is to find that maternal dimension of God which was "withdrawn" from her at an early age. Ann is specific about this in one of her self-reflections in which she takes a passage from Erikson's <u>Young Man Luther</u> and paraphrases it to fit her experience:

". . .the deepest search in life, it seemed to me, the thing that in one way or another was central to all living was (woman's) search to find a (mother), not merely the (mother) of (her) lost youth, but the image of strength and wisdom external to (her) need and superior to (her) hunger, to which the belief and power of (her) own life could be united."

Yet as one reads closely Ann's history it becomes apparent that her religious struggle is not one that can be "solved" simply by restoring her relationship with her mother, either in flesh or in fantasy. Ann's experience pushes us to consider the "double paradox of faith" which I discussed in my analysis

240

of the work of William Meissner (Chapter Two). What Ann becomes clear about in the aftermath of her depressive episode is "that vital reality that you are indeed separate." She is forced up against the awareness that there can be no return to health simply by reconnecting with parents, husband or family. The meaning of her life is seen to require a relationship to the transcendent and not simply to the transference God of her youth. In effect she is now moving through what Kierkegaard called the movement of infinite resignation, a "return to trust to go beyond it" (Meissner, 1969, p. 65). The end point of the separation individuation process is to bring Ann to confront ultimate separation and final aloneness, and faced with that her relationship to her God enters a new phase. It is premature to say what the final shape of this new relationship will be. In truth the last word will not be said until Ann says her last word. However, one can begin to see something of the emergent form of Ann's object representation of God as she describes the changes that have taken place in her life since the depression. Her sense of God is more intimate, immediate and unmediated. [14] The forms and structures which were necessary to connect her to God earlier in life are now seen as incidental to the pervasive reality of God.

> ". . . .I no longer need to work at establishing contact. Special rituals, forms, inspirational routines, even Church itself, are almost irrelevant, except as responses to what is. The presence is total and constant. I seldom experience being out of communication."

Stacy and the Child of the Dream

From the data of the research interview we have hypothesized that Stacy's early interpersonal experience precipitated the defensive formation of what Winnicott referred to as a False Self system "organized around and built out of introjects" (Meissner, 1978b, p. 555).In addition to the parental introjects we have proposed the special case of a False Self system which utilizes the transitional object representation of God. In the case of Stacy this would be the representation of a God who is swift to punish her if she thinks well of herself. This same God also does not tolerate the deception she had to practice as a child for the sake of maintaining some tenuous sense of self esteem. I would suggest that for Stacy, as for Ann, the mitigation of this False Self system also involves development in her relationship to her representations of God. Further, Stacy, like Ann, appears to have been moved along the way of this psychic integration by an

241

experience of constructive regression. The experience is not nearly as sustained or as severe as Ann's depressive episode, but precisely because it is focused and delimited it offers an excellent opportunity to observe the operation of the representational world in the process of faith. I would like to consider the possible relationship between the reported events in Stacy's adult life, the dream sequence she calls "the dream of the truncated child," and the retreat experience which I shall call simply "the cedar bark experience."

Fairbairn makes the point that dreams are usefully regarded as "state of the nation" reports on the vicissitudes of an individual's object relations (Fairbairn, 1952). This attention to the manifest content of dreams as an indicator of the inner representational world has been picked up by a number of researchers studying object relations (Brenneis, 1971; Langs, 1966; McCandlish, 1976). Following this same line of analysis we may consider Stacy's recurrent dream of the truncated child to be a reflection of the organization of introjects aligned to the False Self system. The interesting coincidence of the appearance of this dream sequence with Stacy's daughter's stormy negotiation of adolescence has already been commented on. The elements that reappear in each dream are significant.

(1) There is always a child who in the dream is not an actual baby but a little girl that has been "truncated," either cut down or squished into infant size;

(2) The child has been seriously neglected, either unfed or unchanged;

(3) The child never protests or cries;

(4) Stacy as the mother in the dream realizes to her surprise and horror that while she was elsewhere involved she has forgotten about the baby. In the dream she feels that if the child had only cried she would have gone to it.

The truncated baby we may take to be a representation of Stacy's neglected and depressed True Self. The abandoned infant symbolizes those aspects of Stacy which she has disparaged, ignored or forgotten about while aligning herself with the cause of the parental powers. I suspect that the child does not cry or protest because the dream itself is an expression of the hope that Stacy may still find the sort of good-enough mothering which anticipates needs in advance of their expression. Another way of understanding this "state of the psyche" message is that the truncated baby is also that self which was neglected while Stacy raised and cared for her own three children. Appropriately then the dream first appears at the time Stacy's youngest child is negotiating adolescent separation. If the dream is an indicator of Stacy's capacity to attend to her True Self, then developments in the dream should be some sign of a process of growth towards the realization of an integral self. Such growth would be a reflection of faith development. The event which Stacy identifies as key in her own spiritual life and connected with a significant change in this recurrent dream took place while she was on retreat about two and a-half years prior to the research interview.

In the retreat experience Stacy was walking outdoors making a concerted effort to "attend" to her surroundings and feeling just a bit foolish. While walking a leaf fell off a tree and landed on her breast. The thought that immediately came to her was that the leaf has chosen her and that it was her leaf. The association leaf-breast-baby suggested itself naturally. Stacy felt herself to be at once the bountiful mother and good breast _and_ the child specially loved and selected. "You have not chosen me, I have chosen you" (John 15-16). The experience triggered a release of the kind of unselfconscious reaching out and engagement characteristic of the True Self's creative involvement with the world. "The spontaneous gesture is the True Self in action" (Winnicott, 1965, p. 148). The child-like quality of her experience is even displayed in her oral investigation of her surroundings. She peels a piece of cedar bark and chews it, whereupon there is unleashed a flood of childhood memories (les temps retrouve!). The spell of play is only broken when contemplating a barrier erected on the trail she entertains the intrusive question of her childhood superego, "would it be wrong to cross this barrier?"

In the immediate aftermath of this experience Stacy reconnects with the darker side of her childhood experience, her sense of shame at the fictions she had to live with in order to defend the core of the True Self. She mourns for the little girl who pretends to laugh with her parents when they joke about her earnest attempt to help support the family by working at the church. She cries for herself as a child of thirteen constructing elaborate deceptions to cover the painful fact of her parents' divorce. In the process of this crying Stacy is beginning to come to terms with ambivalence.

The overcoming of ambivalence involves the withdrawing of projections. This means two things: first, accepting those undesired and undesirable aspects of oneself which had been

243

located elsewhere, and second, the gradual ability to see others, especially parents, as "whole objects," composites of good and bad. In the first instance this is a compassionate acceptance of the child she necessarily had to be in order to survive, a child she both hates and loves. Arthur Miller in his play After the Fall beautifully describes this process of acceptance that has begun in Stacy (Miller, 1964, p. 22):

> I dreamed I had a child, and even in the dream I saw it was my life, and it was an idiot, and I ran away. But it always crept on to my lap again, clutched at my clothes. Until I thought, if I could kiss it, whatever in it was my own, perhaps I could sleep. And I bent to its broken face, and it was horrible . . . but I kissed it. I think one must finally take one's life in one's arms, Quentin.

For Stacy to take her life in her arms means to embrace both her True Self and the forms of False Self organization which were necessary in order to protect that inner core of selfhood. The capacity for that is underwritten by an emergent sense of God that is free of some of the transference aspects of her relationship to her own father and mother. An image that appears during the time of the retreat suggests that this process may be experienced as something akin to a new birth:

> On that retreat I had this little fantasy. . .experiencing myself in the birth canal, and it was God's birth canal. A good feeling. I was feeling good. Just went on walking as though a burden had been lifted. It was kind of a new birth.

An indication that a rearrangement of the representations supportive of faith is underway is found in the subsequent changes that appear in the dream of the truncated baby. In the months that follow the retreat experience Stacy finds herself again dreaming of a baby, but this time she is able to care for the child adequately, even in the very midst of her work for the church. An examination of the pattern of Stacy's life over the last several years suggests that she has in fact deepened her ability both to "mother" herself and to allow others to give to her when she is in need of comfort and support. Both are capabilities which will enable her to be fully and fruitfully available as a pastor when and if her church calls her to the ordained ministry.

V. Concluding Reflection

The presentation and analysis of these two cases has served to demonstrate some of the possibilities for a deepened understanding of the phenomenon of faith resident in a psychoanalytic object relations analysis. A final word should be said about the limitations of this approach, or rather about the caveat which must accompany any such effort to examine faith from a psychological perspective. The cases of Ann and Stacy have been presented in greater detail than could be fully explored, let alone exhausted, in the space appropriate to this book. This was done by design to make a point. Even with all the time and data at hand, the psychoanalytic study of faith will never resolve itself into some precise attribution of religious effect to developmental cause. An analysis such as this has necessarily contented itself with a fairly narrow but crucial matter - the role for faith of those object representations which the individual has synthesized into a representation expressly identified as "God." What has not been accounted for and is beyond the competence of this method is how it may happen that God may be a source for the sense of "God."

It is a theological position, which I derive from the work of H. Richard Niebuhr, that wherever we see faith pushing towards inclusive love and genuine charity, and challenging penultimate loyalties and idolatries, we see the activity of God, the One beyond the Many. The healing of "inner manyness" or as we have referred to it, False Self organization, is likewise a sign of the agency of the Divine. An openness to this mystery is not simply a theological import, however. Strictly in psychological terms we must allow ourselves to be humbled but not discouraged by the perpetually elusive and irreducibly complex character of the human drive to create an object of worship from the stuff of vital experience. In the presence of these creative energies it is both good science and true religion to proceed with a measure of modesty and awe. The appropriate last words are therefore given to Martin Dysart, the psychiatrist of Peter Shaffer's play Equus, who speaks for all of us who turn and turn again to the disciplined contemplation of human faith (Shaffer, 1974, p. 88):

> A child is born into a world of phenomena all equal
> in their power to enslave. It sniffs--it sucks--it
> strokes its eyes over the whole uncomfortable range.
> Suddenly one strikes. Why? Moments snap together
> like magnets, forging a chain of shackles. Why? I
> can trace them. I can even, with time, pull them
> apart again. But why at the start they were ever

magnetized at all--just those particular moments of experience and no others--I don't know. And nor does anyone else. Yet if I don't know-if I can never know that--then what am-] doing here? I don't mean clinically doing or socially doing--I mean fundamentally! These questions, these Whys, are fundamental--yet they have no place in a consulting room. So then, do I?. . .This is the feeling more and more with me--No Place. Displacement. . . ."Account for me," says staring Equus, "First account for Me!. . . . ."

FOOTNOTES CHAPTER SEVEN

1. For an instructive discussion of the debate over the role of object relations versus innate factors in the motivated life of the human being, see Gedo, 1979.

2. Useful reviews of this history are slowly becoming available from a number of different theoretical vantages. See Friedman, L.I., 1975; Friedman, L., 1978; Guntrip, 1963; Kanzer, 1979; Mendez & Fine, 1976.

3. For other key discussions of internalization and psychic structure see "On Narcissism" (Freud, 1914) and "Mourning and Melancholia," in which Freud asserts that "the character of the ego is a precipitate of abandoned object-cathexes and that it contains a record of past object choices" (Freud, 1917, pp. 237-260).

4. A neglected anticipation of this insight is Phillipson's book The Object Relations Technique (Phillipson, 1955), in which he draws our hypothesis ,"We do not see - we look for. William Meissner exhaustively examines projection and introjection in his work, The Paranoid Process (Meissner, 1978b).

5. "That which the fond parent projects ahead of him as his ideal in the child is merely a substitute for the lost narcissism of childhood." (Freud, 1914).

6. Two ways in which expectations are communicated that merit mention are naming and birth myths. The Hebrew notion that the giving of a name was the imparting of a destiny or the claiming of a promise is not entirely without psychological foundation. We could examine, for example, the influence on a child's developing sense of self of receiving his father's name, or the name of a deceased and still mourned sibling, or the name of a famous relative or historical-religious figure. The meaning of the name is closely allied to the matter of the stories or myths that surround the birth of the child. The answers the child receives to his first inquiry, "how was it when I was born?" may provide formative images in building the child's sense of self. Stacy, when asked what she remembers being told of her birth, gave two instructive answers with rather different implications for her self-image. She had been born on a cold day and says that for years she thought "Dixie" was written especially for her ("in Dixieland where I was born, early on one frosty morn. . . ."). This birth myth perhaps says something about a story of cosmic specialness which an imaginative child creates for herself.

A more ominous birth story was Stacy's recollection of being told that her mother's labor was long, difficult and dangerous. In the case of Stacy this memory is perhaps a screen for the way in which she was often made to feel responsible for the difficulties and sufferings of her family. Her desire not to be a burden (reflected in the anecdote about wanting to work at a preschool age) may in part be an aspect of the more general need to repair or make reparation for the injury she experiences herself as having inflicted on her mother.

7. As Benedek has insightfully observed, parenting "works" as an interactional system when the child evokes from the parent a constructive regression to the parent's own oral stage of development. Optimally the parent's empathic identification with the child is facilitated by the activation of the parent's own memories of "good-enough" nurturance. Referring specifically to the role of the mother, Benedek writes:

The mother's ability to receive from her child is strongly affected by the confidence which the mother herself has incorporated into her mental structure while receiving from her own mother. Her "giving," her patience and motherliness are derived from the developmental vicissitudes of primary identifications with her mother. These were fantasies before: now with the actuality of motherhood they are tested in reality. (Benedek, 1959)

247

8. In this book I have tried to take note of the fact that when most analysts speak of mothering they mean that adult who is identified by the child as providing the primary nurturance. Hence I have generally attempted to use the term "primary caretaker" or "parent." Chodorow (1978) has pointed out the ways in which exclusive mothering by the female of the species is a sociological artifact nevertheless maintained by psychic factors that can be understood psychoanalytically. Where mothering is an almost exclusively female responsibility, as it was for both our subjects, the role of the father in the developmental process is still significant though only beginning to be studied (Abelin, 1975; Lamb, 1977; Lynn, 1974).

9. Freud also discussed the reappearance of this feeling in adult life as the "oceanic" feeling which he links to the ego's original sense of inclusiveness and mutuality with all that exists (Freud, 1930). Freud did not, however, pursue this pre-oedipal aspect of religious experience nor see how such "regressive" experience might in fact be restorative and finally integrating.

10. Hans Loewald in his brilliant and suggestive paper, "Ego and Reality" discusses how the ego defends its sense of reality (vs. defending itself against reality). In Freud's formulations the father represents a hostile reality (the castration threat). In Loewald's thinking the intervention of the father may very well be on the side of the ego's protecting of a sense of reality against the threat of being overwhelmed by the mother (Loewald, 1951).

11. Benedek's thesis is that "in each 'critical period; the child revives in the parent his related developmental conflicts. This brings about either pathologic manifestations in the parent, or by the resolution of the conflict it achieves a new level of integration in the parent" (Benedek, 1959).

12. It is instructive that when Stacy is asked the interview question, "What kind of animal would it be best to be?" she replies: "A bird. . I think of a bird as very free. . .but also very much in touch with its environment. . .to exercise its freedom it has to know about wind, and that's what keeps it free" (Appendix B). Her wish reflects the same combination of independence and inter-relatedness found in her memory of the injured bird from childhood.

13. No less a figure than Dietrich Bonhoeffer gave eloquent expression to this sense in one of his better known prison poems. In it he ponders the incongruity between the self-assured and comforting pastor he is for his fellow

prisoners and the weary, heart-sick man he knows himself to be. The poem closes with this stanza:

Who am I? This or the other?
Am I one person today, and tommorrow another?
Am I both at once? A hypocrite before others,
And before myself a contemptible, woebegone weakling,
Or is something within me still like a beaten army,
fleeing in disorder from a victory already achieved?
Who am I? They mock me, these lonely questions of mine.
Whoever I am, Thou knowest, O God, I am Thine.

(Bonhoffer, 1953)

14.   A complementary analysis of the transition Ann undergoes could be made from a structural developmentalist perspective. Such an analysis would pay greater attention to a number of factors underplayed in this psychoanalytic discussion, among them: Ann's movement from a universe defined by her caretaking of others to a universe defined by autonomous judgments; the movement from reliance upon the authority and mediation of social structures to a more direct appropriation of religious reality; the guilt she experiences over the conflict of interpersonal loyalties and her loyalty to God (see especially Gilligan, 1977).

The Case of Ann B.: Supplemental Questions

Q: If you could changed into some kind of animal - any animal
   in the whole world - what would be the best animal to be,
   and why?

A: An owl . . . it would be nice to have my own place,
   reasonably high up - though not so far up as to be removed
   from life - but at least a privacy and point of view so I
   could at least observe life. I'm a night person - I'd
   like to be able to observe at night . . . to feel I could
   process all I could observe and people would respect my
   right to do so, because that's what people expect of an
   owl.

Q: What animal wouldn't you want to be at all? Which would
   be the worst, and why?

A: A vulture. They let everyone else do the dirty work -
   they let some other animal do the work of tracking and
   killing the prey - and they're content with what's left.
   I don't want what other people leave. And besides,
   they're ugly to look at.

Q: If you had a chance to be any historical or fictional
   character, who would you most want to be?

A: It changes. . .Queen Elizabeth I. I read widely in that
   period. . . there are things about her I would have
   enjoyed, but mainly what she was involved in.

Q: Why? What was good about being. . . .?

A: Being queen in a very exciting period of time. . .able to
   be a part of the discovery, the moving out into all areas
   of the world. She was the one who made the age of
   discovery possible. There is also Samuel Johnson. For
   some time now - since moving from wanting to manage and
   wanting to use my mind (since my kids got big enough) -
   I've envied people who were able to attract good minds and
   who would come together and regularly deal with their
   thoughts and their ideas, inspire each other. . .just
   enjoying their minds. I admire the way they did their
   work, by coming together, and for women, where does a
   woman get to do that? At least for my generation not with
   other women.

Q: If you could be changed into some kind of thing or object, what would be <u>best</u> to be?

A: A book - it has a life of its own. It not only contains someone's thoughts, but it is also handled, has human contact. Generally kept in a warm part of the building.

Q: What would be the <u>worst</u>, and why?

A: A weapon. Because it is <u>used</u> - and the only reason for it to exist is its own proclivity to hurt, although it can be used to defend.

Q: If you were to go to a masquerade party, what kind of animal or person or character would you most want to go as?

A: I've always had a fantasy of walking in a nineteenth century flowing hoop skirt. Being the queen. . .whatever person would command the most attention.

The Case of Stacy R.: Supplemental Questions

Q: If you could changed into some kind of animal - any animal in the whole world - what would be the best animal to be, and why?

A: A bird. . .I think of a bird as very free, but also very much in touch with its environment. To exercise its freedom it has to know about wind, and that's what helps it to be free.

Q: What animal wouldn't you want to be at all? Which would be the worst, and why?

A: I'd hate to be a warthog. They don't look like they have any fun - doleful looking creatures.

Q: If you had a chance to be any historical or fictional character, who would you most want to be?

A: One of the people I most admire is Mother Theresa - there is such a wholeness about the way she lives and is. It is the Catholic Worker ethos. So simple and direct.

[Note: A day after the interview during which these supplemental questions were asked, Stacy recontacted the interviewer to add two other responses to the preceding question. She spoke of her identification with the fictional heroine Jane Eyre because she was "a tough cookie with a terrible childhood who nevertheless made it," and with Hans Christian Anderson's story, "The Ugly Duckling."]

Q: If you were to be changed into some kind of thing or object, what would be the best to be? Why?

A: I don't identify with objects. . .maybe. . .rocks. I love them. I collect them, play with them, paint them. They have such an intriguing feel. I like to feel them with my eyes shut. Rocks change more than we think they do, these lovely, solid objects.

Q: If you were to go to a masquerade party, what kind of animal or person or character would you most want to go as?

A: The last time I actually went to one I went dressed as an English music hall star. I would probably want to do something extravagant . . .a fantastic hoop skirt or

velvet riding outfit. I might put a name to it. I love
to use different parts of myself that don't ordinarily
come out.

Q: Who would you most want to meet there? A person dressed
    as. . .?

A: If I'm all dressed up, I'd like to meet someone dressed as
    a courtier - so we could play around, really live it up.

BIBLIOGRAPHY

Abelin, E. (1971). The role of the father in the Separation and Individuation Process. In J.B. McDevitt & C.F. Settlage (Eds.), Separation and Individuation. New York: International Universities Press.

Abraham, K. (1924). A short study of the development of the libido. In Selected Papers on Psychoanalysis. London: Hogarth.

Ainsworth, M.D.S. (1969). Object relations, dependency, and attachment: A theoretical review of the infant-mother relationship. Child Development, 40, 969-1025.

_____. (1972). Attachment and dependency: A comparison. In J.L. Gewirtz (Ed.), Attachment and Dependency. Washington: Winston & Sons.

Anthony, E.J. (1976). Freud, Piaget and human knowledge: Some comparisons and contrasts. The Annual of Psychoanalysis, 4, 253-280.

Bakan, D. (1966). The Duality of Human Existence. Boston: Beacon Press.

Balint, M. (1959). Thrills and Repressions. New York: International Universities Press.

_____. (1965). Primary Love and Psychoanalytic Technique. New York: Liveright Publishing Corporation.

_____. (1968). The Basic Fault: Therapeutic Aspects of Repression. London: Tavistock Publications.

Barnett, C. and Baruch, K. (1978). Women in the middle years: A critique of research and theory. Psychology of Women Quarterly, 3, 187-197.

Bart, P. (1971). Depression in middle-aged women. In V. Gornick & K. Moran (Eds.), Women in Sexist Society. New York: Basic Books.

Bass, L.R. and Brown, R. (1973). Generating rules for intensive analysis: Ihe study of transformations. Psychiatry, 36, 172-183.

Baum, G. (1969). Faith and Doctrine: A Contemporary View. New York: Paulist Press.

Becker, E. (1962) The Birth and Death of Meaning: An Interdisciplinary Perspective on the Problem of Man. New York: The Free Press.

_____. (1973). The Denial of Death. New York: The Free Press, Macmillan.

Beit-Hallahmi, B. and Argyle, M. (1975). God as a father projection: The theory and the evidence British Journal of Medical Psychology, 48, 71-75.

Bellah, R. (1964). Religious evolution. American Sociological Review, 29, 352-374.

Benedek, T. (1938). Adaptation to reality in early infancy. Psychoanalytic Quarterly, 7, 200-214.

_____. (1959). Parenthood as a developmental phase. The Journal of the American Psychoanalytic Association, 7, 389-417.

Benson, P. and Spilka, B. (1973). God image as a function of self-esteem and locus of control. Journal for the Scientific Study of Religion, 12, 297-310.

Berger, P.L. (1974). Some second thoughts on substantive versus functional definitions of religion. Journal for the Scientific Study of Religion, 13, 125-133.

Bettleheim, B. (1976). The Uses of Enchantment: The Meaning and Importance of Fairy Tales. New York: Random House.

Blatt, S.J. (1974). Levels of object-representation in anaclitic and introjective depression. Psychoanalytic Study of the Child, 29, 107-157.

Blatt, S., Wild, C. and Ritzler, B. (1975). Disturbances of object representations in schizophrenia. In D. Spence (Ed.), Psychoanalysis and Contemporary Science, Vol. 4. New York: International Universities Press.

Blos, P. (1967). The second individuation process of adolescence. Psychoanalytic Study of the Child, 22, 162-186.

Bonhoffer, D. (1953). Letters and Papers from Prison. New York: Macmillan.

Bowker, J. (1973). The Sense of God: Sociological, Anthropological, and Psychological Approaches to the Origin of the Sense of God Oxford: Clarendon.

_____. (1976). Information process, systems behavior and the study of religion. Zygon, 11, 361-379.

Bowlby, J. (1958). The nature of child's tie to his mother. International Journal of Psychoanalysis, 39, 350-373.

_____. (1960). Separation anxiety. International Journal of Psychoanalysis, 41, 89-113.

_____. (1969). Attachment and Loss. New York: Basic Books.

Brenneis, C.B. (1971). Features of the manifest dream in schizophrenia. Journal of Nervous and Mental Diseases, 153, 80-91.

Brown, L.B. (Ed.)(1973). Psychology and Religion. Harmondsworth: Penguin Press.

Brierly, M. (1951). Trends in Psychoanalysis . London: Hogarth.

Bruner, J. (1964). The course of cognitive growth. American Psychologist, 19, 1-15.

Buber, M. (1967). Between Man and Man. (3rd Edition). New York: Macmillan.

Buckley, M., S.J. (1978). Transcendence, truth, and faith: The ascending experience of God in all human inquiry. Theological Studies, 39, 633-655.

Buescher, G.W. (1967). Faith. In New Catholic Encyclopedia, Vol. V. New York: McGraw-Hill.

Bultman, R. (1955). The crisis of faith. In Essays: Philosophical and Theological. London: SCM Press.

Capps, D. (1974). Contemporary psychology of religion: The task of a theoretical reconstruction. Social Research, 41, 362-383.

Chessick, R. (1974). Defective ego feeling and the quest for being in the borderline patient. International Journal of Psychoanalytic Psychotherapy 3, 73-89.

_____. (1977). <u>Great Ideas in Psychotherapy</u>. New York: Aronson.

Chew, P. (1977). <u>The Inner World of the Middle-Aged Man</u>. Boston: Houghton Mifflin.

Chodorow, N. (1978). <u>The Reproduction of Mothering: Psychoanalysis and the Sociology of Gender</u>. Berkeley: University of California Press

Denzinger, H.J. (1957). The sources of Catholic dogma. In <u>Enchiridion Symbolorum</u>, 30th Edition. St. Louis: Herder.

Draper, E. (1969). Psychological dynamics of religion. In E.M. Pattison (Ed.), <u>Clinical Psychiatry and Religion</u>. Boston: Little, Brown.

Ducey, C.P. (1975). Rorschach experiential and representational dimensions of object relations: A longitudinal study. Unpublished doctoral dissertation. Harvard University Graduate School of Arts and Sciences.

Dulles. A. (1971). <u>The Survival of Dogma</u>. New York: Doubleday & Co.

Dunne, J.S. (1973). <u>Time and Myth</u> Notre Dame: University of Notre Dame Press.

Dupre, L. (1972). <u>The Other Dimension: A Search for the Meaning of Religions Attitudes</u>. New York: Doubleday & Co.

Ebeling, G. (1963), <u>Word and Faith</u>. Philadelphia: Fortress Press.

Elkind, D. (1964). Piaget's semi-clinical interview and the study of spontaneous religion. <u>Journal of the Scientific Study of Religion</u>, <u>4</u>, 40-47.

_____. (1970). The origins of religion in the child. <u>Review of Religious Research</u>, <u>12</u>, 35-42.

_____. (1971). The development of religious understanding in children and adolescents. In M. Strommen (Ed.), <u>Research on Religious Development: A Comprehensive Handbook</u>.New York: Hawthorne Books.

Erikson, E.M. (1963). <u>Childhood and Society</u>. New York: W.W. Norton & Co.

_____. (1964). Insight and Responsibility: Lectures on the Ethical Implications of Psychoanalytic Insight. New York: W.W. Norton & Co.

_____. (1968a). The development of ritualization. In Donald R. Cutler (Ed.), The Religious Situation 1968, Boston: Beacon Press.

_____. (1968b). Identity, Youth, and Crisis. New York: W.W. Norton & Co.

Faber, H. (1972). Psychology of Religion. Philadelphia: Westminster Press.

Fairbairn, W.R.D. (1952a). Psychoanalytic Studies of the Personality. London: Routledge & Kegan Paul, Ltd.

_____.(1952b). Theoretical and experimental aspects of psychoanalysis. British Journal ofMedical Psychology, 27, 122-127.

_____. (1955). Observations in defence of the object-relations theory of the personality. British Journal of Medical Psychology, 28 144-156.

Federn, P. (1952). Ego Psychology and Psychosis. New York: Basic Books.

Fleck, J.R., Ballard, S.N. and Reilly, J.W. (1975). The development of religious concepts and maturity: A three stage model. Journal of Religion and Psychology, 3, 156-163.

Fourcher, L.A. (1977). Adopting a philosophy: The case of Roy Schafer's A New Language of Psychoanalysis. Review of Existential Psychology and Psychiatry, 15, 134-149.

Fowler, J.W. (1974a). To See the Kingdom: The Theological Vision of H. Richard Niebuhr. Nashville: Abingdon Press.

_____. (1974b). Faith, liberation and human development. The Foundation, 79. Atlanta: Gammon Theological Seminary.

_____. (1976a). Stages in faith: The structural-developmental approach. In T.C. Hennessy (Ed.), Values and Moral Development. New York: Paulist Press.

_____. (1976b). Faith development and the aims of religious socialization. In G. Durka & J.M. Smith (Eds.), Emerging Issues Religious Education. Paramus: Paulist Press.

_____. (1977). Faith and the structuring of meaning. Paper read at the Annual Meeting of the American Psychological Association, San Francisco, 1977. Unpublished.

_____. (1981). Stages of Faith: The Psychology of Human Development and the Quest for Meaning. New York: Harper & Row.

Fowler, J. W. and Keen, S. (1978). Life Maps: Conversations on the Journey of Faith. Waco: Word Books.

Fraiberg, S. (1959). The Magic Years. New York: Scribners.

Freud, A. (1965). Normality and Pathology in Childhood: Assessments of Development. New York: International Universities Press.

_____.3 (1966). The Ego and the Mechanisms of Defense. New York: International Universities Press.

Freud, S. (1907). Obsessive actions and religious practices. Standard Edition, 9, 115-128. London: Hogarth, 1959.

_____. (1899). Screen memories. Standard Edition, 3, 301-322. London: Hogarth, 1962.

_____. (1901). The psychopathology of everyday life. Standard Edition, 6. London: Hogarth Press.

_____. (1909). Notes upon a case of obsessional neurosis. Standard Edition, 10, 153-259.

_____. (1910). Leonardo da Vinci and a memory of his childhood. Standard Edition, 11, 59-138. London: Hogarth, 1957.

_____ (1911a). Formulations on two principles of mental functioning. Standard Edition, 12, 220-223. London: Hogarth, 1958.

_____ (1911b). Psycho-analytic notes on an autobiographical account of a case of paranoia (dementia paranoides). Standard Edition, 12, 3-84. London: Hogarth, 1958.

_____ (1912). The dynamics of transference. Standard Edition, 12, 97-108. London: Hogarth, 1958.

_____ (1913). Totem and taboo. Standard Edition, 13, 1-162. London: Hogarth, 1955.

_____ (1914). Some reflections on schoolboy psychology. Standard Edition, 13, 241-243. London: Hogarth, 1955.

_____ (1915). Thoughts for the times on war and death. Standard Edition, 14, 274-302. London: Hogarth, 1957.

_____. (1917). Mourning and melancholia. Standard Edition, 18, 2-64. London: Hogarth, 1955.

_____. (1920). Beyond the pleasure principle. Standard Edition, 18, 1-66. London: Hogarth, 1955.

_____. (1921). Group psychology and the analysis of the ego. Standard Edition, 18, 67-145. London: Hogarth, 1955.

_____. (1923a). The ego and the id. Standard Edition, 19, 1-68. London: Hogarth, 1961.

_____. (1923b). A seventeenth-century demonological neurosis. Standard Edition, 19, 69-107. London: Hogarth, 1961.

_____. (1924a). The loss of reality in neurosis and psychosis. Standard Edition, 19, 183-190. London: Hogarth, 1961.

_____. (1924b). The economic theory of masochism. Standard Edition, 19, 155-170. London: Hogarth, 1961.

_____. (1927). The Future of Illusion.(J. Strachey, Ed. and trans.). New York: W.W. Norton & Co., 1961.

_____. (1930). Civilization and its discontents. Standard Edition, 21, 57-145. London: Hogarth, 1961.

_____. (1933). New introductory lectures on psychoanalysis. Standard Edition, 22, 1-182. London: Hogarth, 1964.

_____. (1939). Moses and monotheism. Standard Edition, 23, 1-132. London: Hogarth, 1964.

_____. (1940). An outline of psychoanalysis. Standard Edition, 23, 141-207. London: Hogarth, 1964.

Feuerbach, L. (1957). The Essence of Christianity. new York: Harper and Row. (Originally published 1841)

Friedman, L. (1978a). Trends in the theory of treatment. Psychoanalytic Quarterly, 47, 524-567.

_____. (1978b) Piaget and psychotherapy. Journal of the American Academy of Psychoanalysis, 6, 175-192.

_____. (1975). Current psychoanalytic object relations theory and its clinical implications. International Journal of Psycho-analysis, 56, 137-146.

Fuchs, E. (1977). The Second Season: Life, Love and Sex - Women in the Middle Years. Garden City, N.Y.: Anchor Press/Doubleday.

Gedo J. (1979). Theories of object-relations: A metapsychological assessment. Journal of the American Psychological Association, 27 361-373.

Gedo, J.E. and Goldberg, A. (1973). Models of the Mind: A Psychoanalytic Theory. Chicago: University of Chicago Press.

Geertz, C. (1966). Religion as a cultural system. In M. Banton (Ed.), Anthropological Approaches to the Study of Religion. New York: Praeger.

Gerwitz, J.L. (Ed.)(1972). Attachment and Dependency. Washington, D.C.: V.H. Winston & Sons.

Gilligan, C. (1977). In a different voice. Harvard Educational Review, 47, 481-517. Cambridge: Harvard University Press.

_____. (1982). In Different Voice: Psychological Theory and Women's Development. Cambridge: Harvard University Press.

Godin, A. and Hallez, M. (1964). Parental images and divine paternity. In A. Godin (Ed.), From Religious Experience to a Religious Attitude. Brussels, Belgium: Lumen Vitae Press.

Goethals, G. (1973). Symbiosis and the life cycle. British Journal of Medical Psychology, 46, 91-96.

_____. (1978). A review of some issues relating to intimacy: A memo to Carol Gilligan. Unpublished memo. Department of Psychology and Social Relations, Harvard University, Cambridge, Massachusetts.

Goldman, R.J. (1964). Religious Thinking from Childhood to Adolescence. New York: Seabury Press.

Goody, J. (1961). Religion and ritual: The definitional problem. British Journal of Sociology, 12, 142-164.

Gould, R.L. (1978). Transformations: Growth and Change in Adult Life. New York: Simon & Schuster.

Greenacre, P. (1957). The childhood of the artist: Libidinal phase development and giftedness. The Psychoanalytic Study of the Child, 12, 47-72.

Gross, I. (Ed.)(1956). Potentialities of Women in the Middle Years. East Lansing: Michigan State University Press.

Grossman, W.I. and Simon, B. (1969). Anthropomorphism: Motive, meaning, and causality in psychoanalytic theory. Psychoanalytic Study of the Child, 24, 78-111.

Guntrip, H. (1949). Psychology for Ministers and Social Workers. London: Independent Press.

_____. (1953). The therapeutic faith in psychotherapy. British Journal of Medical Psychology, 26, 115-132.

_____. (1956). Psychotherapy and Religion. New York: Harpers.

_____. (1961). Personality Structure and Human Interaction. New York: International Universities Press.

_____. (1969a). Schizoid Phenomena, Object-Relations and the Self. New York: International Universities Press.

_____. (1969b). Religion in relation to personal integration. British Journal of Medical Psychology, 42, 323-334.

_____. (1971). Psychoanalytic Theory, Therapy and the Self. New York: Basic Books.

Harlow, H.G. (1961). The development of affectional patterns in infant monkeys. In B.M. Foss (Ed.), Determinants of Infant Behaviour, Vol. I. New York: John Wiley & Sons.

Hartmann, H. (1964). Essays on Ego Psychology. New York: International Universities Press.

Helfaer, P. (1972). The Psychology of Doubt. Boston: Beacon Press.

Henderson, J. (1975). Object relations and the doctrine of "original sin." International Review of Psychoanalysis, 2, 107-120.

Hillman, J. (1975). Revisioning Psychology. New York: Harper & Row.

Holder, A. (1975). Theoretical and clinical aspects of ambivalence. Psychoanalytic Study of the Child, 30, 197-220.

Homans, P. (1970). Theology After Freud: An Interpretive Inquiry. New York: Bobbs-Merrill Company, Inc.

Horowitz, M. (1970). Image Formation and Cognition. New York: Appleton-Century-Crofts.

Horton, R. (1960). A definition of religion and its uses. Journal of the Royal Anthropological Institute, 90, 201-226.

Hume, D. (1956). The Natural History of Religion. H.E. Root (Ed.). Palo Alto: Stanford University Press. (Originally published 1757).

James W. (1897). The will to believe. In Pragmatism and Other Essays. New York: Washington Square Press, 1967.

_____. (1904). The Varieties of Religious Experience: A Study in Human Nature. New York: New American Library, Mentor, 1958.

Jones, E. (1926). The Psychology of Religion. London: Hogarth.

Jung, C.G. (1965). Memories, Dreams and Reflections. A. Jaffe (Ed.). R. Winston (Trans.). New York: Vintage.

Kanzer, M. (1979). Object relations theory: An introduction. Journal of the American Psychological Association, 27, 313-325.

Kardiner, A. and Linton, R. (1939). The Individual and His Society New York: Columbia University Press.

Klein G. (1969). On the meaning of God: Transcendence without mythology. In H.W. Richardson and D.E. Cutler (Eds.), Transcendence. Boston" Beacon Press.

_____. (1977). Attachment to God. Andover Newton Quarterly, 17, 259-271.

Kegan, R. (1978). Ego and Truth. Unpublished doctoral dissertation. Harvard Graduate School of Education, Cambridge, Massachusetts.

Kennedy, E.C. (1973). Believing. New York: Doubleday.

Kernberg, O. (1965). Structural derivatives of object-relations. International Journal of Psychoanalysis, 47, 236-253.

_____. (1967). Borderline personality organization. Journal of the American Psychoanalytic Association, 15(3), 641-685.

_____. (1976). Object Relations Theory and Clinical Psychoanalysis. New York: Aronson.

Klauber, J. (1974). Notes on the psychical roots of religion with particular reference to the development of Western Christianity. International Journal of Psychoanalysis, 55, 249-255.

Klein, G. (1976). Psychoanalytic Theory: An Exploration of Essential. New York: International Universities Press.

Klein, M. (1957). Envy and Gratitude. London: Tavistock Publications.

Kohut, H. (1971). The Analysis of the Self. New York: International Universities Press.

_____. (1972). Thoughts on narcissism and narcissistic rage. Psychoanalytic Study of the Child, 27, 260-400.

Kohlberg, L. (1964). Education, moral development and faith. Journal of Moral Education, 4, 5-16.

_____. (1969). Stage and sequence: The cognitive developmental approach to socialization. In D.A. Goslin (Ed.), Handbook of Socialization Theory and Research. Chicago:

_____. (1971). From is to ought: How to commit the naturalistic fallacy and get away with it in the study of moral development. New York: Academic Press.

Kris, E. (1935). The psychology of caricature. In Psychoanalytic Explorations in Art. New York: International Universities Press, 1952.

Krohn, A. and Mayman, M. (1974). Object representations in dreams and projective tests. Bulletin of the Menninger Clinic, 38, 445-466.

Kung, H. (1979). Freud and the Problem of God. E. Quinn (Trans.). New Haven: Yale University Press.

Lamb, M. (Ed.)(1977). The Role of the Father in Child Development. New York: John Wiley & Sons.

Lambert, W. W., Triandis, L.M. and Wolf, M. (1959). Some correlates of beliefs in the malevolence and benevolence of supernatural beings: A cross societal study. Journal of Abnormal and Social Psychology, 57, 162-168.

Langs, R. (1965). Earliest memories and personality. Archives of General Psychiatry, 12, 379.

_____. (1966). Manifest dreams from three clinical groups. Archives of General Psychiatry, 14 634-643.

Levin, D.C. (1969). The self: A contribution to its place in theory and technique. International Journal of Psychoanalysis, 50, 41-51.

Levinson, D. (1978). The Seasons of a Man's Life. New York: Knopf.

Lichtenstein, H. (1974). The malignant no: Instinctual drives and the sense of self. In M. Kanzer (Ed.), The Unconscious Today: Essays in Honor of Max Schur. New York: International Universities Press.

Lifton, R.J. (1967). Boundaries: Psychological Man in Revolution. New York: Vintage Press.

_____. (1976). The Life of the Self: Toward a New Psychology. New York: Simon and Schuster.

Loewald, H. (1951). Ego and reality. International Journal of Psychoanalysis, 32, 10-18.

_____. (1962). Internalization, separation, mourning and the superego. Psychoanalytic Quarterly, 31, 384-504.

Lorand, S. (1962). Psychoanalytic therapy of religious devotees: A theoretical and technical contribution. International Journal of Psychoanalysis, 43, 50-55.

Lubin, A.J. (1959). A boy's view of Jesus. Psychoanalytic Study of the Child, 14, 155-168.

Lynch, W.F. (1974). Images of Hope: Imagination as Healer of the Hopeless. Notre Dame: University of Notre Dame Press.

Lynn, D.B. (1974). The Father: His Role in Child Development. Monterey: Brooks-Cole.

Maas, H.S. and Kuypers, J.A. (1975). From Thirty to Seventy - A Fifty. Year Longitudinal Study of Adult Life Styles and Personality. San Francisco: Jossey-Bass.

Maccoby, E.E. and Masters, J.E. (1970). Attachment and dependency. In P.H. Mussen (Ed.), Carmichael's Manual of Child Psychology, 3rd Edition, Vol. 2. New York: John Wiley & Sons.

Macmurray, J. (1935). Reason and Emotion. London: Faber & Faber, Ltd.

_____. (1957). The Form of the Personal. (Gifford Lectures, 1953-54.) London: Faber & Faber, Ltd.

Mahler, M., Ross, J.R. and DeFries, Z. (1949). Clinical studies in benign and malignant cases of childhood psychosis (schizophrenia-like). American Journal of Orthopsychiatry, 19 295-305.

Mahler, M., Pine, F., and Bergman, A. (1975). The Psychological Birth of the Human Infant: Symbiosis and Individuation. New York: Basic Books.

Mahler, M. (1972). On the first three subphases of the separation individuation process. International Journal of Psychoanalysis, 53, 333-338.

_____. (1968). On Human Symbiosis and the Vicissitudes of Individuation, Vol. I: Infantile Psychosis. New York International Universities Press.

Maritain, J. (1958). Freudianism and psychoanalysis: A Thomist view. In B. Nelson (Ed.), Freud and the Twentieth Century. New York: Meridian Books.

Mayman, M. (1959). Early memories and abandoned ego states. Southwestern Psychological Association, April 1959. Proceedings of the Academic Assembly on Clinical Psychology. Montreal. McGill University Press, 1963, 97-117.

_____. (1967). Object representations and object relationships in Rorschach responses. Journal of Projective Techniques and Personality Assessment, 31, 17-24.

Mayman, M. and Faris, M. (1960). Early memories as expressions of relationship paradigms. American Journal of Orthopsychiatry, 30, 507-520.

Mayman, M. and Krohn, A. (1975). Developments in the use of projective tests in psychotherapy outcome research. In I.E. Waskow & M.B. Parloff (Eds.), Psychotherapy Change Measures. Report of the Clinical Research Branch Outcome Measures Project, NIMH. (DHEW Pub. No. (ADM) 74-120.)

McCandlish, B.M. (1976). Object relations and dream content of bisexual, homosexual and heterosexual women. Unpublished dissertation. Harvard University, Cambridge, Massachusetts.

McKeown. B. (1976). Identification and projection in religious belief: A q-technique study of psychoanalytic theory. In T. Shapiro (Ed.), Psychoanalysis and Contemporary Science, Vol. 5. New York: International Universities Press.

Meissner, W.W., S.J. (1964). Prolegomena to a psychology of grace. Journal of Religion and Health, 3, 209-240.

_____. (1966). foundations for a Theology of Grace. New York: Paulist Press.

_____. (1969). Notes on a psychology of faith. Journal of Religion and Health, 8, 47-75.

_____. (1974). Correlative aspects of introjective and projective mechanisms. American Journal of Psychiatry, 131 (2), 176-180.

_____. (1975). Differentiation and integration of learning and identification in the developmental process. In The Annual of Psychoanalysis, Vol. 2. New York: International Universities Press.

_____. (1976a). Schreber and the paranoid process. The Annual of Psychoanalysis, 4, 3-40.

_____. (1976b). A note on internalization as process. Psychoanalytic Quarterly, 45, 374-393.

_____. (1977a). Faith and identity. In R. Johnson (Ed.), Psycho-history and Religion: The Case of Young Man Luther. Philadelphia: Fortress Press.

_____. (1977b). The psychology of religious experience. Communio, 4i, 36-59.

_____. (1978a). Psychoanalytic aspects of religious experience The Annual of Psychoanalysis, 6, 103-142.

_____. (1978b). The Paranoid Process., New York: Aronson.

_____. (1979). Internalization and object relations. Journal of the American Psychoanalytic Association, 27, 245-359.

Mendez, A.M. and Fine, H.T. (1976). A short history of the British school of object relations theory and ego psychology. Bulletin of the Menninger Clinic, 40 357-382.

Miller, A. (1964). After The Fall. New York: Viking Press.

Miller, D.L. (1974). The New Polytheism: A Rebirth of the Gods and Goddesses. New York: Harper & Row.

Missildine, H.W. (1975). Your Inner Child of the Past. New York: Simon & Schuster.

Moltmann, J. (1974). The Crucified God. The Cross of Christ as the Foundation of Criticism of Christian Theology. New York: Harper & Row.

Murphy, G. (1958). Human Potentialities. New York: Basic Books.

Murphy, G. and Spohn, H.E. (1968). Encounter with Reality. Boston: Houghton Mifflin.

Nagera, H. (1969). The imaginary companion: Its significance for ego development and conflict solution. Psychoanalytic Study of the Child, 24, 165-196.

Nelson, M.O. (1971). The concept of God and feelings towards parents. Journal of Individual Psychology, 27, 46-49.

Neugarten, B.L. (Ed.)(1968). Middle Age and Aging. Chicago: University of Chicago Press.

Niebuhr, H.R. (1941). The Meaning of Revelation. New York: Macmillan Paperbacks.

_____ (1960a). _Radical Monotheism and Western Culture_. New York: Harper Torchbook.

_____ (1960b). Cole Lectures, Vanderbilt University. Unpublished. (Quoted with permission.)

_____ (1961). On the nature of faith. In S. Hook (Ed.), _Religious Experience and Truth_. New York: New York University Press.

_____ (1963). _The Responsible Self: An Essay in Christian Moral Philosophy_. New York: Harper & Row.

Niebuhr, R. (1972). _Experiential Religion_. New York: Harper & Row.

Nunn, C.Z. (1964). Child control through a coalition with God. _Child Development_, 35, 417-432.

O'Donovan, L. (1978). The courage of faith: An essay in honor of William F. Lynch's seventieth birthday. _Thought_, 53, 369-383.

Osgood, C., Suci, E., and Tannenbaum, P. (1957). _The Measurement of Meaning_. Urbana: University of Illinois Press.

Parens, H. (1970). Inner sustainment: Metapsychological considerations. _Psychoanalytic Quarterly_, 39, 223-239.

Parens, H. and Saul, L. (1971). _Dependence in Man: A Psychoanalytic Study_. New York: International Universities Press.

Parks, S. (1981) _Faith Development and the Imagination in the Context of Higher Education_. unpublished Th.D. dissertation, Harvard Divinity School.

Perry, L.H. (1979). Personal communication, October 1979.

Phillipson, H. (1955). _The Object Relations Technique_. London: Tavistock Publications.

Piaget, J. (1929). _The Child's Conception of the World_. New York: Harcourt & Brace.

_____. (1945). _Play, Dreams and Imitations in Childhood_. New York: Norton, 1951.

_____. (1955). The Language and Thought of the Child. M. Gabain (Trans.). Cleveland: The World Publishing Co.

Pitts, V.P. (1976). Drawing the invisible: Children's conceptualization of God. Character Potential: A Record of Research, 8.

Pruyser, P.W. (1960). Some trends in the psychology of religion. Journal of Religion, 40, 113-129.

_____. (1974). Between Belief and Unbelief. New York: Harper & Row.

_____. (1975). What splits in "splitting"? A scrutiny of the concept of splitting in psychoanalysis and psychiatry. Bulletin of the Menninger Clinic, 39, 1-46.

Rank, O. (1914). The Myth of the Birth of the Hero. F. Robbins & S. Jelliffe (Trans.). New York: Journal of Nervous and Mental Disease Publishing Company.

Reiff, P. (1961). Freud: The Mind of the Moralist. New Anchor Books, Doubleday.

Reik, T. (1931). Ritual: Psychoanalytic Studies. D. Bryan (Trans.). New York: Norton, 1946.

Rizzuto, A.M. (1974). Object relations and the formation of the image of God. British Journal of Medical Psychology, 47, 83-94.

_____. (1976). Freud, God the Devil and the theory of object representation. International Review of Psychoanalysis, 3, 165-180.

_____. (1979). The Birth of the Living God: A Psychoanalytic Studies. Chicago: University of Chicago Press.

Rahner, K. (1960). The theological concept of concupiscentia. In Theological Investigations, Vol. 1. Baltimore: Helicon Press.

_____. (1961). Concerning the relationship between nature and grace. In Rahner, K. (C. Ernest, Trans.). Theological Investigations, Vol. 1. Baltimore: Helicon press.

_____. (1966). Nature and Grace. In Rahner, K. (K. Smyth, Trans.). Theological Investigations, Vol. 4. Baltimore: Helicon Press.

_____. (1967a). Reflections on the problem of the gradual ascent to Christian perfection. In Rahner, K. (H. Kart & B. Kruger, Trans.). Theological Investigations, Vol. 3. Baltimore: Helicon Press.

_____. (1967b). Reflections on the experience of grace. In Theological Investigations, Vol. 3. Baltimore: Helicon Press.

_____. (1968). Faith. In K. Rahner (Ed.), Sacramentum Mundi, Vol. 2. New York: Herder & Herder.

_____. (1969). Anonymous Christians. In Theological Investigations, Vol. 6. Baltimore: Helicon Press.

Robinson, E. (1983). The Original Vision: A Study of the Religious Experience of Childhood. New York: Seabury

Rogers, W.R. (1974). Dependence and counterdependency in psychoanalysis and religious faith. Zygon, 9, 190-201.

_____. (1977). The dynamics of psychology and religion: Teaching in a dialogical field. Paper delivered at Annual Meeting of the Society for the Scientific Study of Religion, Chicago, 1977.

_____. (1978). The theology of Freud. Paper delivered at the Annual Meeting of the American Psychological Association, Toronto, 1978.

Rubenstein, R. L. (1963). A note on the research lag in psychoanalytic studies of religion. Jewish Social Studies, 25, 133-144.

Saffady, W. (1976). New developments in the psychoanalytic study of religion: A bibliographic review of the literature since 1960. Psychoanalytic Review, 63, 291-300.

Sandler, J. (1960). The background of safety. International Journal of Psychoanalysis, 41, 3352-356.

Sandler, J. and Joffe, W.G. (1968). Comments on the psychoanalytic psychology of adaptation with special reference to the role of affects and the representational world. International Journal of Psychoanalysis, 49, 445-454.

Sandler, J. and Rosenblatt, B. (1962). The concept of the representational world. Psychoanalytic Study of the Child, 17, 128-148.

Sales, E. (1977). Women's adult development. In I. Frieze, et. al. (Eds.), Women and Sex Roles: A Social Psychological Perspective. New York: W.W. Norton.

Sartre, J.P. (1964). B. Frechtman (Trans.). The Words. New York: George Braziller.

Saul, L.J. (1970). Inner sustainment: The concept. Psychoanalytic Quarterly, 39, 215-222.

Schafer, R. (1960). The living and beloved super-ego in Freud's structural theory. Psychoanalytic Study of the Child, 15, 163-188.

_____. (1967). Ideals, the ego ideal and the ideal self. Psychological Issues, 5 (2-3), 131-174.

_____. (1968). Aspects of Internalization. New York: International Universities Press.

_____. (1976). A New Language for Psychoanalysis. New Haven: Yale University Press.

Siegman, A.W. (1961). An empirical investigation of the psychoanalytic theory of religious behavior. Journal for the Scientific Study of Religion, 1 (1), 74-78.

Schecter, D.E. and Carman, H. (1979). The birth of a family. Contemporary Psychoanalysis, 15 (3), 380-406.

Schlossman, H. (1972). God the father and his sons. American Imago, 8, 35-51.

Schoenfeld, C.G. (1962). God the father - and mother: Study and expansion of Freud's conception of God as an exalted father. American Imago, 19, 213-234.

Searles, H. (1960). The Nonhuman Environment in Normal Development and Schizophrenia. New York: International Universities Press.

Sears, R.R. (1972). Attachment, dependency, and frustration. In J.L. Gewirtz, (Ed.), Attachment and Dependency. Washington: Winston & Sons.

Selman, R.L. (1974). The Developmental Conceptions of Interpersonal Relations, Vols. I and II. Publication of the Harvard-Judge Baker Social Reasoning Project.

Shaffer, P. (1974). Equus. New York: Avon.

Shands, H.C. (1963). Conservation of the self. Archives of General Psychiatry, 9, 311-323.

Sheehy, G. (1976). Passages: Predictable Crises of Adult Life. New York: E.P. Dutton.

Smith, H. (1969). The reach and the grasp. Transcendence today. In H.W. Richardson & D.R. Cutter (Eds.), Transcendence. Boston: Beacon Press.

Smith, J.E. (1961). The permanent truth in the idea of natural religion. The Harvard Theological Review, 54, 1-19.

Smith, W.C. (1962). The Meaning and End of Religion: A New Approach to the Religious Traditions of Mankind. New York: Macmillan Company

_____. (1977). Belief and History. Charlottesville: University of Virginia Press.

_____. (1979). Faith and Belief. Princeton: Princeton University Press.

Sperling, O. (1944). On appersonation. International Journal of Psychoanalysis, 25, 128-132.

Spilka, B., et. al. (1964). The concept of God; A factor-analytic approach. Review of Religious Research, 6, 20-35.

Spilka, B., Addison, J., and Rosensohn, M. (1975). Parents, self and God: A test of competing theories of individual-religion relationships. Review of Religious Research, 16, 154-165.

Spilka, B., Rosensohn, M. and Tener, S. (1973). Freud revisited: God and father, or is it mother or me. Paper presented at convention of the Rocky Mountain Psychological Association, May 9, 1973, Las Vegas, Nevada.

Spiro, M. (1966). Religion: Problems of definition and explanation. In M. Banton (Ed.), Anthropological Approaches to the Study of Religion. London: Tavistock.

Spiro, M.E. and D'Andrade, R.G. (1958). A cross cultural study of some supernatural beliefs. American Anthropologist, 60, 456-466.

Spitz, R. (1965). The First Year of Life: A Psychoanalytic Study of Normal and Devian Development of Object Relations. New York: International Universities Press.

Squire, A. (1973). Asking the Fathers: The Art of Meditation and Prayer. New York: Paulist.

Stapleton, R.C. (1979). The Experience of Inner Healing. New York: Bantam.

Sugerman, A. (1977). Object relations theory: A reconciliation of phenomenology and ego psychology. Bulletin of the Menninger Clinic, 41 (2), 113-130.

Sugerman, S. (1976). Sin and Madness: Studies in Narcissism. Westminster Press.

Sullivan, H. S. (1953). H. S. Perry and M. L. Gawel (Eds.), The Interpersonal Theory of Psychiatry. New York: W.W. Norton.

Stephenson, W. (1953). The Study of Behavior. Chicago: University of Chicago Press.

Sutherland, J.D. (1963). Object relations theory and the conceptual model of psychoanalysis. British Journal of Medical Psychology, 36, 109-124.

Suttie, I. (1935). The Origins of Love and Hate. New York: The Julian Press, Inc.

Taylor, G. (1978). Demoniacal possession and psychoanalytic theory. British Journal of Medical Psychology, 51, 53-60.

Thornton, M. (1965). The Rock and the River: An Encounter between Traditional Spirituality and Modern Thought. New York: Morehouse Barlow Co.

Tillich, P. (1952). The Courage Io Be. New Haven: Yale University Press.

_____. (1967). Systematic Theology, Vols. I-III. Chicago: University of Chicago Press.

Tylor, E.B. (1871). Primitive Culture: Researches into the Development of Mythology, Philosophy, Religion, Art and Custom. Gloucester, Mass: Smith.

Urist, J. (1973). The Rorschach Test as a multidimensional measure of object relations. Unpublished doctoral dissertation. University of Michigan.

Vaillant, G.E. (1977). Adaptation to Life. Boston: Little, Brown.

van Beeck, F.J. (1979). Christ Proclaimed: Christology as Rhetoric. New York:: Paulist Press.

Vergote, A., Tamayo, A., Pasquali, L., Bonami, M., Pattyn, M., and Clusters, A. (1969). Concept of God and parental images. Journal of the Scientific Study of Religion, 8, 79-87.

Vergote, A. and Tamayo, A. (1981).The Parental Figures and the Representation of God: A Psychological and Cross-Cultural Study. New York: Mouton.

Vergote, A. and Aubert, C. (1972). Parental images and representations of God. Social Compass, 19, 431-444.

Werner, H. and Kaplan, B. (1963). Symbol Formation. new York: John Wiley & Sons.

Wheelis, A. (1958). The Quest for Identity: The Decline of the Super-ego and What is Happening to American Character as a Result. New York: W.W. Norton & Co., Inc.

Whitehead, A.N. (1926). Religion in the Making. New York: Meridian, 1960.

Whiting J.H.M. and Child, I.L. (1953). Child Training and Personality: A Cross Cultural Study. New Haven: Yale University Press.

Williams, D.D. (1968). The Spirit and the Forms of Love. Welwyn: Nisbet.

Williams, J.P. (1962). The nature of religion. Journal of the Scientific Study of Religion, 2, 2-14.

Williams, R. (1971). A theory of God-concept readiness: From the Piagetian theory of the child artificialism and the origin of religious feeling in children. Religious Education, 66, 62-66.

Winnicott, D.W. and Khan, M. (1953). Review of Fairbairn's Psychological Studies of the Personality. International Review of Psychoanalysis, 34, 329-333.

Winnicott, D.W. (1960). The theory of the parent-infant relationship. International Journal of Psychoanalysis, 41, 585-595.

_____. (1965). The Maturational Processes and the Facilitating Environment. Studies in the Theory of Emotional Development London: Hogarth Press.

_____. (1971). Playing and Reality. New York: Basic Books.

Wolff, P. (1960). The developmental psychologies of Jean Piaget and psychoanalysis. In Psychological Issues, Vol. 2. New York: International Universities Press.

Zilboorg, G. (1962). Psychoanalysis and Religion. New York: Farrar, Straus & Giroux.